The Ultimate Guide to Search Engine Marketing

Pay Per Click Advertising Secrets Revealed

By Bruce C. Brown

"If you greatly desire something, have the guts to stake everything on obtaining it."
—Brendan Francis, Playwright

"Politics is not a bad profession. If you succeed, there are many rewards. If you disgrace yourself you can always write a book."
—Ronald Reagan, 40th President of the United States

The Ultimate Guide to Search Engine Marketing
Pay Per Click Advertising Secrets Revealed

ISBN-13: 978-0-910627-99-3   ISBN-10: 0-910627-99-1

Library of Congress Cataloging-in-Publication Data

Brown, Bruce C. (Bruce Cameron), 1965-
  The ultimate guide to search engine marketing : pay per click advertising secrets revealed / by Bruce C. Brown.
      p. cm.
  Includes bibliographical references and index.
  ISBN-13: 978-0-910627-99-3 (alk. paper)
  ISBN-10: 0-910627-99-1 (alk. paper)
  1. Internet marketing. 2. Internet advertising. 3. Search engines. I. Title.
  HF5415.1265.B767 2007
  658.8'72--dc22

                    2007005629

LIMIT OF LIABILITY/DISCLAIMER OF WARRANTY: The publisher and the author make no representations or warranties with respect to the accuracy or completeness of the contents of this work and specifically disclaim all warranties, including without limitation warranties of fitness for a particular purpose. No warranty may be created or extended by sales or promotional materials. The advice and strategies contained herein may not be suitable for every situation. This work is sold with the understanding that the publisher is not engaged in rendering legal, accounting, or other professional services. If professional assistance is required, the services of a competent professional should be sought. Neither the publisher nor the author shall be liable for damages arising herefrom. The fact that an organization or Web site is referred to in this work as a citation and/or a potential source of further information does not mean that the author or the publisher endorses the information the organization or Web site may provide or recommendations it may make. Further, readers should be aware that Internet Web sites listed in this work may have changed or disappeared between when this work was written and when it is read.

EDITOR: Marie Lujanac • mlujanac817@yahoo.com
PROOFREADER: Angela C. Adams • aadams@atlantic-pub.com
ART DIRECTOR: Meg Buchner • megadesn@mchsi.com

Printed in the United States

Printed on Recycled Paper

CONTENTS

Chapter 4: How to Generate Web Site Traffic   73

Chapter 5: Establishing an Online Marketing Strategy   79

Chapter 6: How to Budget for Your PPC Advertising Campaign and Choose Effective Keywords & Keyword Phrases 85

Chapter 7: Google™ AdWords 99

Chapter 8: Yahoo!® Search Marketing 125

Chapter 9: Microsoft® adCenter   141

Chapter 10: How to Identify and Combat Fraud   151

Chapter 11: Increase Profits With Google™ AdSense   167

Chapter 12: How To Increase Sales With Affiliate Marketing   175

Increase Profits With an eBay Store Front   193

With more than a billion people worldwide using the Internet and millions of search queries being initiated every day in the major search engines, no business can afford not to have a well-executed marketing plan linked to search engines.

In the last four years, pay-per-click (PPC) advertising on the major search engines has become an integral part of any successful business's online marketing strategy. In a matter of minutes, you can reach potential customers who are actively searching for the products or services that you sell. This phenomenon has brought about a new paradigm in advertising, one that evened the playing field for small and large advertisers seeking to reach new clients. Suddenly, mom 'n pop stores and startups with limited marketing budgets are able to compete alongside Fortune 500 firms. Companies serving niche markets are now able to reach target clients with a minimum of effort.

> *Half the money I spend on advertising is wasted. The trouble is I don't know which half.*
>
> *—Retailer John Wanamaker, 1886*

Despite amazing technological advances in all facets of advertising and business, Wanamaker's struggle to track the effectiveness of his advertising continues today, making for sleepless nights for marketers and advertisers around the globe. For businesses that engage in a variety of advertising media—billboards, TV, radio, print, and online— it is nearly impossible to separate the efficient from the wasted efforts. PPC advertising is strikingly more powerful. For the first time, smart advertisers are able to see the precise results of each dollar they spend, tracking individual keywords searched to the specific sale, lead, or even phone call that results. Advertisers can cut out inefficient media from their campaign and focus dollars on the most profitable areas.

However, with small and large firms alike diving headlong into PPC advertising—more than 250,000 advertisers now use Google™ and Yahoo!® PPC advertising—the market has become increasingly competitive, driving costs up and forcing advertisers to be far more savvy than ever before. For anyone launching a search engine marketing campaign today, it is imperative to be as knowledgeable about search engine marketing as possible. Unfortunately, with a bewildering array of Web sites, manuals, so-called gurus, and books on the topic, individuals and businesses looking to learn about search engine marketing face an uphill battle just getting started.

Bruce C. Brown's *Ultimate Guide to Search Engine Marketing* is an invaluable tool to anyone looking for a concise and well-written introduction to all aspects of search engine marketing. He provides instructions on launching campaigns in Google™ and Yahoo!®, case studies, information on click fraud, tools to calculate ROI, and tips to generate high performing keywords. He skillfully covers everything you need to know to get started in the profitable and dynamic world of search engine marketing and PPC advertising.

Michael Mothner, President and CEO, Wpromote, Inc.
1650 Pacific Coast Highway, Suite 310
Redondo Beach, CA 90277
Phone: 310-421-4844
Fax: 310-356-3228
Company E-mail: **sales@wpromote.com**
Mike Mothner's E-mail: **mike@wpromote.com**

Biography:

Michael Mothner is President and CEO of Wpromote, Inc., one of the world's leading search engine marketing firms. Wpromote has served more than 10,000 clients in more than 50 countries and is one of a handful of firms worldwide to be a Google™ Qualified Company and a Yahoo!® Ambassador. Michael also provides online advertising consulting services to the financial services industry and serves on the Google™ Advertiser Research Council. Prior to founding Wpromote, he worked at Redpoint Ventures in Los Angeles, evaluating venture capital business opportunities in the Internet and software sector. He graduated *cum laude* from Dartmouth College with a Bachelor of Arts degree in economics and computer science.

INTRODUCTION

"When I took office, only high energy physicists had ever heard of the World Wide Web. Now even my cat has its own page."

Bill Clinton, 42nd president of the United States

As I design and develop Web sites for my clients, I am usually asked if their Web site will be number one in all major search engines, such as Google™, Yahoo!®, and MSN®. Obviously, the ultimate goal we strive to achieve in all cases is to be number one, but the reality is quite different so that the answer is not simple. Being number one is a combination of many factors that start with Web site design and use an effective Web site marketing strategy to maximize chance for high rankings, increased revenues, and Web site traffic, while spending very little money.

Seriously, the truth is that there is no secret formula to obtaining the highest possible search-engine rankings. If there were, everyone would be number one!

In my book *How to Use the Internet to Advertise, Promote, and Market Your Business or Web site with Little or No Money,* I revealed design techniques and marketing tools you can implement for free or with little investment to achieve the best possible search-engine rankings, increase Web site functionality and visibility in all the major search engines. You will find a wealth of resources for your online success in my book.

In this book, we will discuss the often mysterious and misunderstood world of Pay Per Click (PPC) Advertising, which is simply a marketing and advertising technique that allows you to place ads on Web sites and major search-engines results pages, usually for free. We will discuss all aspects of the PPC marketing campaign, including all the relevant methodology to ensure your campaign gets the maximum results for the money.

In the case of PPC advertising, you simply pay for the "clicks." A click occurs when a Web site browser sees your ad and clicks on it. Typically, your Web site opens where you hope the person will buy a product from you. You pay for that "click," based on a pre-determined dollar amount per click (cost per click), whether that "click" results in a sale on your Web site or not. You are simply paying for the ad and the resulting traffic that is generated through the ad to your Web site. There is no guarantee that PPC advertising campaigns will increase sales or revenue. Therefore, this book will maximize your potential for success by taking you through each step of the process.

Who Can Use This Book?

This book is for anyone who has a Web site, is considering developing a Web site, companies with an established online presence that wish to expand their marketing campaigns, the small business, large business, and sole proprietor. In short, it is for you if you are interested in making money, increasing Web site traffic, driving up revenue, and improving your own or your organization's financial posture. This book goes well beyond the basics of PPC marketing and provides you with the essentials of marketing, search-engine optimization, PPC marketing, and other highly successful revenue generating programs.

How This Book Is Organized

We will provide you with the following:

- **History of Online Marketing** — This is a brief history of the evolution of online marketing and the different types of campaigns/marketing strategies employed by Web site operators to promote their business through search engines, free marketing, and PPC marketing programs, and how each of them — or all of them — may be the right solution for your online business.

- **What is PPC advertising?** — This is a general overview of PPC advertising, how it works, how it compares to other marketing techniques, and how to design a PPC campaign for maximum returns. This chapter will include an in-depth introduction to PPC, a comparison to other marketing techniques, and a walkthrough from start to finish to show you how to increase your Web site traffic by 1,000 percent or more. In addition, we will discuss what happens when a visitor clicks on an ad, how it is tracked, and how the click can generate Web site traffic and increased revenue.

- **Search-Engine Optimization** — To get the most of out your Web site marketing campaigns, you need to ensure your Web site is optimized for search engines. I will guide you to design your site for maximum search-engine optimization. I will arm you with industry proven tips and tricks to garner the most from site visitors, increasing revenues and improving Web site design effectiveness. I will also provide detailed instructions about how to improve site design to maximize revenue in conjunction with PPC advertising campaigns.

- **How to Generate Web Site Traffic** — I will provide you with tips and tricks to generate Web site traffic, increase visibility in search engines, and improve Web site rankings in all major search engines. These techniques include all areas of site design, META tags, and page content relative to keyword ranking effectiveness. They will dramatically improve your search-engine rankings and ensure that your marketing campaigns are as cost-effective as possible, while returning the best possible results.

- **How to Choose Effective Keywords and Key Phrases and Develop a Budget for Your PPC Advertising Campaign** — This is the most neglected area in developing a PPC campaign. I will include instructions for using available tools to evaluate keywords, effectiveness, and pricing schemes for maximum keyword cost per click effectiveness — within your ad budget.

- **Google™ AdWords** — I will provide you with a comprehensive introduction to all components of Google™ PPC applications, including detailed set up, campaign design, and management of Google™ campaigns. We will delve into Google™ advertising campaigns to reveal a multitude of proven tips and secrets for maximizing the effectiveness of PPC campaigns using Google™. After you finish this chapter, you will be ready to launch your own Google™ AdWords campaign.

- **Yahoo!® Search Marketing** — I will provide you with a comprehensive introduction to all components of Yahoo!® Search Marketing, including detailed setup, campaign design, and management of Yahoo!® Search Marketing campaigns. We will explore Yahoo!® Search Marketing ad campaigns. When you finish this chapter, you will have all the tools and skills to launch your own Yahoo!® Search-Engine Marketing campaign.

- **Microsoft® adCenter, Multi-Tier, and other PPC Providers** — I will provide you with a comprehensive introduction to the newly released Microsoft® adCenter PPC program, the biggest threat to both Google™ AdWords and Yahoo!® Search Marketing. We will also look at other commercially available PPC applications as we discuss bid management to ensure you have an understanding of the variety of PPC options available to you.

- **How to Identify and Combat Fraud** — This is a comprehensive guide to help you understand fraud, identify it, combat it, and preserve the integrity and financial stability of your PPC campaign. Fraud is the number one problem facing PPC marketing campaigns, and I will show you how to combat and defeat it.

- **Increase Profits with Google™ AdSense** — An introduction to Google™'s AdSense program is another opportunity for you to generate income by allowing other advertisers' PPC ads to be placed on your Web site. This program is an excellent tool to generate revenue at no cost! When you complete this chapter, you can start earning Google™ AdSense revenue in less than five minutes!

- **How to Increase Sales with Affiliate Marketing Campaigns** — Affiliate marketing campaigns can be highly effective tools to increase sales and product visibility and generate tremendous revenue. I will provide you with a comprehensive introduction to Affiliate Marketing Campaigns as part of an effective marketing campaign portfolio in conjunction with PPC programs all designed to sell more products, generate more Web site traffic, and increase your sales revenues.

- **eBay Storefronts and Marketing Campaigns** — eBay is for real. It is not just a place to buy and sell your garage sale leftovers. A viable marketing solution, it reaches millions of site visitors daily. I will provide you with a comprehensive introduction to eBay Marketing Campaigns, eBay Stores, and using eBay to increase Web site sales, generate Web site traffic, and generate additional revenue.

- **Case Studies** — Do not just take my word for it that PPC marketing and search-engine optimization can fuel an enormous increase in online sales, generate substantial Web site traffic, and increase your potential customer base. Read about others who ventured into the PPC marketing and search-engine optimization world and succeeded!

- **Hints, Tips, and Advice from the Experts Who Do It Every Day** — We have asked the industry experts to provide us with their best hints, tips, and advice, and have compiled them for you in one simple-to-navigate chapter. Armed with this information, you have the most recent advice from the best of the best!

I will provide you with the tools and knowledge to unlock the secrets of PPC advertising and enable you to use to the Internet to its fullest potential to promote, advertise, and market your business in a cost-effective campaign designed to increase revenue. The Internet is the ultimate marketing tool — giving you immediate access to billions of people worldwide — and by implementing marketing campaigns such as PPC, you will benefit from search-engine technology where your customers are actively being fed links back to your Web site. After reading this book and applying its principles and techniques, you will empower your business and business Web site to operate a cost-effective and highly successful marketing campaign, ensuring the maximum return on investment through the PPC program.

You will have all the tools and knowledge that you need to take to maximize and harness the power of the Internet to promote and market your business and products through PPC advertising, as well as the formulas for success in developing your Web site strategy, design philosophy, search-engine optimization, and alternative marketing strategies. If you follow the guiding principles in this book — you _will_ be successful!

> _"Give a person a fish and you feed them for a day; teach that person to use the Internet and they won't bother you for weeks."_

—Unknown

PPC advertising, as well as every other topic in this book, can be exclusively designed, implemented, and managed by _you!_

You do not need to be a professional Web designer or hire an expensive marketing firm to promote and market your online business! We tell you the secrets, the time-tested methodology, and the tricks of the trade to ensure that your site ranks at the top of the search engines in conjunction with a highly effective PPC advertising campaign. However, if you prefer to seek professional assistance, we provide a reference list of the industry leaders.

The concepts in this book are simple. They are presented to help you reach your potential customers in a way that you could not previously. In fact, PPC allows your potential customers to seek you out through no cost ad placements on Web sites and in search engines' results. We designed this book for the small business that does not have an information technology or Web design staff and is limited on technology budget and knowledge. If you are the owner, proprietor, or manager of a traditional brick and mortar or online business, you need to implement successful marketing campaigns such as PPC advertising to expand your customer sales base. PPC advertising is a low-cost, high yield alternative to traditional marketing campaigns. You will save thousands of dollars compared with traditional marketing programs such as flyers, postcards, or other forms of offline or postal advertising. These antiquated methods only reach a small customer base, are costly to produce and distribute, and typically fail to generate the return to break even.

The key principle to remember with PPC advertising is you are not paying for the ad space or ad listing at all. You are not paying up front fees with no promise of a return. You are only paying for clicks on your ads; therefore, it is the most effective means of online marketing to draw thousands of potential new customers to your Web site every day!

History and Understanding of Online Marketing

Online marketing schemes have been around since the creation of the World Wide Web. As Web sites became online businesses targeting increased revenues for traditional brick and mortar business, the prominence of online marketing became a dominant force in the industry. Today literally thousands of businesses exist solely on the Internet and do not maintain a traditional retail business. Therefore, online marketing, PPC campaigns, and other enterprising marketing schemes have become increasingly prevalent and extraordinarily competitive. New online businesses emerge and grab big pieces of the available market share every day! To understand PPC advertising campaigns, it is important to understand the history of online marketing and the variety of Web-based marketing techniques deployed in the past and present.

> *"The growth of Internet advertising since its 1994 birth has been truly phenomenal. What started out with banners as bland and common as roadside billboards has exploded into a rich media interactive environment that may soon rival the rabbit hole in Alice in Wonderland."*
> *— Just A Click Away: Advertising on the Internet*

Marketing and advertising a traditional brick and mortar business is a costly venture. Postage and mailing costs are high. Return rates on mailings are typically a dismal 1 percent of the total mailing or less! More than 200 million Americans went online and nearly one billion people worldwide used the Internet in 2005. Internet access grew more than 107 percent in 2005 in the United States and more than 165 percent worldwide. The facts speak for themselves as to the potential marketplace on the Internet:

1. The number of online users will reach 231 million in 2009, representing 75 percent of the total U.S. population (© March 2004 Jupiter Research).

2. Online classified spending will nearly double in the next five years... from $1.9 billion in 2004 to $3.7 billion in 2009 (© September 2004 Jupiter Research).

3. On average, Americans spend 14 hours online each month (© Nielsen//NetRatings, February 2005).

4. The preferred research tool of big-ticket purchases is the Internet (© March 2005 Jupiter Research).

According to Internet World Stats, **www.Internetworldstats.com**, worldwide growth on the Internet ballooned a staggering 189 percent between 2000 and 2005, reflecting that the world population is catching up with the phenomenal growth in the United States. Growth in the Middle East has exploded by nearly 500 percent during this same period!

Internet Marketing

According to Wikipedia (**www.wikipedia.com**), Internet marketing is a "component of electronic commerce. Internet marketing can include information management, public relations, customer service, and sales. Electronic commerce and Internet marketing have become popular as Internet access is more widely available and used. More than one third of consumers who have Internet access in their homes report using the Internet to make purchases."

In the early 1990s, Internet marketing was a new frontier in advertising and sales. Typically, commercial Web sites were nothing more than a corporate public relations presence with generalized information about a company and its products and services. As technology improved and understanding of the Hyper Text Markup Language (HTML) grew, the predominant language for the creation of Web sites improved, commercial Web sites evolved into online brochures and catalogs of corporate product lines. They were designed to allow a potential

WORLD INTERNET USAGE AND POPULATION STATISTICS

World Regions	Population (2006 Est.)	Population Percent of World	Internet Usage, Latest Data	Percent Population (Penetration)	Usage Percent of World	Usage Growth 2000–2005
Africa	915,210,928	14.1 percent	23,649,000	2.6 percent	2.3 percent	423.9 percent
Asia	3,667,774,066	56.4 percent	380,400,713	10.4 percent	36.5 percent	232.8 percent
Europe	807,289,020	12.4 percent	294,101,844	36.4 percent	28.2 percent	179.8 percent
Middle East	190,084,161	2.9 percent	18,203,500	9.6 percent	1.7 percent	454.2 percent
North America	331,473,276	5.1 percent	227,470,713	68.6 percent	21.8 percent	110.4 percent
Latin America/Caribbean	553,908,632	8.5 percent	79,962,809	14.7 percent	7.8 percent	350.5 percent
Oceania / Australia	33,956,977	0.5 percent	17,872,707	52.6 percent	1.7 percent	134.6 percent
WORLD TOTAL	6,499,697,060	100.0 percent	1,043,104,886	16.0 percent	100.0 percent	189.0 percent

NOTES: (1) Internet Usage and World Population Statistics were updated for June 30, 2006. (2) Demographic (population) numbers are based on data contained in the World-Gazetteer Web site. (3) Internet usage information comes from data published by Nielsen//NetRatings, by the International Telecommunications Union, by local NICs, and other reliable sources. (4) For definitions, disclaimer, and navigation help, see the Site Surfing Guide. (5) Information from this site may be cited, giving due credit and establishing an active link back to (**www.Internetworldstats.com**). © Copyright 2006, Miniwatts Marketing Group. All rights reserved worldwide.

customer to do research and explore the products online, and then go to the brick and mortar retail outlet or place a phone order to the company. Since there was no security available online for processing credit cards, deployment of online sales was minimal.

Then thousands of companies began to allow customers to place credit card orders using basic HTML order forms, which captured the unencrypted credit card information, recklessly sending potentially harmful personal financial information throughout the Internet. As they became aware of credit card fraud and theft, savvy Web customers stopped placing credit card orders online.

The development of encryption methods and secure site technology changed everything. Data could be captured securely and transmitted over the Internet in an encrypted format to protect data online. Since the development of encryption technology, online purchasing has exploded and is expected to grow exponentially in the future. As a result, small startup companies like Amazon.com have grown into online sales powerhouses.

Atlantic Publishing Company (**www.atlantic-pub.com**) is a classic example of how the Internet has affected business and marketing operations. In the mid-1990s, Atlantic Publishing Company embraced the Internet with a very basic Web site, featuring a full list of their product lines, with pricing and ordering information. The Web site included an online order form that required users to enter the items they wanted manually, calculate the item costs and totals manually, and send the order via a secure Web page to corporate headquarters for processing.

Today, Atlantic Publishing Company features the latest in Web sites, boasting a full featured shopping cart, secure online order processing, advanced search capabilities, and simplified navigation. The Internet transformed them from a catalog-based business into an online publishing powerhouse, producing more than 50 original publications in 2006 on a wide-range of topics including Food Service, Restaurant Management, Real Estate, Human Resources, Customer Service, Internet Sales and Marketing, and Personal Finance.

"The Internet is becoming the town square for the global village of tomorrow."
— Bill Gates

Internet Advertising

Advertising may be defined as any paid form of communication about an organization and its products and services by an identified and typically paid sponsor. As we have previously discussed, online marketing and advertising campaigns were designed to replicate existing advertising, which was designed for traditional advertising outlets including print media (newspapers, books, and magazines), as well as multi-media advertising (television and radio). With expansion of the Internet and realization of the potential impact on customer sales base and revenues, online advertising was born.

By 2007, online advertising and marketing has matured and become refined. We have moved past the dynamic evolution of online advertising and are now tweaking existing advertising techniques to garner the most out of a company's marketing investment. Technology, population growth, and the increasing number of households with broadband Internet access have pushed advances in technology in the advertising world, generating billions of dollars in sales annually. Online advertising is overtaking traditional means of advertising.

The potential for developing highly innovative and unique ads that attract potential customers is practically limitless. As the Internet grew in popularity, the money spent on online advertising increased dramatically, as did the desire to develop cost-effective advertising methods that promised a high return for low investment.

Gizmag.com (**www.gizmag.com**) reported a 26 percent growth of advertising revenues for the first six months of 2005 over the first half of 2004. Internet advertising revenues for the first six months of 2005 were about $5.8 billion, setting a new record. Advertising money targeting ads through search-engines accounts for about $4 in every $10 spent, and double that of traditional advertising (20 percent). They also report that the top 10 ranked Web sites in any search results rake in 74 percent of all revenue, while the Top 25 take in 87 percent and the top 50 take in a whopping 96 percent of all Internet advertising revenue. What is the lesson here? Investing on the Internet has the potential for a tremendous return on your investment. Statistics support the theory that those sites that consistently rank in the top 100 search-engine rankings get the majority of the revenue. This is one of the most important facts to consider when deploying a PPC marketing and advertising campaign since your ads through major Web portals and search engines such as Google™ and Yahoo place your ad with the top search-engine results, based on your keyword, ad placement, and financial investment.

Types of Online Ads

Three major areas that continue to own the majority of the market share are: Paid search ad (PPC), Banner Ads, and Classified ads.

We will discuss each of these in this book but will concentrate on PPC advertising to ensure that you get the most return from your investment in PPC advertising. Additionally, we will discuss a variety of other advertising methods for use in conjunction with your PPC campaign to help promote your online business.

DoubleClick (**www.doubleclick.com**) is a leading provider of solutions for advertising agencies, marketers, and Web publishers to plan, execute, and analyze their marketing programs. DoubleClick's marketing solutions—online advertising, search-engine marketing, affiliate marketing, e-mail marketing, database marketing, data management, and marketing resource management—help clients yield the highest return on their marketing dollar. In addition, the company's marketing analysis tools help clients measure performance within and across channels. We have found DoubleClick to be an invaluable resource for developing online marketing and advertising solutions.

In 2005, DoubleClick produced *1994–2004 The Decade in Advertising*. To learn more about DoubleClick's many free market-education research reports, visit DoubleClick's Knowledge Central at **http://doubleclick.com/knowledge**. To stay up to date on all the new research which DoubleClick publishes, subscribe to their outstanding e-mail newsletter, The Smart Marketing Report, at (**http://www. doubleclick.com/us/knowledge_central/newsletter_archive/**).

Understanding Banner Advertising

Banner advertising is simply a form of online advertising in which Web developers imbed an ad into the HTML code of a Web page. The idea is that the banner ad will catch the attention of Web site visitors and they will click on the ad to get more information about the products or services advertised. When clicked, the banner ad will take the Web browser to the Web site operated by the advertiser. A banner ad can be created in a variety of formats such as .GIF, .JPG or .PNG. Banner ads can be static images, or they can employ a variety of scripting code, Java, or other advanced techniques such as animated GIFs or rollover images to create rotating banner ads that change every few seconds. Over the past five years, Shockwave and Macromedia Flash technology have become increasingly popular for incorporating animation, sound, and action to banner ads. Banner ads are created in a variety of shapes and sizes depending on the site content and design and are designed to appear unobtrusively in the "white" space available in a traditionally designed Web page.

When a page is loaded into a Web browser such as Microsoft® Internet Explorer or Mozilla Firefox, the banner is loaded onto the page, creating what is called an "impression," which simply means that the Web page containing the ad was loaded and possibly seen by someone browsing that Web site. Impressions are important to advertisers to track how many visitors loaded that particular page and banner ad during a set length of time. If the impression count is low, it is logical that the click-through rate, and subsequent sales will also be extremely low. When the Web site visitor clicks on the banner ad, the person is navigated to the Web site that is linked to by the banner ad, and the Web site is loaded into the browser. The process of a site visitor clicking on a banner ad with their mouse is commonly called a "click-through." Click-throughs are important to advertisers to track how many visitors actually clicked on a particular banner ad, and how many sales are generated by the banner ad in a set time. Unfortunately, high click-through rates do not guarantee high sales. We will discuss many techniques about how to design your Web site properly to maximize your search-engine optimization. Banner ads can be static (imbedded within the actual HTML page by the Web marketing) or may be "served" through a central server, which enables advertisers to display a wide variety of banner ads on thousands of Web sites with minimal effort.

As we have already discussed, most banner ads currently work on a per-click system, where the advertiser pays for each click on the banner ad, regardless of whether that click results in a sale. Originally, advertisers simply paid for the ad space on a Web site, usually for a preset period, such as a week or month, and hoped that someone would see the banner ad and click on it to visit their Web site. Banner advertising is typically a very low cost investment per click usually under ten cents. The banner provider or hosting company then bills the advertising on a pre-determined basis such as monthly. The key difference between banner advertising and PPC advertising is that banner ads are placed within the content of Web pages, while PPC advertising is not image based, and may be dynamically generated based on a search results.

Banner Advertising was extremely popular in the 1990s and early 2000s, and is still popular today; however, it is less effective and popular than other advertising techniques, such as PPC advertising. Banner advertising aims to inform potential customers or consumers about the products or services offered by the advertiser, just like traditional print advertising; however, they offer the advantage of allowing advertisers to track individual statistics and performance at a level not possible with print media advertising.

When banner ads were originally created, they were highly successful; however, as Web surfers became Web savvy, banner ads, popup ads, and other ads were seen as annoying and often distracting from the actual Web site content. It was common to have a Web page loaded with hundreds of banner ads or Web sites that were only placeholders for hundreds of banner ads. Today the standard has improved dramatically, and you typically will not find more than one or two unobtrusive banner ads on any Web page. Additionally, Web browsers such as Microsoft®'s Internet Explorer and Mozilla's Firefox contain built-in pop-up blockers designed to suppress many banner ads.

"Internet advertising is without question taking share from the other media at this time and for good reason — marketers have figured out that online advertising is often the most cost-effective medium for influencing both branding and sales results."
— Greg Stuart, President of Interactive Advertising Bureau

The Difference Between Static Versus Dynamic

In the early days of Web site development, Web sites were "static" in content and were easy to build and maintain, but did not offer any "interactive" type of experience. Internet advertising was primarily limited to static server-based banner advertising served up to static Web pages. The development of database driven Web sites created an entirely new experience for Web site visitors, enabling them to enter data into a Web site and receiving dynamically generated content, based on their query. An example of this is **www.Google.com** or **www.tbo.com/classifieds/** which enable the site visitor to search on any topic they wish, based on their query.

The development of Web portals, such as **www.yahoo.com** and **www.MSN.com**, enabled Web visitors to personalize their Web browsing experience. Personalization allows a Web site visitor to enter information such as name, age, zip code, and other personal preferences to deliver customized Web content based on individual preferences. More advanced Web sites, such as **www.amazon.com**, can actually make recommendations to site visitors based on their profile and preferences, thereby possibly increasing sales and revenue.

With most users today surfing the Web on high-speed broadband, Web site developers have been developing what is known as "rich media." Rich media is ads geared towards high-speed Internet browsers and can display video, audio, music, animations, and special effects. The addition of flashy advertising to interactivity has completed the online experiences where advertisers receive interactive and often entertaining ads disguised as music videos, games, and other interactive content, all with the ultimate goal of producing increased Web site traffic and Internet sales. Although Rich media may be the banner ad of the future, it still has quite a way to go to replace traditional banner advertising.

The Web site, **www.e-commercetimes.com**, recently reported that in figures released by Nielsen for the week ending August 6, 2006, rich media ads accounted for only 1.2 percent of the roughly 57.6 million impressions delivered during the period. At the top of the list for the time frame were compound image/text ads with more than 16 million impressions (27.9 percent), followed by sponsored search links with 14.6 million impressions (25.3 percent), standard GIF/JPG with 13.6 million impressions (23.7 percent), and Flash ads with 12.8 million (22 percent). However, it is estimated that 39 percent of Internet ad spending is expected to be on rich media.

Rich media has evolved in the past year into the recycling of television ads and incorporating full TV commercials onto the Internet. Floating and expanding banners are increasingly popular but frustrating to the

Web site visitor. Floating and expanding ads use motion and appear to float across the screen, blocking the view of the actual Web site content, often requiring a click to close the ad. However, most are based on a time interval to disappear. Sound imbedded in banner advertising is becoming increasingly visible, where sound bites are launched with a Web site as an additional attempt to attract site visitors to click on the specific Web site banner. podcasts, blogs, and RSS broadcasts have become extremely popular in recent years. It is anticipated that more than 12 million Americans will access podcasts alone in 2006. Large advertisers such as Best Buy, Acura, and Volvo are already sponsoring podcasts. Mobile or cellular marketing advertising is growing as the population increases the use of Ipods, MP3 players, cell phones, Blackberries, and Trios. Permission based advertising, or "opt-in," continues to grow in popularity, despite strict anti-spam laws in the United States. The effective use of e-mail with imbedded banner ads or HTML-based advertising allows you to target specific demographic groups to promote products they said they want.

> *"No one bill will cure the problem of spam. It will take a combined effort of legislation, litigation, enforcement, customer education, and technology solutions."*
>
> *—David Baker*

E-mail Advertising Versus Spam

We have provided you with a brief history of online advertising, but we cannot leave out the most controversial method of online advertising: e-mail. E-mail campaigns are used to send out ads or promotions to a large audience or consumer group. The obvious advantage of this type of ad is that you deliver the ad to the inbox of the recipient, instead of waiting and hoping they navigate to your Web site. Unfortunately, e-mail advertising is an extremely volatile subject, as many feel that the unwarranted distribution of bulk e-mail is a violation of their rights, and an illegal invasion of privacy. Thus, the dilemma for online advertisers is how to use e-mail campaigns legally without offending potential customers, eroding their customer base or facing potential legal action.

The key difference between operating legal permission-based e-mail campaigns and spam is the use of permission-based or "opt-in" e-mail lists. Spam or junk e-mail is e-mail that goes to one or more recipients who did not request it. The CAN-SPAM Act of 2003 (Controlling the Assault of Non-Solicited Pornography and Marketing Act) establishes requirements for those who send commercial e-mail, spells out penalties for spammers and companies whose products are advertised in spam if they violate the law, and gives consumers the right to ask e-mailers to stop spamming them. The law, which became effective January 1, 2004, covers e-mail whose primary purpose is advertising or promoting a commercial product or service, including content on a Web site. A "transactional or relationship message" e-mail that facilitates an agreed-upon transaction or updates a customer in an existing business relationship may not contain false or misleading routing information, but otherwise is exempt from most provisions of the CAN-SPAM Act according to the Federal Trade Commission.

The Federal Trade Commission (FTC), the nation's consumer protection agency, is authorized to enforce the CAN-SPAM Act. CAN-SPAM also gives the Department of Justice (DOJ) the authority to enforce its criminal sanctions. Other federal and state agencies can enforce the law against organizations under their jurisdiction, and companies that provide Internet access may sue violators as well.

The CAN-SPAM Act:

- **Bans false or misleading header information.** Your e-mails' "from," "to," and routing information—including the originating domain name and e-mail address—must be accurate and identify the person who initiated the e-mail.

- **Prohibits deceptive subject lines.** The subject line cannot mislead the recipient about the contents or subject matter of the message.

- **Requires that your e-mail give recipients an opt-out method.** You must provide a return e-mail address or another Internet-based response mechanism that allows a recipient to ask you not to send future e-mail messages to that e-mail address, and you must honor the requests. You may create a "menu" of choices to allow a recipient to opt out of certain types of messages, but you must include the option to end any commercial messages from the sender. Any opt-out mechanism you offer must be able to process opt-out requests for at least 30 days after you send your commercial e-mail. When you receive an opt-out request, the law gives you 10 business days to stop sending e-mail to the requestor's e-mail address. You cannot help another entity send e-mail to that address, or have another entity send e-mail on your behalf to that address. Finally, it is illegal for you to sell or transfer the e-mail addresses of people who choose not to receive your e-mail, even in the form of a mailing list, unless you transfer the addresses so another entity can comply with the law.

- **Requires that commercial e-mail be identified as an ad and include the sender's valid physical postal address.** Your message must contain clear and conspicuous notice that it is an ad or solicitation and that the recipient can opt out of receiving further commercial e-mail from you. It also must include your valid physical postal address.

Penalties for each violation of the CAN-SPAM Act are subject to fines of up to $11,000. Deceptive commercial e-mail also is subject to laws banning false or misleading advertising. Additional fines are provided for commercial e-mailers who not only violate the rules described above, but also:

- "Harvest" e-mail addresses from Web sites or Web services that have published a notice prohibiting the transfer of e-mail addresses for sending e-mail.

- Generate e-mail addresses using a "dictionary attack"—combining names, letters, or numbers into multiple permutations.

- Use scripts or other automated ways to register for multiple e-mail or user accounts to send commercial e-mail.

- Relay e-mails through a computer or network without permission—for example, by taking advantage of open relays or open proxies without authorization.

The law allows the DOJ to seek criminal penalties, including imprisonment, for commercial e-mailers who do—or conspire to:

- Use another computer without authorization and send commercial e-mail from or through it.

- Use a computer to relay or retransmit multiple commercial e-mail messages to deceive or mislead recipients or an Internet access service about the origin of the message.

- Falsify header information in multiple e-mail messages and initiate the transmission of such messages.

- Register for multiple e-mail accounts or domain names using information that falsifies the identity of the actual registrant.

- Misrepresent themselves as owners of multiple Internet Protocol addresses that are used to send commercial e-mail messages.

The FTC has issued additional rules under the CAN-SPAM Act involving the required labeling of sexually explicit commercial e-mail and the criteria for determining "the primary purpose" of a commercial e-mail. See the FTC Web site at (**www.ftc.gov/spam**) for updates on implementation of the CAN-SPAM Act. Source: Federal Trade Commission (FTC).

Most recipients of bulk e-mail, spam, or unsolicited ads view them as unwelcome, unpleasant, or offensive. However, many mailing lists deliver solicited (opt-in) useful information to recipients based on subjects that they have given their permission to companies to add their e-mail address to bulk mailing lists. The key to using e-mail as a tool for marketing or advertising is to build your customer lists using opt-in methods (or double-opt in) to ensure that your e-mail lists comply with the requirements of the CAN-SPAM Act. Our recommended permission-based application for the creation and distribution of e-mail ads and management of permission based/opt-in mailing listing is Topica, who may be found online at **www.topica.com**.

According to **Wikipedia.com**, "The California legislature found that spam cost U.S. organizations alone more than $10 billion in 2004, including lost productivity and the additional equipment, software, and manpower needed to combat the problem. Spam's direct effects include the consumption of computer and network resources, and the cost in human time and attention of dismissing unwanted messages. In addition, spam has costs stemming from the kinds of messages sent, from the ways spammers send them, and from the race between spammers and those who try to stop or control spam. In addition, there are the opportunity cost of those who forgo the use of spam-afflicted systems. There are the direct costs, as well as the indirect costs borne by the victims — both those related to the spamming itself and to other crimes that usually accompany it such as financial theft, identity theft, data and intellectual property theft, virus, and other infection, child pornography, fraud, and deceptive marketing."

PPC advertising is thought to be the most efficient and effective method of online advertising today — enabling you to promote your business quickly online in a cost-effective program. Additionally, it is one of the secrets to get your Web site listed at the top of major search engines without having to do any Web site search-engine optimization. (We do think that search-engine optimization is critical to the success of your advertising and marketing campaign and will give you the tools to complete it successfully later in this book.)

PPC is the most successful online advertising technique now and for the foreseeable future, and the concept could not be simpler. Advertisers bid on keywords and promise to pay a certain amount of money each time someone clicks on their ad. The ad pops up in response to a search-engine query performed by a Web site surfer and is displayed because it is relevant to the search query.

With the history we have provided in online marketing and advertising, you should have a good understanding of the variety of ad campaigns in existence, as well as a brief history of how we got to PPC advertising.

Introduction to PPC Advertising

The key concept you need to understand regarding PPC advertising is that, unlike other paid advertising campaigns where you pay for the campaign itself in hopes of generating customers and revenues, you are not paying for any guarantees or promises of sales, Web site traffic, or increased revenue. You are not paying for traditional advertising campaigns hoping for a 1–2 percent return on your investment, and you are not paying for placing a banner ad on a Web site in the hope that someone will see it, is interested in it, and clicks on it. Remember, banner advertising was the largest kind of advertising on the Internet, and it still holds a significant market share. However, the main disadvantage of banner advertising is that the ads are imbedded within pages, and you have to rely on a Web designer to put your banner ad on a page that has similar or complementary content, and rotate it to keep it dynamic, relevant, and appealing. A banner ad for dog food will likely not do well if it is placed on a Web site that talks about computer repairs. Additionally, banner advertising turns off many Web surfers, and not only will they discount the ad, but typically the entire Web site with it. Enter the beauty of PPC advertising! You do not pay to have your ad loaded on a Web page, you do not pay to have your ad listed at the top of search engines, and you ONLY pay for results! In other words, PPC advertising is entirely no cost (minus minimal setup costs), even if your ad is viewed by millions of Web site visitors.

"Forget the schemes and empty promises – there is only one way to guarantee your Web site will get visibility at the top of all major search engines – and it is through hard work combined with PPC advertising."

— Bruce Brown

You will pay only when someone actually "clicks" on your ad. At that point, your PPC company charges your account, based on a formula price per keyword (which we will discuss in later chapters), and the person will be navigated to the Web page on your Web site which you preset when you created your PPC ad.

Keep in mind that the "click" in no way guarantees you any sales (or conversions). It merely means that someone has clicked on your ad. Do not underestimate the importance of having a user-friendly, information rich Web site to capture the attention of the site visitor and close the deal! Not all PPC campaigns must result in a purchase — many advertisers use PPC advertising to sell products, but many more use them to sell services, promotional material, news releases, or draw visitors to their Web sites.

Goto.com started PPC advertising in 1998. It eventually become **Overture.com** and was then purchased by Yahoo. The original concept was that anyone with a brick and mortar or online business could manage and determine their own search-engine ranking based on pre-selected keywords and how much money they were willing to pay for the resultant "click" on their ad.

PPC advertising is expected to exceed $15 Billion in 2007 and will continue to grow at a staggering 40 percent-plus annually! We will spend significant portions of this book walking you through the major players in the PPC market. Google™ (**www.Google™.com**) is clearly the industry leader in terms of market share, but there are many players such as Yahoo.com (**www.yahoo.com**) and we will spend considerable time with each in later chapters of this book.

You, as an advertiser, Web site owner, or corporate manager, will admire the simplicity and functionality of PPC advertising, which allows you to have significant control over your campaign. Before you forge the path towards implementing a PPC marketing plan, it is critical to understand PPC advertising and develop strategies to design an effective campaign, optimize and monitor ad performance, and employ sound business principles in your campaign. One of the success factors in creating and managing a PPC campaign is the effective selection and use of keyword and advanced statistical reporting tools from the PPC provider, as well as your Web hosting company. To ensure the potential for success of a PPC campaign, you must choose the most effective keywords; design an effective, captivating ad; and have a well-designed, information rich Web site with easy navigation.

PPC Advertising Walk Through

You, as the advertiser, pay a rate you specify for every visitor who clicks through from the search-engine site to your Web site. Every keyword has a "bid" price, depending on the popularity of the keyword in search engines. You set your own budget and financial limitations, and you are done. Here is a step by step walkthrough:

- You, as the advertiser, join a PPC program and with a credit card put money on your account to get started.

- You create your ad as you want it to appear with your own selected keywords you wish to target.

- Based on the keyword value, you set how much you are willing to spend on each keyword. Obviously, the more popular keywords are more costly per click than the less popular ones.

- Upon completion—your ad is now ready to appear in search engines.

- When someone searches through a search engine, such as **www.Google.com** by using one of your keywords, the ad is matched to the keyword query and the ad is displayed in the search engine results.

- If the person "clicks" on your ad, they are navigated to your Web site and you are "charged" for the click.

The search engine will return a rank-ordered list of the most popular Web sites matching your search criteria, and it may display your ad if it also matches the search criteria and keyword. Remember, one of the benefits of PPC advertising is that your ad will be placed right up there with the top ranked Web sites in your search category.

Throughout this book, we will use Profit Strategies and Solutions, Inc., (**www.restaurantprofits.com**) as one of our case studies. Profit Strategies and Solutions is a nationally recognized, independent food service profit strategies firm, dedicated to the successful conceptualization and implementation of maximizing the profits of food service companies.

Located in Lake Oswego, Oregon, their team of restaurant consultants, restaurant accountants, and food service experts help their clients realize their maximum profit potential. Profit Strategies and Solutions is a recognized food service consulting firm that helps their clients maximize profits through the implementation of ChefTec Recipe

Software and Restaurant Consulting Services. Profit Strategies and Solutions works to increase the profitability of restaurant businesses because they understand the unique challenges and pitfalls associated with the hospitality industry. Their implementation saves the end user upwards of 70 hours of their time initially entering and creating customized databases for food and alcohol recipe and inventory control.

In general, the rules for most PPC search-engine applications operate on the same principle and rule: the advertiser with the highest bid gets top billing in the search engine return. It is a combination of experience, knowledge of the market, and some trial and error that lets you balance keywords and phrases to deliver optimal results.

I have dedicated an entire chapter of this book to choosing the most appropriate keywords to maximize the potential return on your ad. Additionally, I will recommend a variety of Web-based keyword suggestion applications to assist you with your ad creation.

PPC Benefits:

- PPC advertising is instantaneous and easy to implement.

- PPC advertising results are clearly measurable.

- PPC advertising is cost effective in comparison to other types of traditional and online advertising programs.

- PPC advertising is for both large and small businesses.

- PPC advertising is ideal for testing out market response to new products or services.

- PPC advertising gives you full control over your budget. You can set systematic budgetary limits to minimize your financial risk and investment.

- PPC advertising is more effective than banner advertising.

- PPC advertising delivers a higher click-through rate than banner advertising.

- PPC ads are ideally placed with top search-engine results.

- PPC advertising is delivered only to your potential customers when they are actually searching on keywords related to your products or services contained in your PPC ad.

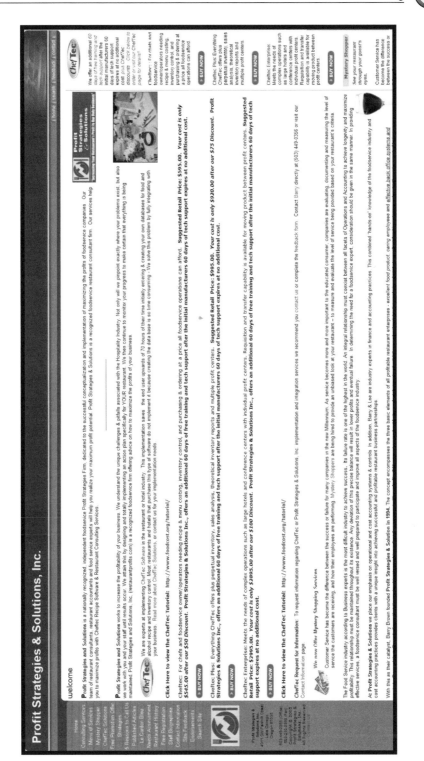

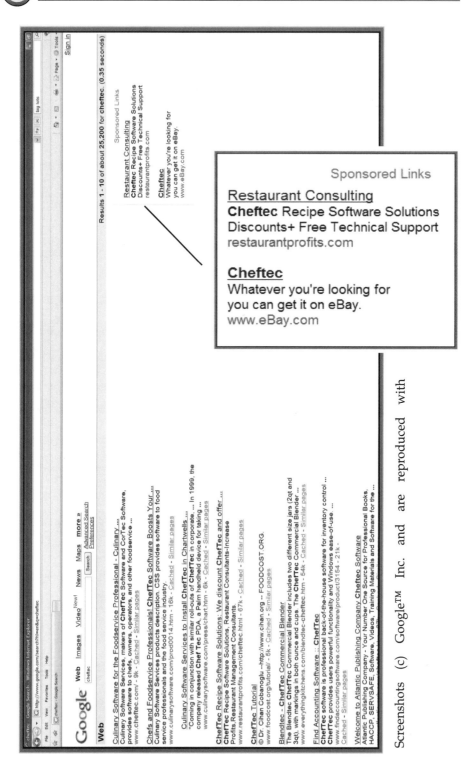

Screenshots (c) Google™ Inc. and are reproduced with

- PPC advertising is delivered based on keyword searches and it is delivered immediately, meaning the chances of turning one of those potential customers into an actual customer is dramatically increased!

- PPC advertising allows you do design your ads and place them in a prominent location on the Web site, as opposed to those flashy, annoying banner ads that turn off potential customers.

- PPC advertising can be delivered in search-engine results (which is the most common) or they can be delivered within the content of a Web page.

Since we are using Profit Strategies and Solutions, Inc (**www.restaurantprofits.com**) as our primary case study, we performed a search as a potential customer might on **Google.com** looking for "ChefTec." ChefTec software is professional back-of-the-house software for inventory control, recipe and menu costing, purchasing and ordering, and nutritional analysis. Innovative technology provides cost and time savings for all food service operations. ChefTec provides users powerful functionality and Windows ease-of-use. Integrated functions allow users to update prices with the touch of a button, track fluctuating food costs, keep accurate nutritional information on menu items, calculate bids using highest, lowest, or average price for inventory items, and more. We did search on the term "cheftec" and a screen shot of the results is on the previous page. You will notice in the search field is our search term of "cheftec." The top eight rankings in Google™ are listed along with "sponsored links" on the right hand side of the screen. You will notice the Number One sponsored search ad is from Profit Strategies and Solutions (**www.restaurantprofits.com**). This is an example of a PPC ad.

If I were to click on this ad, Profit Strategies and Solutions would be charged a fee for this "click."

You should also notice that Profit Strategies and Solutions is the number four ranked company in the Google™ search engine rankings (the top three are the manufacturer of ChefTec Software). The number eight ranked company is Atlantic Publishing Company (**www.atlantic-pub.com**), publisher of this book and publisher and distributor of a wide range of award-winning professional books and products relating to food service, restaurant management, hospitality, real estate, personal finance, and internet marketing.

You may have noticed also that there is one other PPC ad listed for **eBay.com** in the search-engine results from the previous pages. Interestingly, you will discover that sometimes PPC advertising may not deliver the results the Web site visitor expects or the results the advertiser wants

> **Cheftec**
> Whatever you're looking for you can get it on eBay.
> www.eBay.com

Screenshot (c) Google™ Inc. and is reproduced with permission.

to deliver. In this case, when you click on the PPC ad for "ChefTec" on eBay, you will get listings for "Chieftec," which is a manufacturer of computer cases. Regardless of whether the PPC ad is effective and promotes the product I was actually looking for (in this case it did not), the advertiser will still pay for the "click" that I used to navigate to their Web site.

When I click on the PPC ad for Profit Strategies and Solutions, I am properly navigated to their Web page that promotes the sale of ChefTec Solutions software. Profit Strategies and Solutions will be charged for that "click." It is important to note that if I click on the search engine link in the search results for Profit Strategies and Solutions, I am also brought directly to the Web page that promotes the sale of ChefTec Solutions software. Of course, Profit Strategies and Solutions is not charged for this click since this is not a paid advertising listing, but merely a search-engine results page. Remember, in this case the PPC ad is on the right hand side of the page, and the search-engine results links are completely free. It is worth noting that the search-engine results link for Atlantic Publishing Company also returns a link directly to the ChefTec sales page on their site (**www.atlantic-pub.com/cheftec.htm**), which typically means that both Web sites have effectively implemented search-engine optimization plans to ensure maximum visibility with relevant links in major search engines.

Content-Match PPC Advertising

As we have shown, PPC advertising can be delivered in search-engine results, or they can be delivered within the content of a Web page. The screen shot on the next page is an example of "content-match," meaning that your PPC ad is inserted among Web pages with similar content type. For example, Search Guild deals primarily with search-engine optimization, and the PPC ads are also related to the same subject.

Another primary benefit of a PPC campaign is that you have fully customizable advertising solutions in your toolbox. You can create dozens of separate PPC ads with different wording, based on different keywords, all within a single advertising campaign. Having a variety of ads offers tremendous flexibility to target a wide array of potential customer segments. It is a critical component of content-match, where delivery of PPC ads is based on a variety of keywords. However, keep in mind that you still pay per click, and an advertising campaign with a wide target group can quickly consume your marketing budget.

Cost of PPC Advertising

PPC advertising is limited by your advertising budget. You will know in advance how much you will pay per click, and most start out with a minimum price per click, such as $.10. The price can quickly escalate to more money, even as much as $100 per click, depending on the keyword.

The concept is simple — for example, you want to sell Atlantic Publishing Company's award-winning book *The Restaurant Manager's Handbook*, and decide to use the keyword phrase "restaurant management" in your pay-per-click ad. Restaurant management is a common topic, and there are many others who also want to use restaurant management as the keyword phrase in their PPC ads. All of us want to be the top ranked listing. Essentially, we "bid" with our competitors with the amount we are willing to pay for each click on our ad.

It may be cost prohibitive to be the top bidder, since your advertising budget will be consumed much quicker than if you were a number two or number three bidder. However, there are times when it is more critical to be the number one bidder, regardless of the financial impact. Your bid is the maximum amount you are willing to pay for the Web site visitor to click on your ad. Therefore, be careful about the amount you are willing to bid per click, as you may have to pay it! We will discuss bidding in detail later in this book.

Tips, Tricks, and Secrets for PPC Advertising

- Design ads so they target potential customers who are ready to buy — rarely will banner ads or PPC ads draw in the curious Web site browser and result in a sale.

- Ensure your ad is very specific in nature.

- Target one product for each ad if possible, instead of placing a generic ad that targets a large market segment.

- Make your ad link directly to the product page with a link to buy the product on that page, rather than linking to a generic page or the Web site home page.

- If your ads target a very specific product, you may see a reduction in actual clicks because your advertising segment is very narrow. However, those clicks are most likely extremely profitable since you are only getting clicks from individuals seeking information on your specific product. This means your advertising cost may actually be reduced while your sales go up!

- Use reputable PPC engines. If no one uses that search engine, how well do you think your PPC advertising campaign will do?

- Be willing to bid for a good position. If you are trying to save money and are willing to settle for the bottom of the bids, no one is going to see your ad.

- Bid enough to gain the exposure you need, but balance exposure to stretch your advertising budget. It is typically not worth the cost to have the number one bid, and it is often significantly less costly if you are in positions two through ten.

- Know how your favorite search-engine displays results — if the top 10 results are displayed after a search, you do not necessarily need to pay the extra money for the top bids. Most people scroll through the various PPC ads before clicking on the one that most closely matches their interests, allowing you to stretch your advertising budget.

- Being the number one listing on search engines may not be all it is cracked up to be! The top listing is the one that is clicked the most often, but is also has worst percentage of converting clicks into actual sales. Many "click happy" people click on the top listing without ever converting a sale. Those clicks will quickly eat up your advertising budget. You may have better luck by being below the number two listing, since you have the potential for better qualified clicks. Potential customers screen all the ads — not just the first one.

- Use the provided tracking tools to monitor performance and adjust keywords and bidding as necessary.

- Choose very specific keyword phrases and you will lower your costs while increasing the potential conversion rate. Choose multiple, highly targeted words or phrases instead of generic terms in an attempt to get tons of traffic. For example, use "Crystal River Florida Vacation Rental Home," instead of "Florida Rental".

- Expand your advertising campaign with other techniques such as Affiliate Marketing.

- Implement a sound search-engine optimization plan. (See the next chapter.)

- Use capital letters for each word in the Title and in the Description fields of your PPC ad.

- Use demographic targeting with your ads. If your intended audience is in the United States, there is no sense in allowing your PPC ad to be viewed elsewhere, eating up your advertising budget with worthless clicks.

- Use Ad Filtering, if available, to cut down on fraudulent clicks and to save your ad budget by blocking Web sites or regions you do not want your ad displayed on.

- Use Google™ Ad Targeting if you are trying to specify a geographic area, such as Washington, D.C.

- Use the Google™ Keyword Suggestion Tool (more details in the Google™ Chapter) to help you determine which keywords are most effective for your campaign.

- Understand Match Levels — Most PPC providers have levels of matching which you can customize so your ad will be displayed on an exact keyword match only or on a partial keyword match.

- Keep an eye out for fraud. Most PPC providers have some degree of fraud detection and prevention. If you suspect your competition is clicking on your ads, you may want to invest in additional protection such as **http://www.whosclickingwho.com**.

- Check the spelling in your ads to ensure it is correct.

- Imbed keywords within your actual PPC ad. Doing this may help them stand out among competitor ads when potential customers scan them.

We have provided you with an in depth introduction to PPC advertising, how it works, and what it looks like, and we have armed you with the most effective tips, tricks, and secrets to get the most out of your campaign. In the next few chapters, we will concentrate on how to prepare your site to attract the most Web site traffic and ensure your site is optimized for search-engine traffic.

Search Engine Optimization

I feel one of the most critical steps in designing and implementing a successful PPC campaign is to invest in a search engine optimization plan for your Web site to ensure that will work with all major search engines. Search engine optimization does not need to be completed before you begin a PPC campaign. However, it should be an ongoing process that you begin and consistently re-evaluate on a periodical basis. There are more than two billion Web pages on the Internet. Many Web sites are directly competing with yours for potential customers. You need to take realistic and time-proven measures to ensure that your online business gets noticed and obtains rankings within search engines that will deliver the results you desire both with and without PPC advertising campaigns.

We are going to concentrate on some of the most popular search engine optimization techniques, which you can easily implement on your Web sites:

- Basic search engine optimization
- Proper META tag formatting and inclusion
- Proper use of ALT tags
- Search engine registration and submission
- Search engine services
- Privacy policies
- About and feedback pages to improve search engine visibility
- Copyright pages

- Other proven Web site marketing techniques

Search engine optimization (SEO) consists of a variety of proven techniques that you can use to push up the ranking of your Web site within your target market on the Internet by using keywords that are relevant and appropriate to the product or services that you are selling on your Web site and in your PPC advertising campaigns.

"The Internet is like a vault with a screen door on the back. I do not need jackhammers and atom bombs to get in when I can walk through the door."

—Unknown

When you implement a search engine optimization plan, you use a methodology that allows you to make sure that your Web site is "visible" in search engines and is subsequently found by potential customers. Search engine optimization accomplishes this by taking the keywords that people may use to search for your products or services on the Internet using a search engine and placing these keywords in title pages, META tags, and into the content of your Web site, as well as in your PPC advertising campaigns.

When you use SEO properly and optimize your Web site based on sound Web site design principles, you know that your Web site is ready to be submitted to search engines and that you will increase the ranking in search engines, driving potential customers to your Web site for your business success. Focus on the content on each Web page and be sure to include at least 200 content related words on your site's pages. Integrate your keywords into the content you place on each page but be cautious of "keyword stuffing," which happens when you overload the pages with keywords. Doing so may result in your being blacklisted from major search engines.

Successful Search Engine Optimization

Understanding the concepts and actions necessary for successful search engine optimization can be hard to grasp when you start out using SEO techniques. You need to follow several steps to ensure you get the most from your search engine optimization. Some of these steps include:

- Make sure that your Web site is designed correctly and set up for optimal search engine optimization.

- Choose the right keywords that are going to bring the most hits to your Web site.

- Use the right title tags to identify you within search engines.

- Ensure appropriate content writing on your Web site.

- Use properly formatted "META tags" on your Web site.

- Choose the right search engines to which you submit your Web site and understand the free and paid listing service options available.

When you know where to focus for successful search engine optimization, you will discover your ranking in search engines will increase dramatically.

Search engine optimization requires time and patience. It will not get immediate visibility in search engines; whereas PPC advertising will. You need to be realistic in your expectations and expect it to take months to see tangible results.

META Tag Definition and Implementation

META tags are a key part of the search engine optimization program that you need to implement for your Web site. There is some controversy about the use of META-tags and whether they truly impact your search engine rankings. However, I am convinced they can be an integral part of a sound search engine optimization plan and some search engines do use these tags in their indexing process. You do need to be aware that you are competing against potentially thousands of other Web sites often promoting similar products, using similar keywords, and employing other SEO techniques to achieve a top search engine ranking. META tags have never guaranteed top rankings on crawler-based search engines. However, they do offer a degree of control and the ability for you, as the Web site or business owner, to affect how your Web pages are indexed within the search engines.

When it comes to using keywords and key phrases in your META keywords tag, you want to use only those keywords and phrases that you have actually included within the Web content on each of your Web pages. It is also important that you use the plural form of keywords so that both the singular and the plural will end up in any search that people do in search engines. Other keywords that you should include in your META keyword tags are any words that are the misspelling of your keywords and phrases since many people commonly misspell certain words, and you want to make sure that search engines can still find you despite these misspellings.

Do not repeat your most important keywords and key phrases more than five times in a META keyword tag. Another thing to keep in mind is that if your product or service is specific to a certain location geographically, you should mention this geographical location (i.e., Washington D.C., District of Columbia) in your META keyword tag.

META tags comprise formatted information that is inserted into the "head" section of each page on your Web site. To view the "head" of a Web page, you must view it in HTML mode, rather than in the browser view. In Internet Explorer, you can click on the Toolbar on the VIEW menu and then click on SOURCE to view the source of any individual Web page. If you are using a design tool such as Microsoft® FrontPage, Adobe Dreamweaver, Microsoft® SharePoint Designer 2007, or Microsoft® Expression Web Designer, you will need to use the HTML view to edit the source code of your Web pages. You can also use Notepad to edit your HTML source code.

Here is a simple basic layout of a standard HTML Web page:

```
<!DOCTYPE HTML PUBLIC "-//W3C//DTD HTML 4.01//EN"
<HTML>
  <HEAD>
    <TITLE>This is the Title of My Web Page</TITLE>
  </HEAD>
  <BODY>
    <P>This is my Web page!
  </BODY>
</HTML>
```

Every Web page conforms to this basic page layout, and all contain the opening <HEAD> and closing </HEAD> tags. META tags will be inserted between the opening and closing head tags. Other than the page title tag, which is shown above, no other information in the head section of your Web pages is viewed by Web site visitors as they browse your Web pages. The title tag is displayed across the top of the browser window and is used to provide a description of the contents of the Web paged displayed. We will discuss each META tag that may be contained within the "head" tags in depth.

The Title Tag

Whatever text you place in the title tag (between the <TITLE> and </TITLE>) will appear in the reverse bar of an individual's browser when they view your Web page. In the example on the previous page, the title of the Web page would read to the page visitor as "This is the Title of My Web Page."

The title tag is also used as the words to describe your page when someone adds it to their "Favorites" list or "Bookmarks" list in popular browsers such as Microsoft® Internet Explorer or Mozilla Firefox. The title tag is the single most important tag in regard to search engine rankings. The title tag should be limited to 40–60 characters of text between the opening and closing HTML tags. All major Web crawlers will use the text of your title tag as the text they use for the title of your page in your listings as displayed in search engine results. Since the title and description tags typically appear in the search results page after completing a keyword search in the Web browser, it is critical that they be written precisely to attract the attention of site visitors. Not all search engines are alike: some will display the title and description tags in search results but use page content alone for ranking.

The Description Tag

The description tag enables you to control the description of your individual Web pages when the search engine crawlers, which support the description tag, index and spider the Web site. The description tag should be no more than 250 characters.

Look at the "head" tag from the Web site **www.crystalriverhouse.com**, which is a site designed to promote the rental of a Florida Gulf Coast vacation house on a secluded canal located in Crystal River, Florida. The tag that says "name=description" is the description tag. The text you want to be shown as your description goes between the quotation marks after the "content=" portion of the tag (typically up to 250 characters) is allowed for search engine indexing. However, the full description tag may not be displayed in search results (see next page for HTML coding).

It is important to understand that search engines are not all the same, and that they index, spider, and display different search results for the same Web site. For example, Google™ ignores the description tag and generates its own description based on the content of the Web page. Although some major engines may disregard your description tags, it is highly recommended that you include the tag on each Web page since some search engines rely on the tag to index your site.

```
<head>
<META http-equiv="Content-Type" content="text/html; charset=windows-
1252">
<title>Beautiful Crystal River Florida Vacation Rental Home
</title>
<META name="keywords" content="Crystal River rental, Florida, Citrus County,
Grouper, Fishing, vacation home, Gulf Coast rental, florida vacation, florida gulf
coast">
<META name="description" content="Casa Dos Crystal River vacation rental
house and resort paradise. Located on beautiful canal off Crystal River. Crystal
River, Florida, is famous for its manatee watching, diving, grouper and other
world class fishing trips, world class golfing and many more activities.">
<META name="language" content="en-us">
<META name="robots" content="ALL">
<META name="rating" content="SAFE FOR KIDS">
<META name="distribution" content="GLOBAL">
<META name="copyright" content="(c) 2007 APC Group, Inc.">
<META name="revisit-after" content="30 Days">
<META http-equiv="reply-to" content="info@crystalriverhouse.com">
<style>
<!--
.sitecredits { color: #FFFFFF}
-->
</style>
</head>
```

The Keywords Tag

A keyword is simply defined as a word that may be used to search for information on the Internet, and it is also a critical component to developing your PPC campaign, which we will discuss in great detail in later chapters of this book. Using the best keywords to describe your Web site helps get those searchers to find your site in search engines. The keywords tag allows you to provide relevant text words or word combinations for crawler-based search engines to index. Again, although we maintain that the keyword tag is vitally important and should be included on every page, many crawler-based engines may use your page content for indexing instead of the contents of the keywords tag. In truth, the keywords tag is only supported by a few Web crawlers. Since most Web crawlers are content based (in other words, they index your site based on the actual page contents, not your META tags), you need to incorporate as many keywords as possible into the actual content of your Web pages. For the engines that support the description tag, it is beneficial to repeat keywords within the description tag with keywords that appear on your actual Web pages. This increases the value of each keyword in relevance to your Web site page content. You need to use some caution with the keywords tag for the few search engines that support it since repeating a particular keyword too many times within a keyword tag may actually hurt your Web site rankings.

If you look at the example earlier, you will notice that the keywords tag is the one that says <META name="keywords" content=." The keywords you want to use should go between the quotation marks after the "content=" portion of the tag. It is generally suggested that you include up to 25 words or phrases, with each word or phrase separated by a comma.

To help you determine which keywords are the best to use on your site, visit **www.wordtracker.com**, a paid service that will walk you through this process. Wordtracker's suggestions are based on more than 300 million keywords and phrases that people have used over the previous 130 days. A free alternative to determining which keywords are best is Google™ Rankings **http://Google™rankings.com/dbkindex.php**.

The Robots Tag

The robots tag lets you specify that a particular page within your site should or should NOT be indexed by a search engine. To keep search engine spiders out, add the following text between your tags: <META NAME="ROBOTS" CONTENT="NOINDEX">. You do not need to use variations of the robots tag to get your pages indexed since your pages will be spidered and indexed by default; however, some Web designers include the following robots tag on all Web pages: <META name="robots" content="ALL">.

Other META Tags

Many other META tags exist, but most provide amplifying information about a Web site and its owner and do not have any impact on search engine rankings. Some of these tags may be used by internal corporate divisions. In our example earlier, you can see some examples of other META tags that can be incorporated. (*Note:* This is not a complete list of all possible META tags):

```
<META name="language" content="en-us">
<META name="rating" content="SAFE FOR KIDS">
<META name="distribution" content="GLOBAL">
<META name="contentright" content="(c) 2005 APC Group, Inc">
<META name="author" content="Gizmo Graphics Web Design">
<META name="revisit-after" content="30 Days">
<META http-equiv="reply-to" content="info@crystalriverhouse.com">
<META name="createdate" content="4/8/2005">
```

You may also use the "comment" tag, which is primarily used by Web designers as a place to list comments relative to the Web site design, primarily to assist other Web developers who may work on the site in the future. A comment tag looks like this:

```
<!-begin body section for Crystal River Vacation House>
```

ALT Tag

The ALT tag is an HTML tag that provides alternative text when non-textual elements, typically images, cannot be displayed. The ALT tag is not part of the "head" of a Web page, but proper use of the ALT tag is critically important in Search engine Optimization. ALT tags are often left off Web pages. However, they can be extremely useful for a variety of reasons, including:

- They provide detail or text description for an image or destination of a hyperlinked image.

- They enable and improve access for people with disabilities.

- They provide information for individuals who have graphics turned off when they surf the Internet.

- They improve navigation when a graphics-laden site is being viewed over a slow connection, enabling visitors to make navigation choices before graphics are fully rendered in the browser.

Text-based Web content is not the only thing that increases your ranking in the search engines: images are just as important because these images can also include keywords and key phrases that relate to your business. If any visitors to your Web site should happen to have the image option off when hitting your site, they can still see the text that is associated with your images. Place ALT tags anywhere there is an image on your Web site. It is key to remember not to use too lengthy descriptions of your images but do include accurate keywords within the ALT tag. The keywords and key phrases that you use in the ALT tag should be the same keywords and phrases that you used in META description tags, META keyword tags, title tags, and in the Web content on your Web pages. A brief description of the image, along with one or two accurate keywords and key phrases is all you need to optimize the images on your Web pages for search engines.

Most major Web design applications include tools to simplify the process of creating ALT tags. For example, in Microsoft® FrontPage 2003, right click on the image, choose "properties" and the general tab, and you can enter ALT tag text information. To enter ALT tag information directly into a Web page, go to the HTML, view, and enter them after the IMG tags in the following format:

```
<img border="0" src="images/cftec.jpg" width="300" height="103"
alt="Whether you are a chef, restaurant owner, caterer, multi-unit manager or
other foodservice professional, ChefTec Software helps you stay on top of your
business"></b></font></p>
```

How to Use the Correct Keywords

When it comes to keywords, you need to choose the word or word combinations for which your potential customers are searching when they look for products or services using a search engine on the Internet. If you start to optimize keywords that are incorrect, you may be wasting your time as your potential customers search using keywords that do not put you up there in the top rankings of search engines. You will need to do some market research to find out what keywords are being used by people in search engines to find products or services similar to those you are selling. There are software tools on the market that you can use to find out just what these keywords are so that you can implement them into your Web content and into your META tags. As we stated earlier, the importance of the keyword META tag has faded over the years; however, using keywords within the content of your individual Web pages is the key to high Web site rankings. The use of keywords in your PPC advertising campaign, however, is critical. (We will discuss PPC keywords in depth later in this book.)

Search engine optimization means that every page of your Web site will be optimized to the greatest extent possible for search engines. Keywords will vary based on the individual Web page content. By using the wrong keywords, you risk sending your potential customers in an entirely different direction than to your Web site. Always keep in mind that if you are not listed in the top rankings of search engines, your customers may have difficulty finding you, and your competition will have an edge over you. Unfortunately, there is no magic formula to developing search engine-optimized and effective search phrases.

As I mentioned previously, you will need a different list of keywords and key phrases for each Web page that you are optimizing for the Internet, based on the content of that individual page. Keywords that work for some of your Web pages may not work for others. This is why you need to assess how your search engine optimization campaign is progressing and be prepared to make changes along the way.

A good way to keep on top of keywords is to keep an eye on your competition. Use a search engine yourself and use some of the keywords and key phrases that you know target your type of product or service. Look at the top-ranking Web sites and view the source HTML code as well as the keywords that they have used in their META tags. The HTML code will show you the keywords that the site's creator used. You will not only be able to come up with more keyword ideas, but you will also be able to keep up with your competition so that you rank at the top of search engines as well.

Optimization of Web Page Content

Web page content is by far the single most important factor that will determine your eventual Web site ranking in search engines. It is extremely important that you have relevant content on your Web pages that is going to increase the ranking of your Web site in search engine rankings. The content on your Web page is what visitors to your Web site are going to read when they find your site and start to browse your Web pages, whether you browse to a page directly or via a search engine. You need to optimize your Web site with all the right keywords within the content of each Web page so that you can maximize your rankings within search engines. You can use software tools to find out what keywords people are using when they search for certain products and services on the Internet, and we will provide some of those to you throughout this book.

Not only are the visitors to your Web site reading the content on these pages, but search engine spiders and Web crawlers are reading the same content and using it to index your Web site among your competitors. This is why it is important that you have the right content so that search engines are able to find you and rank you near the top of the listings for similar products that people want to buy. Search engines are looking for keywords and key phrases to categorize and rank your site; therefore, it is important that you focus on just as many key phrases as you do keywords.

The placement of text content within a Web page can make a significant difference in your eventual search engine rankings. Some search engines will analyze only a limited number of text characters on each page and will not read the rest of the page, regardless of length; therefore, the keywords and phrases you may have loaded into your page may not be read at all by the search engines. Some search engines do index the entire content of Web pages; however, they typically give more value or "weight" to the content that appears closer to the top of the Web page.

Optimize Your Web Site

If you want to get the best results from search engines, here are some tips that you should follow to optimize your Web site.

- Make sure that you have at least 200 words of content on each page. Although you may have some Web pages where it may be difficult to put even close to 200 words, you should try to come as close as you can since search engines will give better results to pages with more content.

- Make sure that the text content that you have on your Web pages contains those important keywords and key phrases that you have researched and know will get competitive rankings and are the most common phrases potential customers might use to search for your products or services.

- No matter how much content you have after incorporating keywords and key phrases, make sure that the content is still understandable and readable in plain language. A common mistake is stacking a Web site full of so many keywords and key phrases that the page is no longer understandable or readable to the visitor — a sure bet to lose potential customers quickly.

- The keywords and key phrases that you use in the content of your Web site should also be included in the tags of your Web site, such as META tags, ALT tags, head tags, and title tags.

- Add extra pages to your Web site, even if they may not seem directly relevant at first. The more Web pages that you have, the more likely it is that search engines will find your pages and link to them. Extra pages can include tips, tutorials, product information, resource information, and any other information that is pertinent to the product or service that you are selling.

Optimizing your Web content and Web pages is one of the most important tips that you can use to ensure the success of your Web site. If you are unable to optimize your Web site yourself, you should hire an expert so that you get the most out of the Web content on your Web site.

Web Site Optimization Tips, Hints, and Secrets

It is critically important that you explore and implement the wide range of tips, suggestions, and best practices we have provided in this book to give your Web site the most competitive edge and obtain the highest possible rankings with search engines. The following pages contain various best practices, tips, and secrets:

- **It is important to use your keywords heavily on your Web pages.** Use key phrases numerous times, placing them close to the top of the page. Place key phrases between head tags in the first two paragraphs of your page. Place key phrases in bold type at least once on each page. Repeat keyword and key phrases often to increase density on your pages.

- **Design pages so they are easily navigated by search engine spiders** and Web crawlers. Search engines prefer text over graphics and also prefer HTML over other page formats. You must make your page easy to navigate by the search engines.

- **Do not use frames.** Search engines have difficulty following them, and so will your site visitors. The best advice we can give on frames is NEVER to use them.

- **Limit the use of Macromedia Flash** and other high-end design applications, as most search engines have trouble reading and following them, hurting you in search engine listings;

- **Consider creating a site map** of all pages within your Web site. While not necessarily the most useful tool to site visitors, it does greatly improve the search engine's capacity to index all of your Web site pages properly.

- Many Web sites use a left-hand navigational bar, standard on many sites; however, the algorithm that many spiders and Web crawlers use will have this read before the main content of your Web site. **Make sure you use keywords within the navigation,** and if using images for your navigational buttons, ensure you use the ALT tags loaded with appropriate keywords.

- **Ensure that all Web pages have links back to the home page.**

- **Use copyright and "about us" pages.**

- **Do not try to trick the search engines with hidden or invisible text** or other techniques. If you do, the search engine will likely penalize you.

- **Do not list keywords in order within the content of your Web page.** It is perfectly fine to incorporate keywords into the content of your Web pages, but do not simply cut and paste your keywords from your META tag into the content of your Web pages. Doing so will be viewed as spam by the search engine, and you will be penalized.

- **Do not use text on your Web page as the page's background color** (i.e., white text on a white background). This is a technique known as keyword "stuffing," and all search engines will detect it and penalize you.

- **Do not replicate META tags.** In other words, you should only have one META tag for each type of tag. Using multiple tags, such as more than one title tag, will cause search engines to penalize you.

- **Do not submit identical pages with identical content** with a different Web page file name.

- **Makes sure that every Web page is reachable from at least one static text link.**

- **Make sure that your title and ALT tags are descriptive** and accurate.

- **Check for broken links and correct HTML.**

- **Try using a text browser such as Lynx to examine your site.** Features such as JavaScript, cookies, session IDs, frames, DHTML, or Flash keep search engine spiders from crawling your entire Web site properly.

- **Implement the use of the robots.txt file on your Web server.** This file tells crawlers which directories can or cannot be crawled. You can find out more information on the robots.txt file by visiting **www.robotstxt.org/wc/faq.html.**

- **Have other relevant sites link to yours.** We will cover the use of cross-linking your Web site with others later in this chapter; however, back linking is an often overlooked but critically important way of increasing your search engine rankings and gaining search engine visibility.

- **Design Web pages for site visitors, not for search engines.**

- **Avoid tricks intended to improve search engine rankings.** A good rule of thumb is whether you would feel comfortable explaining what you have done to a Web site that competes with you. Other useful tests are to ask, "Does this help my users?" or "Would I do this if search engines didn't exist?"

- **Do not participate in link schemes designed to increase your site's ranking.** Do not link to Web spammers as your own ranking will be negatively affected by those links.

- **Do not create multiple pages, sub-domains, or domains with substantially duplicate content.**

- **Do not use "doorway" pages created for search engines.**

- **Consider implementing cascading style sheets into your Web site to control site layout and design.** Search engines prefer CSS-based sites and typically score them higher in the search rankings.

Web Design and Optimization Suggestions

Shelley Lowery, author of the acclaimed Web design course "Web Design Mastery" (**www.webdesignmastery.com**) and "E-book Starter—Give Your E-books the Look and Feel of a REAL Book" (**www.e-bookstarter.com**) offers valuable tips and suggestions for Web design and Web site optimization. You can visit **www.Web-Source. net** to sign up for a complimentary subscription to Etips and receive a copy of the acclaimed ebook "Killer Internet Marketing Strategies" (**www.web-source.net**).

ESTABLISH LINKS WITH REPUTABLE WEB SITES

You should try to find quality sites that are compatible and relevant to your Web site's topic and approach the Webmaster of that site for a link exchange. Doing so will give you highly targeted traffic and will improve your score with the search engines. (*Note*: do not link to your competitors.) Your goal is to identify relevant pages that will link to your site, effectively yielding quality inbound links. You need to be wary of developing or creating a "link farm" or "spam link Web site," which offers massive quantities of link exchanges with little or no relevant content for your site visitors or the search engines.

How to Establish a Reciprocal Link Program (Backlinks)

Begin your link exchange program by developing a title or theme that you will use as part of your link request invitations. Your title or theme should be directly relevant to your site's content. Since most sites use your provided title or theme in the link to your Web site, be sure you include relevant keywords to improve your Web site optimization and search engine rankings. Keep track of your inbound and outbound link requests. Begin your search for link exchange partners by searching a popular engine such as Google™ and entering key phrases such as link with us, add site, suggest a site, and add your link. If these sites are relevant, they are ideal to being your reciprocal link program since they too are actively seeking link partners. Make sure that the Webmaster of other sites actually link back to your site as it is common that reciprocal links are not completed. If they do not link back to you in a reasonable time, remove your link to them as you are only helping them with their search engine rankings.

You may want to use **www.linkpopularity.com** as a free Web source for evaluating the total number of Web sites that link to your site.

Free Link Popularity Report for Atlantic Publishing Company **www.atlantic-pub.com.**

Google™	981 links
MSN®	680 links
Yahoo!®	661 links

ESTABLISH A WEB SITE PRIVACY POLICY

Internet users are becoming more and more concerned with their privacy. You should establish a "privacy" Web page and let your visitors know exactly how you will be using the information you collect from them. This page should include the following.

- For what do you plan on using their information?

- Will their information be sold or shared with a third party?

- Why do you collect their e-mail address?

- Do you track their IP address?

- You should notify site visitors that you are not responsible for the privacy issues of any Web sites you may be linked to.

- Notify them that you have security measures in place to protect the misuse of their private or personal information.

- Provide site visitors with contact information in the event that they have any questions about your privacy statement.

ESTABLISH AN "ABOUT US" PAGE

An "about us" page is an essential part of a professional Web site for a variety of reasons. One reason is that your potential customers may want to know exactly who you are, and secondly, it is a great opportunity to create a text-laden page for search engine visibility. An about page should include the following:

- A personal or professional biography.

- Photograph of yourself or your business.

- Description of yourself or your company.

- Company objectives or mission statement.

- Contact information, including your e-mail address.

ESTABLISH A TESTIMONIALS PAGE

One way to develop creditability and confidence among your potential customers is to include previous customer testimonials. You do need to make sure your testimonials are supportable; therefore, include your customers' names and e-mail addresses for validation purposes.

Establish a Money-Back Guarantee

Depending on the type of Web site you are operating, you may wish to consider implementing a money-back guarantee to eliminate any potential risk to customers purchasing your products. By providing them a solid, no-risk guarantee, you build confidence in your company and your products.

Establish a Feedback Page

There are many reasons to incorporate a feedback page into your Web site. Potential customers may have questions about your products and services or may encounter problems with your Web site, and the feedback page is an easy way for them to contact you. Additionally, it allows you to collect data from the site visitor such as name, e-mail address, or phone number. A timely response to feedback is critical to assure customers that there is a "living" person on the other end of the Web site, and this personal service helps increase the likelihood they will continue to do business with you.

Establish a Copyright Page

You should always display your copyright information at the bottom of each page. You should include both the word Copyright and the © symbol. Your copyright should look similar to this:

Copyright © 2007 Atlantic Publishing Group, Inc.

How Do Search Engines Work?

There are several different types of search engines, including: crawler-based, human-powered, and mixed. We will discuss how each one works so you can optimize your Web site in preparation for your PPC advertising campaign.

CRAWLER-BASED SEARCH ENGINES

Crawler-based search engines, such as Google™, create their listings automatically. They "crawl" or "spider" the Web and index the data, which is then searchable through **Google™.com**. Crawler-based search engines will eventually revisit your Web site, and as your content is changed (as well as those of your competitors), your search engine ranking may change. A Web site is added to the search engine database when the search engine spider or crawler visits a Web page, reads it, and then follows links to other pages within the site. The spider returns to the site on a regular basis, typically once every month, to search for changes. Often, it may take several months for a page that has been "spidered" to be "indexed." Until a Web site is indexed, the results of the spider are not available through the search engines. The search engine then sorts through the millions of indexed pages to find matches to a particular search and rank them in order based on a formula of how it believes the results to be most relevant.

HUMAN-POWERED SEARCH DIRECTORIES

Human-powered directories, like the Open Directory, depend on humans for their listings. You must submit a short description to the directory for your entire site. The search directory then looks at your site for matches from your page content to the descriptions you submitted.

HYBRID OR MIXED SEARCH ENGINES

A few years ago, search engines were either crawler-based or human-powered. Today, a mix of both types of results is common in search engine results.

Using a Search engine Optimization Company

If you are not up to the challenge of tackling your Web site search engine optimization needs, it may be to your benefit to hire an optimization company so that the techniques you use are implemented and monitored properly. There are many search engine optimization companies on the Internet that can ensure that your rankings in search engines will increase when you hire them. Be wary of anyone who can "guarantee" top 10 ranking in all major search engines: these claims are baseless. If you have the budget to hire a search engine optimization company, it may be extremely beneficial for you since (a) you will know that the experts at SEO are taking care of you and (b) you can focus your energies on other important marketing aspects of your business. To find a search engine optimization company, follow these basic rules:

- Look at the business reputation of the SEO companies that you are thinking about hiring. Ask the company for customer references that you can check out on your own. You can also contact the Better Business Bureau in their local city or state to confirm their reputation at **www.bbb.org**.

- Do a search engine check on each company to see where they fall into the rankings of major search engines such as AOL®, MSN®, and Google™. If the company that you are thinking about hiring to manage your own search engine optimization does not rank high in these search engines, how can you expect them to launch you and your business to the top of the ranks?

- You want to choose a search engine optimization company that actually has people working for them—not just computers. While computers are great for generating the algorithms that are needed to use search engine programs, they cannot replace people when it comes to doing the market research needed to ensure that the company uses the right keywords and key phrases for your business.

- You need to make sure that the search engine optimization company uses ethical ranking procedures. There are some ranking procedures that are considered unethical, and some search engines will ban (or penalize) your business Web site from their engines if they find out that you, or the search engine optimization company that you have hired, are using these methods. Some of these unethical ranking procedures include doorway pages, cloaking, or hidden text, as we have discussed previously.

- The search engine optimization company that you decide to hire should be available to you at all times by phone or by e-mail. You want to be able to contact someone when you have a question or a problem to which you need a solution.

After you have decided to hire a search engine optimization company, it is important that you work with the company instead of just handing over all the responsibility to them. How much control of your Web site you should allow your search engine optimization company is an area of debate. However, since you will be controlling your PPC advertising campaign, you must have control over your search engine optimization efforts. Use these tips to work effectively with your search engine optimization provider:

- Listen carefully to the advice of the search engine optimization account manager. This person should have the expertise to provide factual and supportable recommendations. Search engine optimization companies are expected to know what to do to increase your ranking in the search engines; if they fail to deliver, you need to choose another company.

- If you will be making any changes to your Web site design, be sure to you let your search engine optimization account manager know because any changes can have an effect on the already optimized Web pages. Your rankings in search engines may start to plummet unless you work with your account manager to optimize any changes to your Web site design that you feel are necessary.

- Keep in mind that search engine optimization companies can only work with the data and information that you have on your Web pages. This means that if your Web site has little information, it will be difficult for any search engine optimization company to pull your business up in the search engine rankings. Search engine optimization relies on keywords and key phrases that are contained on Web pages that are filled with as much Web content as possible. This may mean adding two or three pages of Web content that contain tips, resources, or other useful information that is relevant to your product or service.

- Never change any of your META tags after they have been

optimized without the knowledge or advice of your search engine optimization account manager. Your search engine optimization company is the professional when it comes to making sure that your META tags are optimized with the right keywords and key phrases needed to increase your search engine ranking. You will not want to change META tags that have already proven successful.

- Be patient when it comes to seeing the results of search engine optimization. It can take anywhere from 30 to 60 days before you start to see yourself pushed up into the upper ranks of search engines.

- Keep a close eye on your ranking in search engines, even after you have reached the top ranks. Information on the Internet changes at a moment's notice, and this includes where your position is in your target market in search engines.

Search engine Registration

It is possible to submit your Web site for free to search engines. However, when you use paid search engine programs, you will find that the process of listing will be faster and will bring more traffic to your site more quickly. Other than PPC and other advertising programs, such as Google™ Adwords, it is not necessary to pay for search engine rankings if you follow the optimization and design tips contained in this book and have patience while the search engine Web-crawling and indexing process takes place. At the end of this chapter, we have provided a wealth of tools and methods to submit your Web site to search engines for fee. If you decide to hire a third-party company to register you with search engines, we have provided some basic guidance to ensure you get the most value for your investment.

SUBMITTING TO HUMAN-POWERED SEARCH DIRECTORIES

If you have a limited advertising budget, make sure that you have at least enough to cover the price of submitting to the directory at Yahoo!® (called a "directory" search engine because it uses a compiled directory). It is assembled by human hands and not a computer. For a one-time yearly fee of about $300, you can ensure that search engines that are crawlers (a search engine that goes out onto the Internet looking for new Web sites by following links) will be able to find your Web site in the Yahoo!® directory. It may seem like a waste of money to be in a directory-based search engine, but the opposite is true. Crawlers consistently use directory search engines to add to their search listings. If you have a large budget put aside for search engine submissions, you might want to list with both directory search engines and crawler search engines, such as Google™. When you first launch your Web site, you may want it to show up immediately in search engines and do not want to wait the allotted time for your listing to appear. If this is the case, you might want to consider using a "paid placement" program. Remember that your PPC advertising campaigns will show up with the top search engine rankings, based your keyword bidding.

SUBMITTING TO CRAWLER SEARCH ENGINES

Submitting to search engines that are crawlers—search engines that look throughout the Internet to seek out Web sites through links and META tags—means that you will likely have several Web pages listed within the search engine. The more optimized your Web site is, as discussed previously in this chapter, the higher you will rank within the search engine listings.

One of the top Internet crawler search engines is Google™, which is extremely popular because it is not only a search engine, it is also the main source of power and information behind other search engines, such as AOL®. The best thing that you can do when getting your Web site listed at Google™ is to make sure that you have links within your Web site. When you have accurate links on your Web site, you ensure that crawler search engines are able to find you. One thing to keep in mind is that if you have good links AND you listed your Web site with a successful directory search engine, such as Yahoo, you may find that crawlers are able to find you easily, thus eliminating your need to list with Google™ in the first place. However, do not let this stop you from building good links into your Web site and constantly updating them.

USING SEARCH ENGINE SUBMISSION SOFTWARE

There are dozens of software applications that can submit your Web site automatically to major and other search engines. We have reviewed most of these products extensively and recommend Dynamic Submission (**www.dynamicsubmission.com**). Dynamic Submission, currently in version 7.0, is a search engine submission software product that claims to be a "multi-award winning, Web promotions software package, the best on the market today." Dynamic Submission search engine software was developed to offer Web site owners the ability to promote their Web sites to the ever-increasing number of search engines on the Internet without any hassles or complications. It helps you submit your Web site to hundreds of major search engines with just a few button "clicks" to drive traffic to your Web site. To use Dynamic Submission, you simply enter your Web site details into the application as you follow a wizard-based system, which culminates in the automatic submission to hundreds of search engines.

Since nearly 85 percent of Internet traffic is generated by search engines, submitting your Web site to all the major search engines and getting them viewed on the search engine list is extremely important, especially in concert with your PPC advertising campaign. It is essential to submit your Web site details regularly to these Web directories and engines. Some search engines de-list you after a time, and others automatically re-spider your site. Dynamic Submission is available in four editions (including a trial edition, which we highly encourage you to try) to fit every need and budget. Here are the major features of Dynamic Submission 7.0:

- Automatic search engine submission.
- Supports PPC (PPC) and pay-per-inclusion (PPI) engines.
- Support for manual submission.
- Keyword library and keyword builder.
- Link popularity check.
- META tag generator.
- Web site optimizer.
- Incorporated site statistics service.

PAYING FOR SEARCH ENGINE SUBMISSIONS

You may choose to use a fee service to have your Web site listed in popular ranking directories. Be sure to submit your site to the Open Directory manually at **www.dmoz.org**, which is FREE. I have provided you with a list of reputable providers of search engine submission services at the end of the book.

Search engine Optimization Checklist

There are many aspects to search engine optimization that you need to consider to make sure that it works. We have covered each of these in depth earlier in this chapter, but the following checklist can serve as a helpful reminder to ensure that you have not forgotten any important details along the way.

- **Title tag**. Make sure that your title tag includes keywords and key phrases that are relevant to your product or service.

- **META tags.** Make sure that your tags are optimized to ensure a high ranking in search engine lists. This includes META description tags and META keyword tags. Your META description tag should have an accurate description so that people browsing the Internet are interested enough to visit your Web site. Remember to use misspelled and plural words in your META tags.

- **ALT tags**. Add ALT tags to all the images that you use on your Web pages.

- **Web content.** Use accurate and rich keywords and key phrases throughout the Web content of all your Web pages.

- **Density of keywords.** Use a high ratio of keywords and key phrases throughout your Web pages.

- **Links and affiliates.** Make sure that you have used links and affiliates, if you are using them, effectively for your Web site.

- **Web design.** Make sure that your Web site is fast to load and easy to navigate for visitors. You want to encourage people to stay and read your Web site by making sure that it is clean and looks good.

- **Avoid spamming.** Double check to make sure that you are not using any spamming offenses on your Web site. Some spamming offenses include cloaking, hidden text, doorway pages, obvious repeated keywords and key phrases, link farms, or mirror pages.

Always be prepared to update and change the look, feel, and design of your Web pages to make sure that you are using search engine optimization techniques wherever and whenever possible.

Free Web Site Search engine Submission Sites

- http://dmoz.org/ Open Directory Project
- http://tools.addme.com/servlet/s0new
- www.submitexpress.com/submit.html
- www.ineedhits.com/free-tools/submit-free.aspx
- www.submitcorner.com/Tools/Submit
- www.college-scholarships.com/free_search_engine_submission.htm
- www.quickregister.net
- www.global.gr/mtools/linkstation/se/engnew.htm
- www.scrubtheweb.com
- www.submitaWebsite.com/free_submission_top_engines.htm
- www.nexcomp.com/weblaunch/urlsubmission.html
- www.submitshop.com/freesubmit/freesubmit.html
- www.buildtraffic.com/submit_url.shtml
- www.mikes-marketing-tools.com/ranking-reports
- http://selfpromotion.com/?CF=Google.aws.add.piyw
- www.addpro.com/submit30.htm
- www.Web site-submission.com/select.htm

Note: There are many other free services available on the Internet, and we make no guarantee as to the quality of any of these free services. We do recommend you create and use a new e-mail account just for search engine submissions (i.e., <search@yourWeb site.com>).

Free Web Site Optimization Tools and Sample Reports

http://www.Websiteoptimization.com/services/analyze/ — Contains a free Web site speed test to improve your Web site performance. This site will calculate page size, composition, and download time. The script calculates the size of individual elements and sums up each type of Web page component. On the basis of these page characteristics, the site then offers advice about how to improve page load time. Slow load time is the number one reason potential customers do not access Web sites.

Sample Report for RESTAURANTPROFITS.COM

TOTAL_HTML — Congratulations, the total number of HTML files on this page (including the main HTML file) is one which most browsers can multithread. Minimizing HTTP requests is key for Web site optimization.

TOTAL_OBJECTS — Warning! The total number of objects on this page is 58. Consider reducing this to a more reasonable number. Combine, refine, and optimize your external objects. Replace graphic rollovers with CSS rollovers to speed display and minimize HTTP requests.

TOTAL_IMAGES — Warning! The total number of images on this page is 38. Consider reducing this to a more reasonable number. Combine, refine, and optimize your graphics. Replace graphic rollovers with CSS rollovers to speed display and minimize HTTP requests.

TOTAL_CSS — Congratulations, the total number of external CSS files on this page is one. Because external CSS files must be in the HEAD of your HTML document, they must load first before any BODY content displays. Although they are cached, CSS files slow down the initial display of your page.

TOTAL_SIZE — Caution. The total size of this page is 96,309 bytes, which will load in over eight seconds on a 56Kbps modem — or 19.39 seconds. Consider reducing total page size to less than 30K to achieve sub eight second response times on 56K connections. Be sure to provide feedback for pages over 30K by layering your design to display useful content within the first two seconds. Consider optimizing your site with Speed Up Your Site or contact us about our optimization services.

TOTAL_SCRIPT — Warning! The total number of external script files on this page is 18, consider reducing this to a more reasonable number. Combine, refine, and optimize your external script files. Ideally you should have one (or even imbed scripts for high-traffic pages) on your pages.

HTML_SIZE — Caution. The total size of this HTML file is 46,510 bytes, which is above 20K but below 100K. With a 10K ad and a logo this means that your page will load in over 8.6 seconds. Consider optimizing your HTML and eliminating unnecessary features. To give your users feedback, consider layering your page or using positioning to display useful content within the first two seconds.

IMAGES_SIZE — Warning! The total size of your images is 48,609 bytes, which is over 30K. Consider optimizing your images for size, combining them, and replacing graphic rollovers with CSS.

CSS_SIZE — Congratulations, the total size of your external CSS is 1,190 bytes, which is less than 4,080 bytes. This will fit into three higher-speed TCP-IP packets.

MULTIM_SIZE — Congratulations, the total size of all your external multimedia files is 0 bytes, which is less than 4K.

www.sitesolutions.com/analysis.asp?F=Form — A free Web site that analyzes your page content to determine if you are effectively using META tags.

www.mikes-marketing-tools.com/ranking-reports — Reveals search engine rankings offering instant, online reports of Web site rankings in seven top search engines, including Google™, Yahoo!® Search, MSN®, AOL®, Teoma (**Ask.com**), AltaVista, AllTheWeb, and the top three Web directories, Yahoo!® Directory, Open Directory (Dmoz), and LookSmart, all for free.

Sample Report for RESTAURANTPROFITS.COM

Your Search engine Ranking Report by Mikes-Marketing-Tools.com

Visit GoDefy.com for the latest search engine ranking, plus hundreds of other quality Internet marketing products and services.

"No" = Not found in top 50. "—" = Engine not selected. "ERR" = No response.

	Google™	Yahoo!® Search	MSN®	AOL®	Alta Vista	AllThe Web	Yahoo!® Direct.	Open Direct.	Look Smart
"cheftec software"	#3	#7	#4	#3	#7	#7	No	No	No
Your most recent checks...									
"cheftec"	#4	#11	#4	#4	#10	#11	No	No	No

www.keyworddensity.com — Free fast and accurate keyword density analyzer.

Sample Report for RESTAURANTPROFITS.COM

http://www.restaurantprofits.com/cheftec.html

HTML	KEYWORDS	TOTAL	PERCENT
Title	2	16	12.5
META_Description	1	10	10
META_Keywords	1	61	1.63
Visible_Text	14	1233	1.13
Alt_Tags	5	92	5.43
Comment_Tags	0	435	0
Domain_Name	1	2	50
Image_tags	13	265	4.9
Linked_Text	10	60	16.66
Option Tags	0	0	0
Reference_Tags	25	302	8.27
TOTAL	72	2476	2.9

ADDITIONAL FREE WEB SITE OPTIMIZATION TOOLS

- **www.hisoftware.com/accmonitorsitetest**
  A Web site to test your Web site against accessibility and usability: Section 508, Complete WCAG, CLF, XAG standards.

- **www.wordtracker.com**
  The Leading Keyword Research Tool. It is not free, although there is a limited free trial.

- **https://adwords.Google™.co.uk/select/KeywordSandbox**
  Gives ideas for new keywords associated with your target phrase but does not indicate relevance or give details of number or frequency of searches.

- **http://inventory.overture.com/d/searchinventory/suggestion**
  Returns details of how many searches have been carried out in the Overture engine over the period of a month and allows a drill down into associated keywords containing your keyword phrase as well.

- **www.nichebot.com** Wordtracker
  This site and Overture-based tools as well as a nice keyword analysis tool, which focuses on Google™'s results.

- **www.digitalpoint.com/tools/suggestion**
  Gives search numbers on keywords from Wordtracker and Overture sources.

Web Site Design and Optimization Tools

- **www.Webmarketingtoolscentral.com**
  A large variety of tools, guides, and other services for Web design and optimization.

- **www.htmlbasix.com/META.shtml**
  Free site that automatically creates properly formatted HTML META tags for insertion into your Web pages.

- **www.coffeecup.com**
  ◊ **HTML Editor** The CoffeeCup HTML Editor 2005 is two editors in one!
  ◊ **Direct FTP** The only drag and drop FTP client that edits HTML, previews images, and more!

◊ **VisualSite Designer** Now anyone can make a Web site . . . no experience needed!

◊ **Flash Firestarter** The fastest and easiest way to make killer Flash effects for your Web site.

◊ **Flash Form Builder** Create Flash e-mail forms without using HTML or scripts!

◊ **Live Chat** Live chat with users on your Web site.

◊ **Flash Web site Search** Add customized search to your Web site in a flash!

◊ **Google™ SiteMapper** Create powerful Google™ site maps in seconds!

◊ **RSS News Flash** Add headlines and news to your Web site fast!

◊ **Flash Blogger** Easily create and modify your own online journal!

◊ **Password Wizard** Password-protect your site quickly and easily with Flash.

◊ **PixConverter** Easily re-size your digital pictures for Web sites, e-mail, CDs, and more.

◊ **MP3 Ripper and Burner** Easily rip MP3s or burn music CDs now!

◊ **Image Mapper** Often imitated — never duplicated — the original image mapper!

◊ **StyleSheet Maker** Create advanced Web sites using cascading style sheets.

◊ **Button Factory** The most popular button software on the Net now makes Flash!

◊ **GIF Animator** The coolest animation software on the planet now does Flash!

◊ **WebCam** Putting live WebCam images on your Web site has never been easier.

◊ **PhotoObjects 10,000** More than 10,000 ready to use graphics that are perfect for Web design.

How to Generate
Web Site Traffic

Web site traffic is the number of visits a Web site receives, determined by the number of visitors and the number of pages they visit. Web sites monitor the incoming and outgoing traffic to see which pages of their site are popular and if there are any apparent trends, such as one specific page being viewed mostly by people in a particular country. Web traffic is measured to see the popularity of Web sites and individual pages or sections within a site.

Your Web site traffic can be analyzed by viewing the statistics found in the Web server log file or by using Web site traffic analysis programs. Any quality Web hosting company will provide free detailed statistics for Web site traffic. A hit is generated when any file is served. The page itself is considered a file, but images are also files. Thus a page with five images could generate six hits—the five images and the page itself. A page view is generated when a visitor requests any page within the Web site—a visitor will always generate at least one page view (the home or main page), but could generate many more as site visitors travel through your Web site. There are many ways that you can increase your Web site traffic—all leading to greater sales and profit potentials. We will discuss a variety of options that will lead to increased Web site traffic.

How To Create Media Exposure And Develop A Marketing Strategy

Media exposure is a key component in your successful marketing profile and strategy. Your customers will form their opinions (positive or negative) based on what they hear and see in print, on television, on the radio, or on the Web. These "media" channels are not to be confused with the common short-form referral to online "multimedia" as media, too. Recognizing the importance of media exposure can boost the sales of your products or services. That positive media exposure is also a major step toward maintaining credibility in your online marketplace and ensuring that you compel visitors to channel more traffic to your Web site.

The first thing you need to keep in mind is that media exposure, as with online marketing campaigns, will take some time to become effective. It is not going to happen overnight, and you will have to take the time to think about the direction in which you want that exposure to take you. Make sure you know the differences between online and offline media exposure. There are several things that you can do to promote your offline media exposure. These may include the following.

- **Approach your local chamber of commerce and request that they write a short article about you and your business**; even if you are an online-only business, the local exposure is great. You can then take that article and publish it on your Web site as another promotion tool or use it in an online e-zine campaign. You will want to make sure that the focus of the article is just as much about you as it is about the business you are promoting. Remember that you want to promote yourself as well as your business. The best local media exposure results if you are viewed as a leader in your community.

- **Offer to be a speaker at a seminar or lead a workshop in your area of expertise.** This is a great way to gain media exposure that is incredibly positive and community oriented, thus gaining credibility and trust among potential clients. Circulate your URL at the seminar and give away a digital report via an auto-responder e-mail. Put your Web site URL on everything you distribute (flyers, promotional items, business cards, letterhead).

- **Follow up any correspondence or phone calls from the media with a letter or phone call.** Make sure to leave your Web site URL on their voice mail. This strategy gains media exposure for you by building a reputation as a conscientious, courteous entrepreneur.

Share your knowledge by writing articles and professional opinions for online publications and upload them to automated, e-zine syndication sites. These syndication sites are perfect for having immediate hotlinks back to your Web site and other specific landing pages. Remember to include your e-mail OR your picture in the byline as well as brief biographical information on yourself and your business. The more exposure you generate, the more successful your business will become.

Develop tactics to make media exposure and coverage work for you. Make media friends wherever and whenever the opportunity presents itself, all in an effort to increase media awareness and promote public relations. You are going to have to earn media exposure, but the time and effort that you spend will be your investment by having a positive public profile both on- and offline.

Keep in mind that most columnists will give their e-mail address at the conclusion of their article. Send them a note with your comments and views, while offering your expertise as a source for future quotes. Optimize your media exposure whenever possible; the returns for your business will be substantial.

> *"Surfing on the Internet is like sex; everyone boasts about doing more than they actually do. But in the case of the Internet, it is a lot more."*
> — *Tom Fasulo*

Media exposure of all kinds is one way that you can boost your Web presence visibly and increase the amount of Web site traffic. Media exposure can also be defined as "promotion and publicity" for the online success of your company. You need to make the media work for you, not against you, so that customers can easily find you, learn to trust you and your product, and keep coming back to your Web site for repeat sales as you develop loyal customers. Your potential and existing customers are only going to buy products and services from a business that they feel is trustworthy. To earn that trust and reliance, you have to make the most of media exposure so that you can build your credibility and find a secure position for your business as an expert in your target market. What is going to work best is a combination of effective online and offline publicity and public relations that is geared toward affirming your corporate trustworthiness, reliability, and credibility.

Many businesses pay thousands of dollars for media exposure, publicity, and advertising. You can get free publicity and public relations for your business Web site by using proven methods that will garner media exposure. Many businesses pay $10,000 for advertising with a rate card. Your company can get that same advertising exposure with little to no money over the Internet. By engaging in Internet media campaigns, or "non-traditional" media methods (such as PPC marketing) for gaining media exposure, you can accomplish two things:

- Save a significant amount of money.
- Be in full control of your own media techniques.

Your customers are going to form negative or positive opinions about your business based on what they see and hear on the radio, on the television, or in print. Mass media, such as radio, television, and print, are often difficult and certainly very costly methods to promote your business, so we will concentrate on less costly methods to grab attention in a big way. By using positive media relations, you will be making enormous strides toward successful search-engine positioning in the Internet marketplace. Positioning will allow you to convert more of the traffic to your Web site into satisfied, paying customers and when implemented in conjunction with a PPC marketing campaign will lead to online success.

Gaining the Trust of Your Clients

Gaining the trust of your customers is extremely critical in developing a continuing relationship that rewards your online business with repeat customer sales. The one-time sale may boost your immediate sales numbers, but returning customers will take your business from mediocre to fantastic profits. Your goal is to build quality customer relationships and maintain them. Gaining media exposure, both online and offline, opens the doors to a potentially long-term relationship with customers by using implied third-party credibility, thus legitimizing you as the expert in your field. Once you attract the prospects, you still have to deliver your goods or services and ensure that the customer is completely satisfied.

Increasing Your Public Profile

The more positive your public profile, the more success you will have both online and offline. Your public profile is your trademark for success and profits. Just as important, your online profile and business rating are critically important for how customers perceive you. Your local and state Better Business Bureaus are great organizations to join and obtain positive ratings. Other online business profile ratings services worth considering are **www.resellerratings.com**, **www.epinions.com**, and **www.consumerreports.org**.

Take some time to determine just what type of public profile you want to project. Most likely, you will want a successful, upbeat profile based on your credibility supported by your products, services, and superior customer satisfaction. You can increase your public profile by taking advantage of opportunities that allow you to use your services and knowledge in a variety of venues, thereby gaining public awareness and online marketing exposure without spending your own funds on relatively expensive advertising. Think outside the box. Do not always stick to convention just because the business market dictates certain protocol.

Positioning yourself, and actually becoming an expert in your market takes time, patience, and personal confidence. Just knowing the advantages of effective marketing is half the battle in getting there. Remember, it is the combination of media and marketing that really communicates the benefits and unique aspects of your business, which in turn drive customers to your Web site.

Your goal when it comes to sharing your expertise is to publish for free, thereby allowing many other organizations, news services, and other publications or magazines to distribute your article throughout their distribution network in return for Web site links back to your Web site and direct product promotions to thousands of potential new customers. There are ways that you can publish a full-page ad promoting yourself and your business without spending a dime. Contact editors of publications and offer them your press release to add content to their next publication. Many editors are looking for useful and relevant content so that they can meet deadlines. You need to take advantage of this opportunity and create the perfect article for publication.

You should target newspapers, magazines, newsletters, Web sites, and Web magazines as ideal opportunities for displaying your article. Keep in mind that magazines that have both an offline and an online image are excellent for increased exposure for driving customers to your Web site. Atlantic Publishing is one example of a company that uses e-zines. They have produced e-zine newsletters for more than four years and have grown a significant subscriber database. They routinely publish articles at no cost to professionals within the industry, providing a variety of hyperlinks, company and product descriptions, and other promotional material all at no cost, driving thousands of potential customers to their Web site.

Establishing an Online Marketing Strategy

Before you can implement a PPC campaign which will work for you, you need to develop and offline and online marketing strategy. For your online strategy, you need to follow some basic rules that will help ensure your PPC campaign is successful. Make sure that your Web site is professional and has a great design. You want your Web site to have a clean, tight look so that customers are compelled to return. Professional site design means having a Web site that is

- Easy to navigate.

- Has appropriate logos.

- Has up-to-date information.

- Answers customer questions.

- Does not look like an amateur site.

- Implements a search-engine optimization plan.

Never hide anything from your customers. Give them all the data that they need to make an informed decision about your product or services. Follow through on what you say you offer at your Web site to maintain credibility and trust. You do not want to be identified and exposed in the media as a poor company, scam site, or rip-off artist. Bad news travels fast, and it travels even faster on the Internet—quickly making your PPC marketing campaign, or any other marketing campaign, a money loser.

Using Press Releases to Generate Exposure

We have already discussed the importance of media exposure, but what about using an online press release to get that same exposure to your customers? An online press release is part of the online medium of communication, and online communication is all about timing. Your press release, whether printed and faxed or online, is one method of communicating with your customers and your industry. It is up to you to make the most of a press release so that it has as much impact as possible.

Most companies use press releases to alert the public about a new product or a new service they offer. These press releases, while informative, tend to be somewhat dry, and consumers typically skim over them, sometimes even missing the key points. In fact, the bottom line is if your release is not newsworthy, it won't be selected by the media for coverage. That said, a press release promoting specific events, specials, or newsworthy items can be very effective. The Silvermine Tavern (**www.silverminetavern.com**) has used effective press releases for years by publishing written press releases, which are printed in the newspaper, as has Atlantic Publishing Company through their Library Books Resource Guide (**www.librarybooks.biz**). Silvermine Tavern publishes press releases online and also disseminates highlights through their online newsletter promotional program, gaining maximum promotional potential at virtually no cost. As an alternative to a written press release, you could try a multimedia approach. If you are giving a live press release, you can incorporate the audio or video files onto your Web site, either to complement a written press release or replace it altogether. It is highly recommended that you have a media section on your Web site to serve reporters, columnists, producers, and editors with your latest press release information. Many people find listening to an audio clip or, better yet, watching a video clip preferential to reading a written press release. There is so much written word on the Internet that trying another medium to get your message across could be just the boost your company needs. You should also think of other Web site owners as another form of media channel since everyone is looking for fresh content and expert advice. You can also use online press releases as an avenue to imbed advertising that can generate revenue for you, such as Google™ AdSense, which is covered in Chapter 11.

Consider using an online press release service, such as www.PRweb.com, to generate successful media exposure for your online business. This free service is another tool to distribute your press release information to thousands of potential new customers or clients. Keep in mind the value of using highly relevant keywords often within the content of your online press release to use the benefits of search-engine optimization (SEO). Including live links within your online press release is another way for you to ensure increased media coverage. Linking to relevant Web sites increases the credibility and functionality of your online business. You may also do your own press release through your own e-zine or e-mail campaigns, which are covered in detail later in this book.

Make sure that you give your customers a reason to visit your site, to spend time browsing it, to interact with it, and most importantly, to return to it. Offer incentives by showcasing featured products or promotions, and use creative, new Internet tools, such as video and audio, to create an interactive experience. For affordable and easy tools, check out www.MyInstantVideo.com or www.audiomarketingon-line.com. You can also import video clips from promotional products, CDs/DVDs or create your own video clips and add them to your Web site.

Publish Customer Testimonials

Using customer testimonials is a great way to promote the quality and reliability of your Web site and, more importantly, promote your products or services. This is an amazingly effective tactic. The media you create and the coverage that you get are a subtle, third-party referral to you. However, the strongest and most effective sales assistance comes from direct customer testimonials. I highly recommend using audio and video testimonials as well as printed quotes on your Web sites. You should include your customer's name, e-mail address, and Web address with each unsolicited testimonial to increase believability. A script that will rotate testimonials on your Web site is available from www.willmaster.com.

Remember that no matter how flashy or impressive your Web site may look, customer service, satisfaction, and reliability keep customers coming back.

Techniques for Generating Web Site Traffic

The following techniques may be employed to increase Web site traffic. These proven methods will help increase your Web site traffic.

- **Create a "What's New" or "New Products" page.** Site visitors like to see what is new, trendy, or just released. Make it easy for them.

- **Establish a promotion program.** The sky is the limit for promotions. You can offer free products, trial samples, or discount coupons. Everyone loves a bargain; give it to them.

- **Establish a contest.** We already discussed Atlantic Publishing Company's Top 50 Restaurant Web sites contest that drew thousands of site visitors. Similar contests cost nothing to create, are simple to manage, and draw visitors back.

- **Add content-relevant professional articles, news events, press releases**, or other topics of interest on a daily basis to draw back visitors to your site.

- **Establish a viral marketing campaign** or imbed viral marketing techniques into your current advertising programs or e-zines. Viral marketing lets you incorporate such things as a "forward to a friend" link within the ad. In theory, if many people forward to many more friends, it will spread like a virus (hence the name viral) and eventually go to many potential customers.

- **Use signature files with all e-mail accounts.** Signature files are basically business cards through e-mail, so why not send your business card to all your e-mail recipients? Signature files are sent with every e-mail you send out and can contain all contact information, including business name and Web site URL. Signature files can be created in Microsoft® Outlook or Outlook Express.

- **Start an affiliate program and market it!** Include your affiliate information in e-mails, newsletters, e-zines, and on Web sites to promote your program. A successful affiliate program will generate a significant increase in Web site traffic.

- **Include your Web site URL on everything** (business cards, letterhead, promotional items, e-mails)!

- **Win some awards for your Web site.** There are quite a few award sites which are nothing more than link exchange factories; however, there are some reputable award sites such as **www.webbyawards.com** and **www.100hot.com**.

- **Everyone loves search engines, so put one on your Web site.** Visit Google™ to add a free search feature to your Web site. This is a great tool that site visitors will love! There are dozens of other free search services you can incorporate free into your Web site. Just do a search on "free Web site search," and you will have plenty from which to choose. You can even earn money by using the search feature outlined in Chapter 11 with Google™ AdSense.

- **Register multiple domain names with search engines** and "point" them to your main Web site. Owning similar or content-related domain names is a good investment to protect yourself from competitors' using similar-sounding domain names and will help you with search-engine rankings.

- **Put your URL into your e-mail signature** so you are constantly advertising your Web site.

- **Put your Web site URL on your business card.**

- **Register your site with online directories** relevant to your content.

- **Write free articles and submit them to other newsletters.**

- **Post often on content related forums and message boards** and post your Web site URL with each entry.

- **Submit content often to content-relevant e-mail discussion groups** on related content and post your Web site URL with each entry.

- **Establish links from other sites to yours (backlinks).** Create a links page or directory on your Web site and offer your visitors a reciprocal link to your site for adding a link to yours on theirs.

- **Create an exciting contest on your Web site to draw in traffic.** Free items and exciting contests are extremely popular and are very appealing.

- **Establish an affiliate program** (We will discuss this in detail in Chapter 12).

- **Develop quality Web site content that is well-organized and captivating.**

- **Use eBay to generate Web site traffic.**

- **List your URL on all offline advertising and printed materials** (i.e., stationery, print ads).

- **Begin a business blog on your Web site.** If it is well done and has relevant content, people will link to it, increasing your site's visibility and ranking in search engines.

- **Implement a PPC advertising campaign** — the purpose of this book!

You may be asking why I included this chapter in this book, as it is not directly related to a PPC campaign. The primary reason is that a PPC advertising campaign by itself is not going to be your business's sole salvation or money maker. It can be highly effective when used in conjunction with search-engine optimization plan and the other techniques I have outlined to generate Web site traffic and increase your business (and Web site's) customer base and revenue.

How to Budget for Your PPC Advertising Campaign and Choose Effective Keywords & Keyword Phrases

Web site traffic is the number of visitors or visits a Web site receives. As we have discussed in detail, more than 80 percent of Web site traffic originates from a search engine. In addition to being vitally important that you implement search-engine optimization techniques to raise the visibility and ranking of your Web site, it is important for you to determine what keywords or key phrases your potential customers may use when seeking out your company, products, or services.

A keyword is a word or phrase that people (consumers or businesses) would employ to locate information on the products, services, or topics that they are interested learning more about or purchasing. When choosing the keywords you will eventually bid on and imbed within your advertising campaign, you need to think like a potential customer, not as the seller or advertiser. You must determine which search terms that a potential customer might use to find you through search engines. Getting high rankings in a search engine and high visibility of your

PPC ad based on keywords is directly related to how "competitive" the keyword is. Remember, you do not own any keywords, and chances are your competitors are targeting the same keywords; therefore, you will find the cost to buy a keyword in a PPC advertising campaign is primarily determined by how many other Web sites are competing for the same keyword or key phrases.

The formula for determine the cost of a keyword varies by PPC companies; however, the primary factor in determining cost is the relationship of the keyword to top 10 rankings within a search engine. If your keywords are not competitive (in other words, not many companies are trying to use the same keywords in their campaign), the cost of the keyword is relatively low, and will yield high search-engine rankings. If you are competing with hundreds or thousands of other companies for the same keywords, the cost of those keywords will escalate dramatically as each company strives to "outbid" the others in the fight to claim one of the top positions — often highly contentious keywords can cost up to $100 each per click, quickly consuming advertising budgets.

Knowing how much a keyword "costs" will be covered in depth throughout this book in later chapters dedicated to the setup and management of your PPC campaign, but it is important that you understand the theory and concepts for the process so that you can determine in advance which keywords are most effective and most cost efficient.

Key to selecting keywords is determining how often someone will actually search the Web using that keyword or key phrase. Logically keywords that are less competitive will typically bring you less traffic simply because the keyword is not used often during a search. Conversely, you can expect more traffic with highly competitive keywords; however, this may not always be the case as the field of competitors typically grows directly in proportion to the keyword competitiveness. When you begin your PPC campaign, you should be provided with in depth analyses on a regular basis to help you monitor, adjust, and evaluate the performance of your marketing campaign.

These reports should tell you exactly which keywords are being used by those who are using search engines with your campaign and helps you determine if your chosen keywords are effective.

Keyword Research Tools

Another method to determine what keywords you should use is to use one of many keyword research tools provided on the Internet. Please note that not all of these tools are free. Some of the keyword research tools are:

- WordTracker **www.wordtracker.com** — Promises to find the best keywords for your Web site. I entered "restaurant consulting" into the generation tool, and the application returned a list of generated keyword suggestions. Here were the top 10: restaurant consulting, consulting, restaurant, Restaurant Consultant, food, consultant, restaurant consultant, restaurants, training, and Restaurant.

You choose the keywords you want to use and the application returns "count" and "prediction reports." *Count* is the number of times a particular keyword has appeared in the wordtracker database, while *prediction* is the maximum total predicted traffic for all of the major search engines/pay per bids and directories today.

Screenshots © Google™ Inc. and are reproduced with permission

Choose data to display	Cost and ad position estimates	

Calculate Estimates using Max CPC:
US Dollars (USD $) | 5.00 | Recalculate

More specific keywords - sorted by relevance [?]

Keywords	Estimated Avg. CPC	Estimated Ad Position	Match Type: [?] Broad
restaurant consulting	$2.67	1 - 3	Add »
restaurants consulting	$1.63	1 - 3	Add »
restaurant consultants	$3.34	1 - 3	Add »
restaurant consultant	$2.96	1 - 3	Add »
restaurant consulting firms	$0.05	1 - 3	Add »
restaurant consulting group	$0.05	1 - 3	Add »
a restaurant consultant	$0.05	1 - 3	Add »
firm restaurant	$0.05	1 - 3	Add »

Add all 8 »

Download all keywords: .csv (for excel), .csv

Additional keywords to consider [?]

Screenshots © Google™ Inc. and are reproduced with permission.

- **Google™ Keyword Tool** — This tool available at **https://adwords.Google.com/select/KeywordToolExternal** generates potential keywords for your ad campaign and reports their Google™ statistics, including search performance and seasonal trends.

The Google™ Keyword Tool can generate a variety of data including; keywords, keyword popularity, cost and ad position estimates, global search positive trends, and negative keywords. Of the tools listed, Google™ is by far the most user-friendly and comprehensive. There are also dozens of other keyword generation tools available on the Internet..

The detailed reports provided by your PPC provider will track each search term used that resulted in someone's clicking on your ad. By analyzing this report, you can determine which keywords were effective and which were not. Since you are able to modify your keywords at any time, it is well worth the analysis on your performance reports to understand how your PPC ad is doing.

How to Develop Keywords

One of the biggest challenges when establishing your PPC campaign is developing your initial list of keywords and key phrases. We have shown you how to perform research with your list of keyword, however you must have a list of "potential" keywords or key phrases to start that process in the first place. Here are some hints and tips about how to develop your initial keywords and key phrases:

- **Brainstorm** — Develop a list of all the possible keywords or key phrases you believe people might use to find your Web site.

- **Screen your employees, friends and customer base** for a list of all the possible keywords or key phrases you believe they might use to find your Web site.

- **Screen your competitors' Web sites** for a list of all the possible keywords or key phrases on their Web site.

- **Take your entire list of keywords and key phrase and use the tools we have provided to refine your list** and identify the most competitive and cost-effective keywords.

The following article entitled "How to Create Keyword Phrases for your PPC Promotions," by Abe Cherian provides insight about how to create keyword phrases.

How to Create Keyword Phrases for Your PPC Promotions

One of the most obvious mistakes Web site owners make when they are launching their PPC campaign is not having a list of credible keyword phrases available. The most common tool to use when searching for keyword phrases is WordTracker (**http://www.wordtracker.com**).

When you use WordTracker to "check" the profitability of your idea, record every keyword phrase that you use in a text file. And use many. Do every search you can possibly think of to solve your problem.

For example; using the advanced golf tactics, you may do the following searches:

- how to become good at golf
- how to beat my competitors in golf
- winning golf matches
- advanced golf strategies
- get better at golf
- advanced golf
- improving golf
- golf advantage
- golf e-books
- advanced golf tips
- golf techniques

- get good at golf
- how to win a golf match
- golf strategies
- winning golf
- being better at golf
- secrets of great golf players
- improving golf ability
- guide to golf
- golf tips
- advanced golf techniques

And so on until you have exhausted absolutely every option.

- Make a list of phrases that describe your proposed product.
- Make a list of phrases that describe the problem that your product solves.
- Make a list of phrases that describe the benefits of your product.
- Make a list of phrases that describe the features of your product.
- Make a list of phrases that describe your competitors, their names, companies, and their products.
- Make a list of phrases that are commonly associated with your product. As soon as a keyword pops into your mind save it in your keyword file. If you are following my advice you should have recorded every remote keyword that you could possibly think of.

How to Create Keyword Phrases for Your PPC Promotions

Even so, as you continue the process, especially when you write your sales copy, create your product, and begin advertising, you will come up with more keywords. Record them in the keyword file immediately because they are pure gold. Even if, for whatever reason, you choose not to use WordTracker it is important that you create and record such a list.

Creating keywords immediately after getting your idea is important for two reasons:

1. Your mind is fresh, excited, and creative because of the passion and emotion you have for your idea. You will most likely do your best work during this time, and you will want to do your best work on this list. It will become evident that keywords are tremendously valuable to your online business.

2. At this point, you are in the exact frame of mind that your prospect will be in when looking for your product   that you have not yet created. Your thinking has not yet been warped by the effort you have put into your product or the pride you have in it.

Do you recognize the immense power in this? Having this list of keywords is important for the following reasons:

- These phrases will be used to drive PPC traffic to your site. The more phrases, the more traffic and the cheaper the traffic.

- The PPC traffic will determine the profitability of certain phrases by allowing you to see which exact keywords your customers—not your visitors—are using.

- You will use your customers' most common phrases as subjects for your search-engine optimization.

- You will use this list when creating your product to give you ideas about how to improve it, what benefits it should offer, and guidance on what to incorporate.

- You will use it when you are writing your sales copy to know what needs you should address. This is also based on the PPC data.

- You will use it for writing articles. It is a wealth of potential topics and you will know which topics your customers are most interested in hearing about.

You will be truly amazed at what you will do with this list of keywords. This list will be referred to many times and will assist you in generating a great

How to Create Keyword Phrases for Your PPC Promotions

deal of wealth if you use it correctly. The investment of time and energy you put into it will be well spent I assure you.

http://www.articlealley.com/article_70185_7.html

Abe Cherian is the founder and Project Manager for Multiple Stream Media, a company that helps businesses and online entrepreneurs generate exponential results from their advertising and marketing.

Web Properties of Multiple Stream Media
http://www.msmedianetwork.com

Advertising network
http://www.imediamarketingtools.com

Marketing Automation & CRM

Keywords are the building blocks of your successful PPC advertising campaign. If you do not invest the time and research to choose the best possible keywords for your campaign, ultimately your PPC campaign will suffer. Keep in the mind that the more specific your keyword or key phrase is, the more likely a potential customer who may be looking for your products or services will be to find them. Careful and repetitive analysis of your keywords is the secret formula for PPC search-engine success. While the time investment is significant, so are the results of refining and improving your keyword effectiveness — ultimately you will be rewarded in revenue sales.

Another article which may be of assistance that is available on Article Marketer is "The Importance of Keyword Marketing for Newbies," by Richard East. This article provides insight into keyword marketing for both PPC and search-engine optimization for your Web site. It is broken into two parts and is available at **http://www.articlealley. com/article_56070_62.html** and **http://www.articlealley.com/article_ 55978_81.html**.

Tips and Tricks When Developing Keywords or Key Phrases

The following is a compilation of the tips, tricks, and best practices that you can employ to assist in the process of creating your keywords and key phrases for your PPC campaign.

- Brainstorm a list of any relevant keyword or key phrase you can think of. Take some time away from the list and over the period of seven to ten days keep adding more potential keywords and key phrases to the list. It is not uncommon to have thousands of keywords initially for your PPC campaign.

- Be sure to incorporate your company name, catch-phrases, slogans, or other recognizable marketing material into keywords.

- Add both the singular and the plural spellings for your keywords.

- Add your domain names to your list of keywords. You will be surprised how many people search for a company by the URL instead of the company name (i.e., atlantic-pub.com instead of Atlantic Publishing Company).

- Take a peak at the META tags on competitors' Web sites, in particular the "keywords" tag. Review this list and add them to your keywords list.

- Avoid trademark issues and disputes. Although there is some degree of latitude about trademarks, my recommendation is to avoid using other companies' trademarks unless you are an authorized distributor or reseller of their products.

- Put keywords in the title of your PPC ad to generate a much higher click-through rate.

- Use bold face font in the title of your PPC ad.

- Find your target audience.

- Incorporate words that add to your PPC ad, such as: amazing, authentic, fascinating, powerful, revolutionary, and unconditional.

- End your ads with words that promote an action on the part of the reader, such as: "Be the First," "Click Here for all the Details," "Limited Time Offer," and "Free Today."

How to Establish a Budget for your PPC Campaign

As we have established, PPC advertising allows you to pay quickly to have your ad listed on major search engines. Since they are considered "sponsored links," they are significantly different than standard search-engine results you might see when you perform a search in a search engine. These links will ultimately affect your advertising budget as pay for each "click." Sponsored links, or PPC ads, usually appear at the top, bottom, or right side of the results page following a search with any search engine.

You may see PPC ads called Paid Listings, Sponsored Links, Sponsored Listings, or Featured Listings. PPC advertising allows you to have your ad listed on search engines with the agreement that you will pay for each "click" on your ad based on bids you have placed on your chosen keywords. When your ad is clicked, depending on the keyword used to perform the search and the value of that keyword, you pay a fee to your PPC provider.

The relative placement with a search engine is based on the keyword bidding system. Your competitors and your maximum cost per click determine your relevant placement in the search-engine results. It is important to note that there are additional factors, depending on the search engine, that will determine your actual ad placement beyond just the cost per keyword. Google™ uses a formula to calculate your PPC ad position that is calculated by multiplying your bid amount by your ad's click-through rate. It is not uncommon that ads with a higher click-through rate may appear higher in the "sponsored listings" than other ads with a higher bid amount. Overture uses your bid amount as the determining factor for position.

As the advertiser embarking on your first PPC advertising campaign, there is a wide-variety of PPC companies available, with Google™ and Yahoo being the biggest and most recognized. Choosing which company is a difficult process, and you may choose multiple companies (such as both Google™ and Yahoo). Your financial constraints are one of the primary factors in developing your PPC campaign. All PPC advertising campaigns require you to pay "per click" based on pre-negotiated costs per keyword. PPC campaigns are set up with a credit card, and you must pre-load funds into your account, such as $150. Since you have no control over who will click on your PPC ad, or how often, you are taking a financial risk based on the keyword costs times the number of clicks on your PPC ad. You do have some significant control over your budget since you can:

- Establish a Maximum Cost Per Click

- Establish a Maximum Daily Total

- Establish a Maximum Monthly Total

You will need to make a decision in regard to how to launch your PPC campaign, your choices are typically:

- **Exact Match** — The most precise matching that requires an exact match of all keywords. This is a good program since you will have only highly qualified results, and there is less impact on your budget. We recommend you only start with an Exact Match PPC campaign.

- **Content Match** — A less restrictive matching which allows your ad to appear whenever your exact keywords appear in that exact order. If the person searching includes additional words before or after the keyword phrase or if the general "content" of your keyword phrases are a close match, your ad will be displayed. We do not recommend that you implement a Content Match campaign until your campaign is refined and tested, and then only if your budget allows.

PPC Budget Planning

You need to give some thought to determining a manageable budget before starting your PPC campaign. Establishing a monthly budget for PPC advertising is difficult because pricing is based on keyword bids, which change in value often, and typically go up in cost over time. Most businesses shift advertising funding from traditional marketing programs (print media, radio) toward PPC advertising. An alternative method is to estimate your increased revenue based on your PPC campaign and establish a percentage-based budget (percent of anticipated or realized increased revenue due to the PPC campaign). The advantage of this type of budget is that you can scale the percentage up or down based on your actual sales derived from the PPC campaign. Google™ provides you with a Budget Optimizer for AdWords, which helps you, the advertiser, receive the highest number of clicks possible within your specified budget.

Measuring Return on Investment

You can measure the Return On Investment (ROI) for a PPC campaign. If you exceed your budget, you can cancel your PPC campaign at any time. To determine what your starting budget should be, you will need to decide how much a PPC conversion (a visitor becomes a customer) is worth in profit to your business, how many additional sales leads your company is ready to handle, your conversion rate (provided by your PPC company), and what your conversion goal is. The formulas below will help you to establish your PPC budget:

Sales leads per day X Percent of conversion X 20 work days in month = Number of Conversions	$ in Profits per conversion X Number of conversions = PPC Budget Maximum	Total Profit from PPC campaign — Total Budget for PPC = PPC Profit

Here we do the math. Assume that you make an average of $100 net profit per conversion, you can process 100 sales leads per day, and your conversion rate is 20 percent (20 percent of all click-throughs culminate in a sale). Based on an average 20-work-day-month, this gives you a net profit of $4,000 per month that can be spent on your PPC advertising campaign.

If you then pay out $2,000 for your PPC advertising campaign for one month of PPC service and receive 500 leads that convert into 100 conversions (20 percent conversion rate), you are realizing $8,000 profit on your advertising campaign costs, resulting in a 400 percent Return On Investment.

Number of Conversions	PPC Budget Maximum	PPC Profit
100	$100	$10,000
X	X	—
20%	400	$2,000
X	=	=
20 work days in month	$4,000	$8,000
=		
400		

Keep in mind your actual sales figures will change monthly, based on actual conversions.

"Selecting the Right Search-Engine Keywords" by John Hayward is another article from Article Alley that would be helpful to read. In this article Hayward explains factors that should help you decide which keywords you should choose for your campaign.. This article is available at **http://www.articlealley.com/article_73532_6.html**.

Google™ AdWords

Google™ is the most popular search engine in the world today, and it also boasts the number one PPC advertising program; Google™ AdWords. As I stated in earlier chapters, to advertise in all major search engines you will want to consider using Google™ AdWords in concert with Yahoo! ® Search Marketing. We will provide you with a detailed guide to Google™ AdWords in this chapter, and Yahoo!® Search Marketing in the next chapter.

What is Google™ AdWords?

Google™ AdWords is a user-friendly, quick, and simple way to purchase highly targeted cost-per-click (CPC) or cost-per-impression (CPM) advertising. AdWords ads are displayed along with search results on Google™, as well as on search and content sites in the growing Google™ Network, including AOL ®, EarthLink, HowStuffWorks, and Blogger. When creating an AdWords keyword-targeted ad (PPC ad), you choose keywords for which your ad will appear and specify the maximum amount you are willing to pay for each click and you only pay when someone clicks on your ad. Google™ Adwords also features the AdWords Discounter that automatically reduces the actual CPC you pay to the lowest cost needed to maintain your ad's position on the results page.

When you create an AdWords site-targeted ad, you choose the exact Google™ Network content sites where your ad will run and specify the maximum amount you are willing to pay for each thousand page views on that site. You pay whenever someone views your ad, whether the viewer clicks or not. As we mentioned in earlier chapters, we recommend you start out with Google™ Adwords keyword targeted ad, and do not allow content-matching. There is no minimum monthly charge with Google™ Adwords, but there is a one-time activation fee for your account. Although your campaign can literally start in minutes, we highly recommend you invest the time to identify the best keywords possible and follow our guidance on creating your ad.

Where Will My Google™ AdWords Ad Appear?

Your Google™ Adwords ad could appear on all of the search and content sites and products in the Google™ Network. The Google™ global search network includes Froogle and Google™ Groups and the following:

Screenshots © Google™ Inc. and are reproduced with permission.

Google™'s Adwords Content network of high-quality consumer and industry-specific Web sites and products includes:

How Are Google™ AdWords Ranked?

CPC
X
Quality Score
=
Ad Rank

Keyword-targeted ads are ranked on search result pages based on their maximum cost-per-click (CPC) and Quality Score on **Google™.com**. The Quality Score is determined by the keyword's performance history on Google™: its click-through rate (CTR), relevance of ad text, historical keyword performance, landing page quality, and other relevancy factors.

Google.com states that having relevant keywords and ad text, a strong click-through rate on Google™, and a high cost-per-click will result in a higher position for your PPC ad. One of the main advantages of this system is that you cannot be locked out of the top position, as you would be in a ranking system based solely on price.

For a keyword-targeted ad's position on a content page, Google™'s system considers two things:

- The Ad Group's content bid or, if content bids are not enabled, its maximum CPC.

- The ad's past performance on this and similar sites.

As we have shown you in earlier chapters, your PPC ad will be displayed in search-engine results.

When you have completed the account setup process, you will be required to activate your account through an opt-in e-mail that is sent to your specified e-mail account. Once this is confirmed, your account is activated and you can log into your new Google™ AdWords account. At this point, you will be required to enter your billing information. Upon completion of your billing information, your ad typically appears within minutes. Google™ Adwords is set up to operate with three distinct levels. They are Account, Campaign, and Ad Group. The chart below shows the account structure and the settings that are applied at each level. In summary:

Screenshots © Google™ Inc. and are reproduced with permission.

- Your account is associated with a unique e-mail address, password, and billing information.

- At the campaign level, you choose your daily budget, geographic and language targeting, distribution preferences, and end dates.

- At the Ad Group level, you create ads and choose keywords. You can also select a maximum cost-per-click (CPC) for the Ad Group or for individual keywords.

- Within each Ad Group, you create one or more ads and select a set of keywords to trigger those ads. Each Ad Group runs on one set of keywords. If you create multiple ads in an Ad Group, the ads will rotate for those keywords.

- When you log into your account, you can see your ads' click-through rates (CTRs) listed below each of the ads. If a particular ad is not performing as well as the others (if it has a low CTR), you can delete or refine it to improve the performance of your Ad Group.

How Much Will Google™ AdWords Cost?

You will pay a $5 fee to set up your Google™ AdWords account. Each keyword has a minimum bid based on the quality of the keyword specific to your account. If your keyword or Ad Group's maximum cost-per-click (CPC) meets the minimum bid, your keyword will be active and trigger ads. If it does not, your keyword will be inactive for search and not trigger ads on Google™ or its partner search sites. Remember to use the tips we provided regarding how to bid successfully on keywords! When you review your account, your keywords will be listed as "active" (which will trigger PPC ads), or "inactive" (which will not trigger PPC ads). Some key cost factors to remember:

- The position of an ad is based on the maximum CPC and quality.

- The higher the Quality Score, the lower the CPC required to trigger ads, and vice versa.

- There is no minimum spending requirement.

- The activation fee is a one-time $5 charge.

- You set the daily limit on how much you are willing to spend.

- You set how much you are willing to pay per click or per impression.

- You only pay for clicks on your keyword-targeted ad.

- You only pay for impressions on your site-targeted AdWords ad. We recommend you start out with keyword targeted ad until your campaign is well established.

Establishing and Managing Your Google™ Account

Google™ provides a wide variety of tools to help you establish your account, choose keywords, manage your budget and manage your account in detail. The Google™ Keyword Tool generates potential keywords for your PPC campaign and tells you their Google™ statistics, including search performance and seasonal trends. You simply enter potential keyword phrases or a specific URL that will generate suggested keywords for you based on the Web site content. You can then add new keywords to your campaign. The screen shot below depicts the Keyword tool:

Screenshots © Google™ Inc. and are reproduced with permission.

The screen shot depicts the Site-Related tool. Remember, if you are targeting products or a certain page on your Web site, enter that URL to generate keywords, instead of your home page.

Screenshots © Google™ Inc. and are reproduced with permission.

You may wish to incorporate Negative Keywords into your campaign. Negative keywords prevent your ads from appearing for queries containing the Negative keyword. Google™ offers a tool that simplifies the process of creating negative keywords and incorporating them into your campaign. A screen shot of the Negative Keyword tool is above:

Screenshots © Google™ Inc. and are reproduced with permission.

Google™ Traffic Estimator

The Google™ Traffic estimator tool provides a wealth of data relevant to your chosen keywords and helps you determine expected traffic, daily budget, costs per keyword, and campaign success. Remember, this is simply a tool; it is not a guarantee of performance; however, it is based on the best data in Google™ and should be representative of what you may expect.

Average CPC: $8.19 (at a maximum CPC of $17.32) Estimated clicks per day: 17 - 20 (at a daily budget of $150.00)				Estimates are based on your bid amount and geographical targeting selections. Because the Traffic Estimator does not consider your daily budget, your ad may receive fewer clicks than estimated.		
Maximum CPC:	Daily budget:	Get New Estimates				
Keywords ▼	Search Volume	Estimated Avg. CPC	Estimated Ad Positions	Estimated Clicks / Day		Estimated Cost / Day
Search Total		$6.54 - $9.87	1 - 3	17 - 20		$80 - $150
chefsc		$0.71 - $0.99	1 - 3	0		$1
recipe software		$10.05 - $15.09	1 - 3	1		$6 - $20
restaurant consulting		$1.69 - $2.53	1 - 3	6		$10 - $20
restaurant management		$5.93 - $8.90	1 - 3	10 - 13		$70 - $120
Estimates for these keywords are based on clickthrough rates for current advertisers. Some of the keywords above are subject to review by Google and may not trigger your ads until they are approved. Please note that your traffic estimates assume your keywords are approved.						

Screenshots © Google™ Inc. and are reproduced with permission.

You simply enter keywords into the appropriate fields, along with some optional entries such as maximum cost per click, daily budget limits, as well as targeted languages and locations, and click "continue" to see the results. The results provide you with an average cost per click, volume, estimated ad position, estimated number of clicks per day, and estimated cost per day.

Google™ AdWords Campaign Setup

The first step you must complete to create a new Google™ AdWords campaign. Remember—you can have many campaigns within a Google™ AdWords account. To create a new campaign, click on the Create a New Campaign Link on the Google™ AdWords Campaign Management Screen.

All Campaigns
+ Create a new campaign : keyword-targeted | site-targeted [?]

Screenshots © Google™ Inc. and are reproduced with permission.

You may choose "Keyword-Targeted" (target customers by keywords), or "Site-Targeted" (target customers by Web sites). We recommend you choose "Keyword-Targeted." Keyword-targeted campaigns will appear on Google™ Search Engine results pages where site-targeted will appear on Web sites that you have selected in the Google™ network. You must name your campaign. Choose a name that will help you identify which campaign it is easily and quickly. This is important if you create multiple campaigns in your account.

Create a campaign and an Ad Group

Name your campaign: [Restaurant Profits]   Example
A campaign is the top level of account organization for all your ads. [?]

Name your new Ad Group: [Profit]   Example
An Ad Group connects your ad and its related keywords, which you'll create in a few moments. This name is for your use; it won't be seen by customers. [?]

Your Account	
Campaign	
Ad Group	Ad Group
Ad(s)	Ad(s)
Keywords	Keywords

Target customers by language

What language(s) do your customers speak?

Hold down the *control* or *command* key to select multiple languages.

English
Chinese (simplified)
Chinese (traditional)
Danish
Dutch
Finnish
French
German

Target customers by location

How large is the area where you'd like your ad to appear? Choose one:

◉ **Countries and territories** - Your ads will appear for searches made anywhere in the locations you select.

○ **Regions and cities** - Your ads will appear for searches made in the regions and cities you choose.
(Not available for all locations or ad formats.)

○ **Customized** - Your ads will appear for searches made within a specific distance from your business or other location you choose.
(Not available for all ad formats.)

[Continue »]

New Campaign Setup

Target customers > Create ad > Choose keywords > Set pricing > Review and save

Target customers by country or territory

Highlight the countries or territories on the left where you'd like your ad to appear, then click 'Add.' Select as many as you like. Your ads will appear to users anywhere in each location you select.

Available Countries and Territories

All Countries and Territories

United States
Australia
Austria
Belgium
Brazil
Canada
China
Denmark

[Add »]
[« Remove]

Selected Countries and/or Territories

United States

[« Back]   [Continue »]

You will also have to choose the Ad-Group name. The Ad-Group name contains one or more ads that target one set of keywords or sites. You will set your maximum cost per click or cost per thousand impressions (CPM) for all the keywords or sites in the Ad Group. You may also set prices for individual keywords or sites within the Ad Group. Again, if you are setting up a keyword-targeted campaign, you need to set up the maximum cost-per-click only for the keywords, not the sites, which are used for site-targeted campaigns. Additionally, you will choose the targeted customers by language and location.

Next, you will create the actual ad that will be displayed in the search-engine results page. Google™ AdWords has multiple ad options including:

- **Text Ad**

- **Image Ad**

- **Local Business Ad** — Local business ads are AdWords ads associated with a specific Google™ Maps business listing. They show on Google™ Maps with an enhanced location marker. They also show in a text-only format on Google™ and other sites in our search network.

- **Mobile Text Ad** — Your ads will appear when someone uses Google™ Mobile Search on a mobile device.

- **Video Ad** — Video ads are a new ad format that will appear on the Google™ content network. Your video ad will appear as a static image until a user clicks on it and your video is played.

Screenshots © Google™ Inc. and are reproduced with permission.

You can see samples of these types of ads on the next page.

We recommend you start out your campaigns with the Text Ad. Google™ AdWords provides you with a simple form to create your text ad. As you enter data, the example is updated with your data. In the screen shot below, notice that we have capitalized each keyword in each line, as well as providing the display URL, and the actual destination URL, which as we discussed in earlier chapters, may be different depending on your campaign.

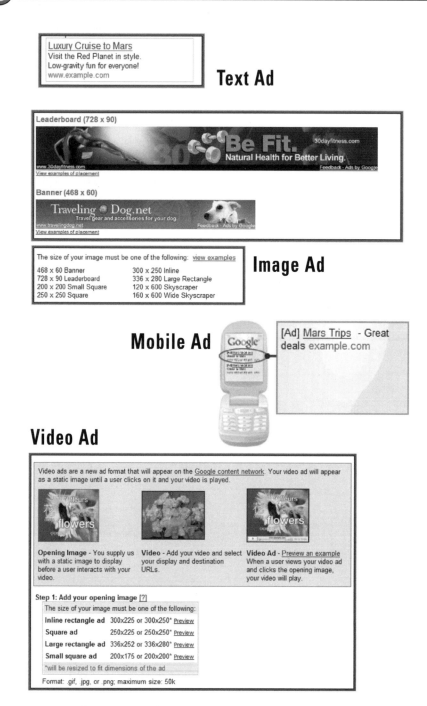

Screenshots © Google™ Inc. and are reproduced with permission.

You will need to give some extra time and attention to the wording of your ad. Wording can be tricky because of the limited space on each line of the ad, as well as the restrictions imposed by Google™. While Google™ AdWords has a clear policy about how to create the ad, Yahoo is even more restrictive and can present a challenge in creating an ad that says what you want it to say and still passes the review of the PPC provider.

On page 115 you will find an ad for a fictitious business we created to help you create ads called Gizmo Auto Sales, **www.gizmoautosales.com**. You may not be able to use superlatives such as finest, best, biggest, nor are they recommended. You are also restricted from promotional punctuation such as the "!" and "$" symbols. You are limited on the number of words capitalized, and you cannot use all caps.

This ad will NOT pass review:

Lowest Used Auto Price Quotes — Get them NOW!
Save $$CASH$$ with Discount Prices
www.gizmoautosales.com

This ad will pass review:

Used Automobile Price Quotes — Free all the Time
Save money with Discount Auto Prices
www.gizmoautosales.com

It is critical to load the title (first line of your PPC ad) with keywords. PPC programs may have different rules that apply concerning the Title line; however, you should strive to load it with keywords, while maintaining readability, and strive to make it captivating to a potential customer. Your goal is simply to capture the attention and interest of a potential customer. If you can do that, your ad is successful. If no one is interested in your ad, it will not get clicks, and will not draw customers to your Web site. Test multiple versions of ad to see which works best and change keywords to help you analyze which is most effective. Review the ads of competitors. You may find they are outperforming you simply because their ad is better written, more captivating, or has more customer appeal.

The use of free, rebate, bonus, and cash are perfect for attracting attention of Web site surfers. Other words that may encourage Web

Site visitors to click through your ad should be used as long as your ad message is concise and clear. Do not overload them with words that will lose the meaning of your ad. Remember that both Google™ and Yahoo must review and approve your ad, and if your ad does not pass their review, you will be notified.

You should also consider the domain name listed in your ad, as it may have an effect on your ability to draw in potential customers. Your domain name should be directly related to your product or services and be professional in nature. The domain name **reallycheapcars.com** may not impart a perception of quality in your automobiles that you are striving to achieve. Perhaps the domain name **qualitycars.com** would be a better choice. Be wary of domain names that are overly promotional in content, as they may drive away potential customers (i.e., **freecars.com**).

You will find an abundance of companies that offer Search Engine Copywriting services, a good option if you are having problems developing successful ad campaigns.

Some recommended sources for Copywriting include:

- **www.searchenginewriting.com/**
- **www.grantasticdesigns.com/copywriting.html**
- **www.roncastle.com/web_copywriting.htm**
- **www.futurenettechnologies.com/creative-copywriting.htm**
- **www.tinawrites.com/**
- **www.brandidentityguru.com/optimized-copywriting.html**

Search-engine copywriting is critical to a successful PPC advertising campaign. While we have recommended professional services for this task, it is not overly difficult to achieve if you apply some basic discipline and rules. While I have repeatedly stressed the insertion of keywords into an ad, simply cramming keyword after keyword into your PPC ads may be counter-productive, and doing so is not search-engine copywriting. Successful search-engine optimization copywriting takes planning, discipline, analysis, and some degree of trial and error. Below are some general guidelines for successful search-engine optimization copywriting.

- **Use no more than four keywords per ad.** Four keywords

provide a wide variety without saturating the ad with keywords and losing the meaning of the ad.

- **Use all of your allowed characters in each line of the ad.** The length depends on the PPC provider; however, use the space you have been provided. There is no incentive for white space.

- **Write In Natural Language where possible.** "Natural language" is a popular term used extensively with copywriting. It simply means that the reader should not be able to detect the keywords the ad is targeting. The best ads are written for an individual to read and understand, imbedded with subtle keywords, projecting a clear message so that it reads "naturally." The opposite of this is a keyword-crammed ad that is nothing more than a collection of keywords, and is entirely "unnatural" to read.

- **Use Keywords in the Title and Description lines** — However, use common sense and follow the rules we provided so that

you do not overload them with keywords.

- **Test and Tweak** — Test your ad and analyze your reports and results. Your ad may need tweaking and improvements, or it may be entirely ineffective and may need to be replaced.

Google™ will check your ad and Web site for content, functionality, and to ensure the ad complies with editorial guidelines.

Google™ AdWords will extract keywords from your site based on a scan of the Website URL and propose them to you as potential keywords to use on your campaign. You may choose any keywords suggested or enter any of your own into the campaign window. Google™ recommends a maximum of 20 keywords per ad for best results. Once you have selected keywords that closely match your products or services, click the "continue" button. (See first screenshot on next page).

Restaurant Consulting
Reduce Costs + Increase Profits!
Discount Prices + Free Tech Support
www.restaurantprofits.com
Edit - Delete

You can create additional ads for this Ad Group, if you choose. [?]
+ Create new ad

Choose keywords

Who will see your ad?
When people search Google for the keywords you choose here, your ad can show. Keywords must be directly related to your ad. (Don't enter 'real estate' when you're selling cars.) Enter 20 or fewer keywords for best results. Example list

Enter as many specific words or phrases as you like, one per line:

```
liquor inventory control
cheftec
inventory control
inventory control systems
job costing
job costing software
food costing software
project costing
costing
recipe costing
menu costing
```

Sample keywords based on a scan of your site
If they describe your product or service, click 'Add'. (See our disclaimer.)

Click categories to view keywords:

▼ Category: inventory control

  « Add all in this category

  « Add inventory control system

  « Add retail inventory control software

  « Add inventory control software

  « Add warehouse inventory control

  « Add inventory control database

  « Add simple inventory control

  « Add inventory control program

  « Add retail inventory control

  « Add quickbooks inventory control

  « Add basic inventory control

▶ Category: inventory

Want more?
Enter any word to see related keywords:

[   ] [Search]

▶ Advanced option: match types

Important note: Please note that we cannot guarantee that these keywords will improve your campaign performance. We also reserve the right to disapprove any new keywords you add. Keep in mind that you alone are responsible for the keywords you select and for making sure that your use of the keywords does not violate any applicable laws, including any applicable trademark laws. For more details, please review our Terms and Conditions.

[« Back] [Continue »]

Screenshots © Google™ Inc. and are reproduced with permission.

What is the most you would like to spend, on average, per day?

The daily budget [?] controls your costs. When the daily limit is reached, on average, your ad will stop showing for that day. (The budget controls the frequency of your ad, not its position.) Raise or lower your budget as often as you like.

Enter your daily budget: $ [   ]

What is the maximum you are willing to pay each time someone clicks on your ad?

You influence your ad's position by setting its maximum cost per click (CPC) [?]. The max CPC is the highest price you're willing to pay each time a user clicks on your ad. Your max CPC can be changed as often as you like.

Enter your maximum CPC: $ [   ] (Minimum: $0.01)
Higher CPCs lead to higher ad positions, which usually get more clicks.

Want to purchase the most clicks possible?

▶ View Traffic Estimator - Enter a CPC and see the estimated rank, traffic, and costs for your keyword(s).

Three things to remember:

- You can always change your CPC and budget, or pause your account entirely.
- Your budget controls your spending. If your daily budget is $5.00 and there are 30 days in a month, you'll never be charged more than $150 in that month.
- Lower your costs by choosing more specific keywords, like *red roses* instead of *flowers*. Specific keywords are more likely to turn a click into a customer. Edit your keyword list.

[« Back] [Continue »]

Screenshots © Google™ Inc. and are reproduced with permission.

You must now enter your budgetary constraints and limitations, such as the daily budget. When the daily limit is reached, your ad will stop showing for that day. The budget controls the frequency of your ad, not its position. You may raise or lower your budget amount as often as you like. Additionally, you must choose your maximum cost per click, which is the highest price you are willing to pay each time a user clicks on your ad. Your maximum CPC can be changed as often as you desire.

Screenshots © Google™ Inc. and are reproduced with permission.

You may discover that the costs can escalate quickly without setting daily and monthly budget limitations. Keep in mind that limits on your daily/monthly budgets will also affect your ad performance because your ad will not be displayed after you hit your budget limits. Google™ recognizes when your ad is bumping against its budget constraints and may suggest you increase your budget amount to increase visibility of your ad:

Screenshots © Google™ Inc. and are reproduced with permission.

The Google™ Campaign Summary

The Campaign Summary screen is where you will control all your Google™ AdWords campaigns. At this screen you will be presented with an overview of each campaign, including Campaign Name, Status, Budget, Clicks, Impressions, Click-Through Ratio, Average Cost per Click, and Total Cost. Note that the data are presented based on the reporting period selected.

To drill down into each campaign, simply click on the Campaign Name to view detailed status based on keywords and ad variation performance. This module will help you determine the effectiveness of each keyword, as well as add or remove keywords. Your keywords may be marked "inactive for search" in the "status" column, and stop showing on search results if they do not have a high enough Quality Score and maximum cost-per-click (CPC). In other words, your keyword or Ad Group's maximum CPC does not meet the minimum bid required to trigger ads on Google™ or its search network partners. This typically occurs when keywords are not as targeted as they could be, and the ads they deliver are not relevant enough to what a user is searching for, which ultimately means you need to refine your keywords or your ad.

Keywords marked inactive for search are inactive only for search. They may continue to trigger ads for content sites if you have the Google™ content network enabled for that campaign. Again, we recommend that you turn off this feature initially and only use keyword searches because a keyword marked as inactive for search may continue to generate clicks and charges on the content network. If your keyword is inactive for search, you may increase your keyword's Quality Score by optimizing for relevancy. Optimization is a technique for improving the quality of your keywords, ad, and campaign to increase your keyword's performance without raising costs. Try to combine your keyword with two or three other words to create a more specific keyword phrase. This will result in better targeting and potentially better performance.

Screenshots © Google™ Inc. and are reproduced with permission.

You may also increase your keyword's maximum Cost per Click to the recommended minimum bid. Your keyword's minimum bid is the amount required to trigger ads on Google™ and is determined by your keyword's Quality Score. When your maximum CPC falls below the minimum bid, your keyword will be inactive for search. For this reason, you can simply increase your maximum CPC to the minimum bid to re-activate your keywords. You may also choose to delete all your keywords that are inactive for search.

Screenshots © Google™ Inc. and are reproduced with permission.

Screenshots © Google™ Inc. and are reproduced with permission.

The Ad Variations link allows you to review performance for each ad within a selected campaign. It is common to have multiple ads created for the same or different keyword combinations within the same campaign. In the example below, it is clear by the percent served that the first ad is served considerably more than the second ad, which is rarely served. The reasons for this may vary, depending on the keywords chosen or the campaign settings.

If you click on the Edit link, under the Actions column, you can tweak your campaign ads to improve your statistics.

Remember, for each Ad Group you create, you can create up to 50 ad variations. The variations can be in any of the formats offered for AdWords, including text, image, and video ads. When you first sign up for an account, you will be offered the chance to create additional ad variations immediately after you create your first ad. You can also create ad variations later, after your account is running. Sign into your account and choose the Ad Group you want to work with. Click the Ad Variations tab, find the line reading "Create new ad," and then select

Edit Keyword Settings

This optional feature helps you track individual keywords and their costs. You may enter individual Max CPCs or destination URLs for any keyword. Fields left blank will take the default Ad Group CPC or URL. To enter an entire list of keywords, URLs, and bids all at once, try the Edit Keywords and CPC page.

Default bid:$ 2.00 Max CPC [?]

Keyword	Status [?]	Search Bid Max CPC	Destination URL		Clicks	Impr.	CTR	Avg. CPC	Cost	Avg. Pos
restaurant consulting	Active	$ 3.50	http:// www.restaurantprofits.com		248	10,161	2.44%	$0.81	$200.74	5.5
restaurant management	Active	$ 3.25	http:// www.restaurantprofits.com		28	4,599	0.60%	$0.51	$14.24	14.3
cheftec	Active	$ 3.25	http:// www.restaurantprofits.com/cheftec.html		103	3,301	3.12%	$0.50	$51.30	1.8
recipe software	Active	$ 3.00	http:// www.restaurantprofits.com/cheftec.html		7	4,872	0.14%	$0.83	$5.83	12.8
chef tec	Active	$ 3.00	http:// www.restaurantprofits.com/cheftec.html		52	2,624	1.98%	$0.49	$25.72	2.3
restaurant consultants	Active	$ 2.00	http:// www.restaurantprofits.com		101	6,157	1.64%	$0.93	$93.65	9.8
restaurant consultant	Active	$ 2.00	http:// www.restaurantprofits.com		79	4,609	1.71%	$0.86	$68.19	8.6
restaurant accountant	Active	$ 2.00	http:// www.restaurantprofits.com		65	3,798	1.71%	$0.73	$47.75	5.0
hospitality management	Active	$ 2.00	http:// www.restaurantprofits.com		0	1,168	0.00%			19.8
increase profits	Active	$ 2.00	http:// www.restaurantprofits.com		3	846	0.35%	$0.82	$2.46	5.0
Restaurant Recipe Software	Active	$ 2.00	http:// www.restaurantprofits.com		3	416	0.72%	$0.83	$2.48	10.2
food service expert	Active	$ 2.00	http:// www.restaurantprofits.com		1	39	2.56%	$0.19	$0.19	2.2
restaurant management consultants	Active	$ 2.00	http:// www.restaurantprofits.com		0	29	0.00%			14.6
Cheftec Consulting	Active	$ 2.00	http:// www.restaurantprofits.com/cheftec.html		0	0	-	-	-	-
Cheftec Recipe Software	Active	$ 2.00	http:// www.restaurantprofits.com/cheftec.html		0	0	-	-	-	-
Cheftec Sales	Active	$ 2.00	http:// www.restaurantprofits.com/cheftec.html		0	0	-	-	-	-
recipe inventory software	Active	$ 2.00	http:// www.restaurantprofits.com/cheftec.html		0	0	-	-	-	-
restaurant management consultant	Active	$ 2.00	http:// www.restaurantprofits.com		0	0	-	-	-	-
restaurant history	Active	$ 2.00	http:// www.restaurantprofits.com		0	0	-	-	-	-
restaurant profitability	Active	$ 2.00	http:// www.restaurantprofits.com		0	0	-	-	-	-
customer profitability	Active	$ 1.00	http:// www.restaurantprofits.com		0	0	-	-	-	-
foodservice news	Active	$ 1.00	http:// www.restaurantprofits.com		0	0	-	-	-	-

Screenshots © Google™ Inc. and are reproduced with permission.

the type of ad you want to create. All ad variations in a single Ad Group are triggered by the same set of keywords. You can choose to have ads optimized automatically, so that the best-performing ad variations show most often, or you can choose to show them evenly regardless of their performance. You may choose to have ads optimized to show better-performing ads more often (and is the default selection), or rotate, which shows all ads equally. If you want different ads to appear for different keywords, you can create multiple Ad Groups or campaigns.

Screenshots © Google™ Inc. and are reproduced with permission.

The Edit Keyword Settings page helps you track individual keywords and their costs. You may enter individual maximum cost-per-click or destination URLs for any keyword.

Based on your current keywords, your recommended budget is **$8.00 / day**.

If the recommended amount is too high, try raising your budget to a comfortable amount. Or, to make the most of your budget, try refining your ads and keywords.

Screenshots © Google™ Inc. and are reproduced with permission.

Editing Your Campaign Settings

In the "Edit Campaign Settings" menu, you have the ability to modify your campaign settings including campaign name, budget options, ad scheduling, keyword bidding, networks (which specify keyword search or content search), target audience, and ad serving (which allows you to optimize the ads or rotate them evenly).

Google™ AdWords will suggest the recommended budget amount for your campaign by clicking on the View Recommended Budget link in the Edit Campaign Settings screen, as shown at right.

Ad scheduling lets you control the days and times your AdWords campaigns appear. Your AdWords ads normally are available to run 24 hours each day. Ad scheduling allows you to set your campaigns to appear only during certain hours or days of each week. For example, you might set your ads to run only on Tuesdays or from 3 until 6 p.m. daily. With ad scheduling, a campaign can run all day, every day, or as little as 15 minutes per week.

To determine when you want your ads to show, you may want to run an hourly report. Ad scheduling can be used with both keyword-targeted and site-targeted AdWords campaigns. If you select the advanced setting, the bid multiplier will apply to both cost-per-click (CPC) and cost-per-thousand-impressions (CPM) bids. Ad scheduling will not raise or lower your budget. The AdWords system will try to reach your usual daily budget in whatever number of hours your ad runs each day. Learn more about ad scheduling and your AdWords budget.

Position preference lets you tell Google™ where you would prefer your ad to show among all the AdWords ads on a given page. Whenever you run a keyword-targeted ad, your ad is assigned a position (or rank) based on your cost-per-click (CPC) bid, your keyword's Quality Score, and other relevant factors. There may be dozens of positions available for a given keyword, spread over several pages of search results. If you find that your ad gets the best results when it is ranked, for example, third or fourth among all AdWords ads, you can set a position preference for those spots. AdWords will then try to show your ad whenever it is ranked third or fourth and avoid showing it when it is ranked higher or lower. If your ad is ranked higher than third for a given keyword, the system will automatically try to lower your bid to place your ad in your preferred position.

You can request that your ad be shown only when it is:

- Higher than a given position (such as above seven)
- Lower than a given position (such as below four)
- Within a range of positions (such as from two to eight).
- In a single exact position (such as position two).

Position preference does not mean that your ad will always appear in the position you specify. The usual AdWords ranking and relevance rules apply. If your ad does not qualify for position number one, setting a position preference of "one" will not move it there. Position preference simply means AdWords will try to show your ad whenever it is ranked in your preferred position and to avoid showing it when it is not. Position preference also does not affect the placement of AdWords ad units on the left, right, top, or bottom of a given page. It only affects your ranking relative to other ads across those units.

Google™ AdWords allows you to track Conversions. In online

advertising, a conversion occurs when a click on your ad leads directly to user behavior you deem valuable, such as a purchase, sign up, page view, or lead. Google™ has developed a tool to measure these conversions, and ultimately, help you identify how effective your AdWords ads and keywords are for you. It works by placing a cookie on a user's computer whenever the person clicks on one of your AdWords ads. Then if the user reaches one of your conversion pages, the cookie is connected to your Web page. When a match is made, Google™ records a successful conversion for you. Please note that the cookie Google™ adds to a user's computer expires in 30 days. This measure and the fact that Google™ uses separate servers for conversion tracking and search results protect the user's privacy. You may select Conversion Tracking under your campaign main menu, and there are some minimal setup requirements for Conversion Tracking to work.

Google™ AdWords Reports

Google™ provides full online statistical, conversion, and financial reporting for the Google™ AdWords program. You can view all your account reports online 24 hours a day, 7 days a week, and you can also have them set up to be e-mailed to you on a scheduled basis. You have a variety of advanced reports available, including:

- **Statistical Reporting**: displays the average actual cost-per-click (CPC), the number of times your ads were shown (impressions), how many times users clicked on your ads (clicks), and your ad and keyword click-through rates (CTR). This reporting is available for each of your keywords, ad variations (such as text

Campaign ▼	Ad Group	Keyword	Keyword Matching	Keyword Status	Keyword Min CPC	Current Maximum CPC	Keyword Destination URL	Impressions	Clicks	CTR	Avg CPC	Cost	Avg Position
ProfitStrategies	RestaurantConsulting	Restaurant Recipe Software	Broad	Active	$0.05	$2.00	http://www.restaurantprofits.com	6	0	0.00%	$0.00	$0.00	6.0
ProfitStrategies	RestaurantConsulting	Total - content targeting	Content					1,196	0	0.00%	$0.00	$0.00	4.2
ProfitStrategies	RestaurantConsulting	chef tec	Broad	Active	$0.10	$2.00	http://www.restaurantprofits.com/cheftec.html	77	0	0.00%	$0.00	$0.00	2.7
ProfitStrategies	RestaurantConsulting	cheftec	Broad	Active	$0.10	$2.00	http://www.restaurantprofits.com/cheftec.html	49	1	2.04%	$0.13	$0.13	1.1
ProfitStrategies	RestaurantConsulting	food service expert	Broad	Active	$0.10	$2.00	http://www.restaurantprofits.com	3	0	0.00%	$0.00	$0.00	1.7
ProfitStrategies	RestaurantConsulting	hospitality management	Broad	Active	$0.20	$2.00	http://www.restaurantprofits.com	14	0	0.00%	$0.00	$0.00	19.3
ProfitStrategies	RestaurantConsulting	increase profits	Broad	Active	$0.15	$2.00	http://www.restaurantprofits.com	33	0	0.00%	$0.00	$0.00	1.7
ProfitStrategies	RestaurantConsulting	recipe software	Broad	Active	$0.40	$2.00	http://www.restaurantprofits.com/cheftec.html	53	0	0.00%	$0.00	$0.00	8.7
ProfitStrategies	RestaurantConsulting	restaurant accountant	Broad	Active	$0.04	$2.00	http://www.restaurantprofits.com	93	1	1.08%	$0.24	$0.24	3.0
ProfitStrategies	RestaurantConsulting	restaurant consultant	Broad	Active	$0.04	$2.00	http://www.restaurantprofits.com	233	5	2.15%	$1.60	$8.01	3.9
ProfitStrategies	RestaurantConsulting	restaurant consultants	Broad	Active	$0.04	$2.00	http://www.restaurantprofits.com	272	13	4.78%	$1.71	$22.19	4.9
ProfitStrategies	RestaurantConsulting	restaurant consulting	Broad	Active	$0.03	$2.00	http://www.restaurantprofits.com	481	8	1.66%	$1.18	$9.48	3.8
ProfitStrategies	RestaurantConsulting	restaurant management	Broad	Active	$0.10	$2.00	http://www.restaurantprofits.com	15	0	0.00%	$0.00	$0.00	12.1
Totals and Overall Averages:								2,495	28	1.12%	$1.43	$40.05	4.2

Screenshots © Google™ Inc. and are reproduced with permission.

ads, image ads, video ads, mobile ads, and local business ads), Ad Groups, campaigns, and account.

- **Financial Reporting**: review a detailed billing summary and itemized payment details that include invoice dates, invoice numbers, specific and summary campaign costs, and billing adjustments.

- **Conversion Reporting**: track your AdWords conversions (successful sales, leads, or submissions).
  Screenshots © Google™ Inc. and are reproduced with permission.

Google™ AdWords Tips and Hints

Here is a compilation of some tips and hints which will help you to develop and manage a highly effective Google™ Adwords Campaign, which in turn will generate higher click-through rates, lower your cost per click, and get conversions (i.e., click-throughs that result in sales of your products).

- **Define your target audience and narrow the scope of your ad to potential customer markets**; that is, if you do not sell overseas or in foreign speaking countries — do not pay to have your ad listed there.

- **Develop multiple ads for each campaign and run them at the same time.** You will quickly determine which is effective and which is not. Do not be afraid to tweak ads or replace poor performing ads.

- **Monitor and use Google™ Reports** by tracking your costs, return on investment, and the click-through ratios for each ad. Implement Google™ Conversion Tracking to track the effectiveness of completing a sale.

- **Include Targeted Keywords in the Headline and Description lines** of your ad. Keywords stand out in search-engine results and help to attract attention of potential customers, as well as increase your ad effectiveness. Be very specific in your keywords. Being too generic will draw in traffic but not sales!

- **Make your ad stand out by announcing the advantage your company product has that others do not!** For example, in addition to selling Cheftec Software, Profit Strategies and

Solutions, Inc., "offers an additional 60 days of free training and tech support after the initial manufacturer's 60 days of tech support expires at no additional cost."

- **Include words that stand out and grab the attention** of potential customers, such as Free, New, and Limited Offer.

- **Do not just link to the homepage of your Web site.** Link directly to the relevant landing page for your specific product or service. Doing so will help you convert the "visit" to a "sale."

- **Free may not be good for you!** If your ad says "free," you can expect lots of traffic by folks who just want the "free" stuff but will never buy anything. They will only increase your costs. Remember, they click on your ad, but you pay! Consider limiting the use of "free" to cut back on traffic that will never culminate in a sale.

An article from Article Alley which may be helpful to you when working on your Google™ AdWords campaign is "Guide to Google™ Adwords — Target your Adwords ads for Motivated Visitors," by Peter Bergdahl. This article is available for you at **http://www.articlealley.com/article_92745_6.html**.

The Best Advice for Managing Your Google™ AdWords Account

- **Google™ provides you with Conversion Tracking if you choose to implement it** and I highly recommend you take the time to install it. However, I recommend you track your own conversion rates as well. If Google™ is not reporting conversions, yet you have been paying for thousands of clicks, there is a problem. You are the victim of fraud, the conversion tracking HTML code is not working properly, or your PPC campaign is generating traffic, but your Web site is not converting sales (which indicates a problem with your site content—you have to have good, relevant content to "finish" the sale).

- **Monitor your daily and monthly budget on a regular basis.** This is even more important if your campaign becomes successful which means it will cost more. Most companies set daily and monthly limits and forget about the budget. As your desire to get the top page listings increases, so does your tendency to "bump" up the budget a few dollars a day, or add another $1 per click and before you know it your campaign costs can double or triple.

- **Monitor your daily and monthly budget and number of clicks.** You may find your ads will no longer be served for much of each month if you hit your daily and monthly limits early in the month. It is not uncommon for new AdWords customers to set a monthly limit of $100. It is also not uncommon for the $100 to be used within the first week, meaning your ads are not served for the remaining three weeks of the month. The same applies for daily limits. A low daily limit may minimize the number of hours your ad may be displayed.

- **Use multiple marketing schemes**, including multiple PPC campaigns with multiple PPC providers. Google™ and Yahoo are the biggies, but do not forget about Microsoft® adCenter and others. I will provide you quite a bit of information on other PPC providers and other alternative revenue or sales generating schemes.

- **Google™ AdWords allows you to test multiple ads based on the same keyword group** and do it simultaneously. By creating different ads, you can track each individually and determine which is the most effective. When you determine which are less effective, you can tweak them and change the wording to improve their success.

- **Be realistic in your expectations.** Although your PPC campaign can be established quickly, do not expect your business to quadruple the first day your campaign is established. It takes time, patience, and constant monitoring and modifying your campaign to become highly effective.

- **Spend the time to research your keywords and develop quality keywords**. Unbelievably, the time spent, which can be significant, will result in less cost and better quality click-through rates. Your conversion rates will improve dramatically with highly relevant, targeted, and refined keyword lists.

- **There are plenty of free resources on the Internet about how to manage your AdWords campaigns effectively.** Use them! The advice of experts is valuable when creating and managing your accounts. Become active in PPC discussion forums to exchange ideas and experiences with AdWord, and you will acquire more tips and tricks to improve your campaigns.

- **Create your ad with relevant and targeted keywords and ad copy.** Type "used car" into Google™, and you will get 13,000,000 links and tons of ads. However, this is such a broad category you may never find the used car you are looking for. Now type in "porsche 911" and you get 1,100 links, and many ads, but the ads are much more targeted and relevant. By creating relevant and targeted ads, you can eliminate many clicks—which you pay for—that offer no hope of conversion because you simply do not have the products that the person was looking for. Your goal is to keep costs low by eliminating unnecessary clicks.

As Billy Joel said, "I'm keeping the faith, yeah, yeah, yeah, keeping the faith." You need to do that with Google™ AdWords (or any PPC program). I said in the introduction that there is no magic bullet, secret formula, or hidden code to rocket you to success. It takes time, attention, work, and more work. Eventually, if you following hte principles of this book, you will see increased Web site traffic, a growing customer base, and conversions.

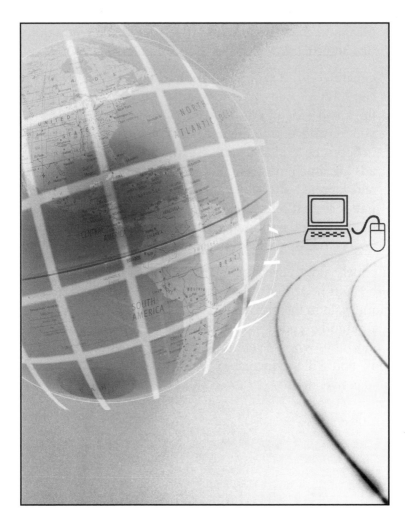

CHAPTER 8

Yahoo!® Search Marketing

Yahoo!® Search Marketing, formerly known as Overture, is similar to Google™ AdWords that we covered in detail in the previous chapter. It has many similarities with Google™ AdWords program; however, it also has some unique differences, and most notably uses a different user-interface. I highly recommend you use both Yahoo!® Search Marketing as well as Google™ Adwords simultaneously to ensure you are reaching all major search engines. You should use this chapter to familiarize yourselves with Yahoo!® Search Marketing, as part of your PPC marketing campaign strategy. Yahoo!® Search Marketing offers a wide-variety of products. They include:

- **Sponsored Search** — Allows you to reach active Internet users on top search-engine sites.

- **Local Advertising** — Allows you to target prospects searching for businesses in your neighborhood.

- **Search Submit** — Allows you to expand your reach and coverage in algorithmic search listings.

- **Product Submit** — Allows you to reach millions of motivated buyers through Yahoo!® Shopping.

- **Travel Submit** — Allows you to promote your offers and deals to eager travelers on Yahoo!® Travel.

- **Directory Submit** — Allows you to include your business in the Yahoo!® Directory.

Yahoo!® Sponsored Search

Yahoo!® Search Marketing is a global leader in commercial search services on the Internet, providing new and more powerful ways for businesses and customers to connect online. Yahoo!® claims that their advertisers can reach more than 80 percent of active Internet users. Yahoo!® Search Marketing's flagship product is Sponsored Search, which lists your site in search results across the Web through major portals and search engines, including; Yahoo!®, MSN®, AltaVista, InfoSpace, Sympatico.ca as well as Search Engines such as DogPile, METAcrawler, webCrawler, Alltheweb. If you use Content Match, your ad may be displayed on content match partners including CNN.com, ESPN.com, and KnightRidder. Yahoo claims that advertising in the top positions for a keyword enables you to appear on more search sites and reach 80 percent of active Internet users, while lower positions reach about 40 percent of users. Therefore, bidding into the top positions on as many keywords as possible will help you establish a successful Yahoo!® Sponsored Search campaign.

Using a Web search engine is a basic, common practice for navigating or finding information on the Internet. More than 98 percent of all Web surfers use a search engine regularly, and incredibly, this service is provided at no cost. Yahoo!® Sponsored Search delivers targeted, relevant text ads as part of search-engine results, very similar to Google™ AdWords. Nielsen/Netratings reported for one week in 2005, search engines displayed more than 13 billion sponsored search results. Yahoo!® Sponsored Search delivers search results from the search engine, along with relevant highly targeted ads, designed to drive qualified Web traffic to their Web sites.

The principles of Yahoo!® Sponsored Search are:

- Delivery targeted and relevant advertiser-provided content (ad) within a set of search-engine results.

- Traffic and ad-serving based on keyword relevance.

- Match advertiser content (keywords) to Web user queries through search engines to delivery relevant, targeted results ads.

- Display ads in rank order based on keyword, bidding, and other algorithms.

- Systematic process that collects data and charges advertisers based on actual clicks on their ads.

Yahoo!® Sponsored Search Listing Guidelines

Yahoo!®-produced Sponsored Search-engine Listing Guidelines help you realize a better return on your investment. The links to the guidelines for each of the following are included below.

KEYWORD SELECTION

There must be a strong, direct relationship between keywords and the content, purpose, and theme of your site. Choose keywords that best describe what is on your site to attract users who want what you offer.

Their specific keyword selection guidelines can be found at **http://help.yahoo.com/l/us/yahoo/ysm/sps/start/editorial/keyword_selection.html**.

TITLES AND DESCRIPTIONS

Use clear, factual, and objective language that accurately describes what you offer on your site.

The entire list of their title and description guidelines, as well as correct and incorrect samples, can be found at **http://help.yahoo.com/l/us/yahoo/ysm/sps/start/editorial/title_description.html**.

SUBMITTED URL

These are what take the users to the page where they can easily find what they are searching. For mor ifnormation on specific guidelines for submitted URLs, see **http://help.yahoo.com/l/us/yahoo/ysm/sps/start/editorial/urls.html**.

UNACCEPTABLE CONTENT

They may not accept listings that relate to certain products or services. They also reserve the right to decline or remove any listing at any time at their discretion. Be sure not to violate Yahoo!®'s Unacceptable Content Policy which can be found at **http://help.yahoo.com/l/us/yahoo/ysm/sps/start/editorial/unacceptable_content.html**.

Setting up a Yahoo!® Sponsored Search Account

You will pay a $5 fee to set up your Yahoo!® Sponsored Search account, which is same cost to establish a Google™ AdWords account. Again, I highly recommend you use both Yahoo!® Sponsored Search and Google™ AdWords together, as they will complement each other and target different search engines. The Account Setup wizard will walk you through the set-up process. The Account Setup screen contains options you can adjust at any time after you establish your account, including:

- **Account On/Off** — Allows you to turn your Sponsored Search Account on or off.

- **Content Match Advertising** — This feature displays your PPC ad when relevant content is viewed on Yahoo!® Partner pages. It is recommended that you leave Content Match OFF when you set up you account.

- **Advanced Match Type** — Allows you to reach even more targeted customers. You go to the Manage Listings page and select the individual listings you would like to opt into this feature and click on the Match Type Options button.

- **Easy Track** — Provides detailed information when analyzing your Web server logs. When enabled, you will receive data that will allow you to determine traffic by keyword, match type, and raw search query.

- **Conversion Counter** — Allows you to measure conversions, conversion rate, and cost-per-conversion; track conversions at the keyword, category and account levels; track conversions for all match types and Content Match, and sort conversion data by day, week or month. This free feature requires you to place some HTML code on your Web site.

Creating Yahoo!® Sponsored Search Account Keywords

According to Yahoo!®, more than 500 million unique keywords appear on their Search Marketing network. As with Google™ AdWords, you should submit and maintain a core number of keywords that are relevant to your Web site while ensuring that you meet the Yahoo!® listing guidelines. Yahoo!® states that the most successful advertisers bid on between 500 and 5,000 keywords. For maximum traffic to your site, Yahoo!® recommends you generate as many keywords as possible; however, I recommend you keep them to a manageable number.

As we have discussed in earlier chapters, one of the best places to look for ideas for developing your keywords is your own business Web site.

The Yahoo!® Search Marketing Keyword Selector Tool is a great resource for finding keywords for your site. The Keyword Selector Tool can be found once you log into your account and click on the Manage Sponsored Search tab or by going to **http://inventory.overture. com/d/searchinventory/suggestion/**.

Screenshots © 2007 Yahoo!® Inc. Yahoo!® and the Yahoo!® logo are trademarks of Yahoo!® Inc.

Keyword Selector Tool

Not sure what search terms to bid on?
Enter a term related to your site and we will show you:

• Related searches that include your term
• How many times that term was searched on last month

Get suggestions for: (may take up to 30 seconds)

restaurant%20consulting

Note: All suggested search terms are subject to our standard editorial review process.

Searches done in August 2006 Count Search Term	
1015	consulting restaurant
118	consulting restaurant service
80	consulting restaurant services
61	consulting design restaurant
60	consulting firm restaurant
51	concept consulting restaurant
33	consulting management restaurant

Your keywords can be single words or phrases that relate to what you are offering. When people search for the keyword you have chosen, your site should show up in the search results. Yahoo!® will also allow you to make categories of your keywords.

The position of your ad will be based on the cost-per-click in the bidding process.

Yahoo!® Keyword Key Cost Factors:

• The placement of your ad will be based on the maximum cost-per-click.

• No spending minimum.

• The $5 one-time activation fee is all you need to get started.

• Daily limits on how much you want to spend are set by you..

Screenshots © 2007 Yahoo!® Inc. Yahoo!® and the Yahoo!® logo are trademarks of Yahoo!® Inc.

The cost-per-click is decided by you depending on how much you want to pay per impression.

- The only clicks you pay for are the ones on your ad.

Creating a Yahoo!® Sponsored Search Ad

Your ad titles and descriptions are of vital importance to your PPC search advertising campaign since they will introduce and entice your potential customers to your company, products, and Web site and will provide the initial impression of your company. Research indicates that users are more likely to click on listings that are tailored, clear, and factual. When writing ads, you should also:

- Include the keyword.

- Choose URLs that have relevant page content to your ad.

- Write titles and descriptions that are accurate.

Screenshots © 2007 Yahoo!® Inc. Yahoo!® and the Yahoo!® logo are trademarks of Yahoo!® Inc.

- Describe what users will find when they go to your site.

You will need to give some extra time and attention to the wording of your ad. Wording can be tricky because of the limited space on each line of the ad, as well as the restrictions imposed by Google™. While Google™ AdWords has a clear policy about how to create the ad,

Yahoo is even more restrictive and can present a significant challenge in creating an ad that says what you want it to say, and still passes the review of the PPC provider.

Below you will find an ad for a fictitious business we created for helping you create ads called Gizmo Auto Sales, **www.gizmoautosales.com**. You may not be able to use (nor are they recommended) superlatives such as finest, best, biggest. You are also restricted from promotional punctuation such as the "!" and "$" symbols as well as being limited on the number of words capitalized and being prohibited from using ALL CAPS.

Ad Example	
This ad will not pass review:	**This ad will pass review:**
Lowest Used Auto Price Quotes— Get them NOW! Save $$CASH$$ with Discount Prices www.gizmoautosales.com	Used Automobile Price Quotes — Free all the Time Save money with Discount Auto Prices www.gizmoautosales.com

It is critical to load the title, the first line of your PPC ad, with keywords. PPC programs may have different rules that apply to the Title line. However, you should strive to load it with keywords, while maintaining readability, and strive to make it captivating to a potential customer. Your goal is simply to capture the interest of a potential customer. If you can do that, your ad is successful. If no one is interested in your ad, it will not get clicks and will not draw customers to your Web site. Test multiple versions of your ad to see which works best and change keywords to help you analyze which is most effective. Review the ads of competitors. You may find they are outperforming you simply because their ad is better written, more captivating, or has more customer appeal.

The use of "free," "rebate," "bonus," and "cash" are perfect for attracting the attention of Web site surfers. Other words that may encourage Web Site visitors to click through your ad should be used as long as your ad message is concise and clear. Do not overload them with words that will lose the meaning of your ad. Remember that both Google™ and Yahoo must review and approve your ad; if your ad does not pass their review you will be notified or your ad may be ignored.

You should also consider the domain name listed in your ad, as it may have an effect on your ability to draw in potential customers. Your domain name should be directly related to your product or services and be professional in nature. The domain name reallycheapcars.com may not impart a perception of quality in your automobiles that you are striving to achieve, perhaps the domain name qualitycars.com would be a better choice. Also, be wary of domain names that are overly promotional in content, as these may drive away potential customers, i.e., freecars.com.

You will find an abundance of companies that offer Search-engine copywriting services, which is a good option if you are having problems developing successful ad campaigns.

Some recommended sources for copywriting include:

- **www.searchenginewriting.com**
- **www.grantasticdesigns.com/copywriting.html**
- **www.roncastle.com/web_copywriting.htm**
- **www.futurenettechnologies.com/creative-copywriting.htm**
- **www.tinawrites.com/**
- **www.brandidentityguru.com/optimized-copywriting.html**

Search-engine copywriting is critical to a successful PPC advertising campaign. While we have recommended professional services for this task, it is not overly difficult to achieve if you apply some basic discipline and rules. While I have repeatedly stressed the insertion of keywords into an ad, simply cramming keyword after keyword into your PPC ads may be counter-productive and is not search-engine copywriting. Successful Search-engine Optimization copywriting takes planning, discipline, analysis, and some degree of trial and error.

Search Engine Optimization Copywriting

Below are some general guidelines for successful Search-engine Optimization copywriting:

- **Use no more than four Keywords per ad.** Four keywords provide a wide variety without saturating the ad with keywords and losing the meaning of the ad.

- **Use all of your allowed characters in each line of the ad.** The length depends on the PPC provider; however, use the space you have been provided. There is no incentive for white space.

- **Write in natural language where possible.** "Natural language" is a popular term used extensively with copywriting. It simply means that the reader should not be able to detect the keywords that the ad is targeting. The best ads are written for an individual to read and understand, imbedded with subtle keywords, and project a clear message so that it reads "naturally." The opposite of this is a keyword- crammed ad that is nothing more than a collection of keywords and is entirely "un-natural" to read.

- **Use keywords in the title and description line.** However use common sense and follow the rules we provided so that you do not overload them with keywords.

- **Test and tweak**. Test your ad and analyze your reports and results. Your ad may need tweaking, improvements. It may be entirely ineffective and need to be replaced.

Yahoo!® Sponsored Search Ad Keyword Bidding

As we have discussed, bidding is often the most complicated and costly factors when managing your PPC campaign, and Yahoo!® Search Marketing is no exception. However Yahoo does provide you with tools to assist you in the process:

- Do not guess at bid levels. Base bids on your business model, business objectives, and supporting metrics.

- Do not bid so high that you will not make a profit.

- Do not bid so low so that your listings dip out of the market. In other words, your ads will never get displayed to anyone.

- Monitor the performance of your account and adjust bids based on what you learn and observe about performance.

Yahoo makes the bidding process easy by using a system based on Maximum Bidding, which allows you to set the maximum you are willing to pay for a click, and the system automatically adjusts your bid to get the best price available. You pay only one cent more than the maximum bid of the listing below yours. For example, if your maximum bid is one dollar and the maximum bid of the listing below you is 56 cents, you pay 57 cents per click. Yahoo!® Search Marketing's systems continually monitor the bid prices to ensure that you never pay more than your maximum bid for a click. Remember to implement the bidding strategies we told you about earlier to stretch your budget and give you the best possible exposure for your PPC ads.

Yahoo!® Recommended Bidding Strategies

Yahoo!® offers three recommended bidding strategies, which are:

- Set all listings to your target maximum bid. This option is best for businesses that want to minimize time spent managing bids. This is definitely the easiest method and ensures that you are not over-spending. This is the recommended method to bidding.

- Set individual bids on all your keywords, managing each one relative to the competitive listings around it. This option is best for businesses that would benefit more from spending a significant amount of time and effort on consistent monitoring than on risking the loss of potential clicks. This method requires a much heavier workload and may cause you to miss opportunities.

- Pick some keywords to bid higher than your average target bid.

- This option is best for businesses that want to compete on specific keywords and/or want to encourage conversion throughout the customers' buying cycle. This method requires careful management to avoid over-spending.

Your Max Bid ($)	Top 5 Max Bids				
2.75	2.75	1.04	1.03	1.02	1.01
2.25	2.25	2.16	2.15	2.05	1.00
2.25	2.25	1.66	1.65	1.60	1.49
1.50	1.50	0.10	-	-	-
1.50	1.50	-	-	-	-
1.50	1.50	0.50	0.12	0.11	-
1.50	1.50	0.10	-	-	-
1.25	1.25	0.52	0.11	0.10	0.05
0.75	0.75	0.60	0.58	0.57	0.50
0.50	0.50	-	-	-	-
0.50	0.50	0.15	0.13	0.10	-

Update Bids

Screenshots © 2007 Yahoo!® Inc. Yahoo!® and the Yahoo!® logo are trademarks of Yahoo!® Inc.

The screen shot at right reveals your current bid, and the top five max bids compared your bid. It is useful to gauge how much you should bid for a keyword. Remember, you pay only one cent more than the maximum bid of the listing below yours.

The Bid Tool can be used to show you the maximum bids, and the ads for those bids.

Screenshots © 2007 Yahoo!® Inc. Yahoo!® and the Yahoo!® logo are trademarks of Yahoo!® Inc.

The account management screen provides you with a wealth of data relative to the performance of your campaign by keyword and category, including the position of your ad, your cost per click, your maximum bid, the top five maximum bids, the click index, number of clicks, average cost, total cost, total conversions, conversion rate, and cost per conversion. The last three will only report results if you have set up this feature. This screen allows you to update your listings, category, bid options, and match type options, as well as update your bidding.

The Money Manager screen lets you set up your daily budget if you

Screenshots © 2007 Yahoo!® Inc. Yahoo!® and the Yahoo!® logo are trademarks of Yahoo!® Inc.

choose to have a daily limit. You may also turn it off and have no limits in place; however, your costs may escalate dramatically. I recommend you set initial daily budgets to contain your costs. The account activity summary screen shows you the current account balance, average daily click charges, and an estimate of how many days before your account is depleted.

Screenshots © 2007 Yahoo!® Inc. Yahoo!® and the Yahoo!® logo are trademarks of Yahoo!® Inc.

The budgeting feature is designed to provide you with financial control by allowing you to determine the approximate amount your account is charged every month. By entering an amount for your approximate daily budget, your target monthly budget is calculated—your approximate daily budget multiplied by 30. Budgeting then automatically adjusts the daily rotation of your listings so that over the course of 30 days, your daily click charges should be close to your target monthly budget. This makes account management easier by eliminating the need to monitor your balance constantly, as well as helping to provide a daily flow of leads to your site.

You can set the approximate daily budget by entering an estimate of the amount of money you would like to spend on the account in the Approximate Daily Budget field. If you want to increase your traffic, consider increasing both your max bids and your budget, because increasing your budget alone does not necessarily increase the number of impressions you will receive. If you click the "Budget Off" button, your account will begin to receive the maximum amount of traffic without regard to a budget. Each time your account balance falls below that amount, Yahoo will charge your credit card the amount you specified until your account balance equals at least three days' worth of click charges.

Budget smoothing is a feature designed to adjust the display of your listings over the course of 30 days based on your approximate daily budget. You may see fluctuations in your actual daily click charges due to changes in search volume. In addition, low daily budgets, particularly those below $10, will see the greatest daily fluctuations. However, over the course of 30 days your total monthly click charges should be close to your target monthly budget. You will need to make sure that your daily budget is proportional to your bid amounts. If you have one or more keywords with high bids and you set a low daily budget you will likely reach your daily budget very quickly and your account will be offline for the remainder of the day.

Yahoo!® Sponsored Search Reports

Yahoo provides a wide variety of highly detailed reports to assist you in managing your PPC campaign effectively. They include:

- **Account Activity Detail** — Access your impressions, clicks, cost per click, and total cost summarized for all keywords in the account.

- **Account Summary** — A look at your account click, and cost totals, and your cost per click summarized for all terms.

- **Billing Transaction Detail** — Historical data of all billing transactions on your account.

- **Category Detail** — Detailed information on each of your categories, including keywords, average bid, average position, total clicks, and total cost.

- **Category Summary** — Information on your categories, including average bid, average position, total clicks, and total cost.

- **Daily Budgeting Report** — Keep track of daily spending against budget.

- **Intra-Day Account Activity** — Updated several times per day with the latest available information for keywords by all bid amounts, positions, number of clicks, cost, and URL.

- **Keyword Activity Detail** — Access the totals for each of your keywords by average position, impressions, total clicks, click-through rate, cost per click, and total cost.

- **Keyword Summary** — Access the totals for each of your keywords by average position, impressions, total clicks, click-through rate, cost per click, and total cost.

- **URL Activity** — Information on a given URL, including keyword, clicks, cost, and URL.

- **Monthly Financial Reports** — Access your Invoices, Account Statements, and Activity Reports. Invoice clients may view past invoices in this section. Information is available for the previous six months.

Yahoo!® Content Match

Yahoo!® Content Match enables you to place your listings on even more locations on the Web and potentially drive more traffic to your site. Content Match is based on relevance and allows your ad to be displayed on potentially thousands of "relevant" Web sites. For example, when a user goes to a site like Yahoo and views content pages (such as articles and product reviews), Content Match provides relevant listings (ads) on the same page. In the example below, we searched on **travel.yahoo. com** for information on Kodiak, Alaska (the birthplace of two of my three children!).

Screenshots © 2007 Yahoo!® Inc. Yahoo!® and the Yahoo!® logo are trademarks of Yahoo!® Inc.

As you can see there are results listed, as well as "content match" results shown on the right hand side of the screen. Content Match listings currently appear on many of Yahoo's content areas (including Entertainment, Finance, and Shopping), MSN® content areas, and other online destinations. We recommend you turn Content Match off until you are comfortable with the result of your PPC campaign and can then decide to implement content match, as the results realized may not match the cost.

Here are some of the benefits of Content Match:

- It offers access to the content of popular, high-quality sites, including **Yahoo.com**, MSN®.com, **WallStreetJournal.com**, **ESPN.com**, and **CNN.com**.

- Sponsored Search advertisers can edit existing listings, while bidding separately and independently, tracking results through proprietary tools, providing more insight into performance and greater control of costs.

- Relevant listings are displayed to interested users, increasing visibility.

Yahoo!® Search Submit

Search Submit is also a PPC advertising program that allows you to submit your Web sites into the Yahoo!® Search Index. Search Submit gives you additional coverage on search results pages by providing inclusion into the Yahoo!® Search Index, which powers standard or algorithmic search results (those appearing in the main body of the page) across Yahoo, AltaVista, AlltheWeb, and other portals. Search Submit provides an easy and timesaving method for submitting Web pages to the Yahoo!® Search Index, eliminating guesswork and chance often associated with standard search results. Web Site URLs that are accepted into the Index are refreshed every 48 hours and receive detailed reporting of search-engine performance.

There are two Search Submit options:

- **Search Submit Express** is offered to customers with 1,000 or fewer URLs and both account enrollment and management occur online. Pricing is on an annual subscription basis per URL. Currently the cost is $49, plus a cost-per-click that depends on what category your Web Site is listed under (typically around $0.15 per click).

- **Search Submit Pro** is a managed account program available to customers with 1,000 or more URLs. Customers provide content via an XML feed. Pricing is on a fixed cost-per-click basis, based on content category, e.g., automotive.

Yahoo!® Search Marketing Tips and Hints

- Invest the time to create an effective keyword list. If you sell multiple items, include those product keywords into your lists and incorporate each into relevant/targeted ads. Use the free keyword tools I have discussed in this book.

- Remember, it is not always necessary to be number one/top position ad, and in fact it is not the most cost-effective position for you. Research reveals that the ad in the first position frequently gets clicked simply because it is the first ad, costly you money with minimal chance for conversion and low return on investment. Target positions two to five, but be on the first page of the ads so that they show without the Web user having to scroll to get to them.

- You can typically get an excellent ad position by bidding just a penny above your competitors. Use the Yahoo bid tool to assist you with bidding and bid position (**http://uv.bidtool.overture. com/d/search/tools/bidtool**/). Unlike Google™ AdWords, Yahoo ads are ranked entirely based on your bid amount.

- Write ads using the guidelines we have provided in this book. Use action verbs, be specific, and target your audience. Do not use generic action statements such as "click now." Instead, use action verbs and factually based content. Be honest in your ad so you will not turn off potential customers.

- Follow the Yahoo!® Search Marketing Ad Guidelines.

- Capitalize the first letter in each word in your title. Include your keywords in your ad title and repeat it in your ad copy.

- Take advantage of the extensive reports in Yahoo!® Search Marketing and monitor your campaign performance. Use the provided conversion counter to track results, conversion, and return on investment.

It all comes down to conversion rates. Tremendous Web site traffic is great, but not without making conversions (sales). Make sure your landing page content is relevant to your ad and can capture the interest of potential customers, providing them with information about your products and can close the deal.

Microsoft® adCenter

Microsoft® adCenter is the latest competition (and biggest threat) to the big two PPC providers; Google™ and Yahoo!® Microsoft® adCenter is the advertising platform which allows you to advertise on Live Search. If you have a Web site and want to promote your business on Live Search, you can bid on keywords that are relevant to your site to secure a placement on the paid listings (Sponsored Sites) section of Live Search.

Like Google™ AdWords and Yahoo, there is a one-time $5 fee to establish a Microsoft® adCenter account. Microsoft® is taking direct aim at the market shared by Google™ and Yahoo in the PPC marketplace.

Microsoft® adCenter is an advertising platform you can use to help build your pay-per-click campaigns. They provide guidelines to help you get your ad on Live Search. According to the site above, the Microsoft® adCenter features include targeting based on geographic location, gender, and day part and day of week. They also provide a list of what their tools will allow you to do:

- Generate keyword lists
- Upload your keywords in bulk
- Build, save, and export reports
- Estimate the rank of your keywords before you spend a dime.

How to Set Up a Microsoft® adCenter Account

After signing up for an account with Microsoft® adCenter, you will then need to set up you campaigns. To do this you will need to follow these steps:

1. **Create** — You will need to create your campaign, name it, and set your preferences for targeting and tracking.

2. **Build** — You will need to then build the actual ad you want to use for the campaign, provide the link to your ad, and customize it for best results.

3. **Keyword** — Using keyword research tools, you will need to create your own keyword list.

4. **Set and Submit** — Figure out what you want to spend, enter your bid amount, and submit your order.

Microsoft® publishes an extensive Web Blog on Microsoft® adCenter that is located at **http://blogs.msdn.com/adcenter**. You should consider using this free resource to assist you with implementing a successful Microsoft® adCenter campaign. To read the press release announcing Microsoft® adCenter, visit **http://www.Microsoft®.com/presspass/press/2006/may06/05-03SAS7PR.mspx**. To register or learn more about this program, visit **http://advertising.MSN®.com**.

The following article entitled "Microsoft®'s Entrance to AdCenter: Google™ and Yahoo, Be Prepared!," by Joseph Pratt is available at **http://www.articlealley.com/article_64157_7.html** and is free to republish.

Microsoft®'s Entrance to adCenter: Google™ and Yahoo, Be Prepared!

Let's welcome Microsoft®'s adCenter to the PPC advertising field. A quick question, though, why is adCenter here? Microsoft®, the juggernaut, sat on the sidelines for quite a while and watched as first Overture (later bought by Yahoo) and then Google™ took online advertising to the level that we see it today.

This business, hardly fully grown, yet quite developed, is still dominated by Yahoo and, in particular, Google™. adCenter is not an entry into the ground floor of a new field of business, but a giant undertaking in a field that, frankly, Microsoft® will likely not dominate. I suppose Microsoft® could get in the microchip processing business, too. I mean they have the money – the point is businesses do not just enter new enterprises because they can. Inexperience taking on experience is rarely a winning proposition. Yet in this case, apparently, Microsoft® is taking on Google™ just because they can – there is enough dough.

Microsoft®'s Entrance to adCenter: Google™ and Yahoo, Be Prepared!

Microsoft® has deep pockets, deeper than Google™ – no matter what Google™'s stock price is, because they have the years of profitability. What kind of deep pockets, you may ask? In Nov. '04 Microsoft® issued a special dividend and paid $3 per share to stockholders. Microsoft® has over ten billion shares outstanding. So, in effect, they dispersed $30 billion from their coffers to their shareholders. Too much money lying around is not a bad problem for a company to have, eh? If you check out Google™ Finance and look at Microsoft®'s balance sheet, you will see that they have money enough to do anything still – and that includes dueling with Google™ adCenter.

The basic aim of Microsoft®'s adCenter is to increase advertising revenue and directly compete with Google™ in the industry share of advertising dollars. Is it green pastures of profit or the lust of competition that has brought Microsoft® into this game? It is tougher to sell the profit motive, honestly. Conventionally speaking, Microsoft®'s scenario today would have been unthinkable only four or five years ago – that Microsoft® would try to become a major provider of online media.

Perhaps Microsoft® is entering into an opportunity, partially by luck, where it can exploit Google™. Google™ has made some quantifiable mistakes and created weaknesses that competition could exploit, possibly. I believe that one key to knocking Google™ off the top of the heap is to go after the advertising base.

I have observed adCenter, advised new users, and even signed up for it myself. The adCenter console is sleeker than Google™ and the reporting (and this is important for advertisers – possibly lost on Google™) is better. Primarily, they offer a Cost Estimator for advertisers to help keep within budget while providing rank, traffic, and cost estimates per keyword. adCenter, on the surface at least, seems intent on ceding information over to the advertiser.

Microsoft®'s adCenter can further drive a wedge between Google™ and its advertising base by raising the click fraud issue. Aside from being notoriously difficult to communicate with, for advertisers with concerns, Google™ has been secretive, almost sneaky, about their click fraud settlement – contacting advertisers to opt-out of the class action settlement with a harmless looking e-mail, some say that resembles spam. Google™ may be creating an environment of mistrust that could ironically, given Microsoft®'s bullying reputation, drive advertisers to Microsoft®'s adCenter.

Microsoft®'s Entrance to adCenter: Google™ and Yahoo, Be Prepared!

I think that if Microsoft® wants to step up their Search-engine Marketing platform above what is available they have a number of duties:

1 Bring more meaningful Web conversion data for advertisers – and that is exactly what they seem to be trying to do with their reporting interface options for advertisers.

2 Seek out partnerships here, there, and everywhere. The Yahoo and eBay announcement had thunderous effects on the search arena – a real blow, perhaps, to Google™'s pride. Has success, as it is known to do in human nature, bred contempt?

3 The toughest trick of all, and one where Google™ is only getting stronger – increase gross user search. This one factor could make adCenter's whole existence futile. Google™ is doing a bang-up job of increasing an already dominant share of search. Just this week Google™ recorded 43.1 percent of searches conducted by U.S. residents in April (2006). This is up from 36.5 percent in April 2005. Google™ has been taking all comers lately with charges of click fraud, secrecy, being hypocrites, even the protectors of child porn – charges do not come much more scurrilous in the corporate world. But Google™'s growing share of search is a magic bullet, impossible for competitors, short-sellers, or even run-of-the-mill ill-wishers to ignore. It confirms that they are the top banana in the world of Internet marketing. Simply put, when people want to find things on the Internet, they are going to Google™ first. The inference is clear: Google™'s search is best. While Google™ grows, the competition claws to keep market share, competition that includes Yahoo!®, a company that only exists right now to bleed search share to Google™, a percentage point at a time, despite an impressive track record and performance in the field. And this is promising to Microsoft®?

Tips and Hints For an Effective Microsoft® adCenter Campaign

Microsoft® adCenter may be the newest competition for Google™ AdWords and Yahoo!® Search Marketing, but you can be assured, it is here to stay and will continue to grow and acquire market share. Use these tips and hints to ensure that your adCenter account is as effective and efficient as possible:

- **Choose your keywords carefully** and invest the time required to optimize your keyword list. Use the Keyword Selection Tool provided to Microsoft® adCenter subscribers to assist you in this process. Invest time in developing an arsenal of effective keyword phrases.

- **Implement what is known as "Split Testing"** which you use with Yahoo!® Search Marketing and Google™ AdWords. The concept is simple: you run multiple ads with slight differences at the same time and compare the click-through rates against each other. Microsoft® adCenter allows you to run multiple ads simultaneously. You can track which ad has a higher click-through rate, try new ads each week to refine your ad effectiveness, and eliminate or modify those that are under performing. There is also a free tool by the name of Split Tester that helps you determine whether you have collected enough data to be sure of the results.

- **Use Landing Pages for your ad.** Do not just direct them to your home page. The home page is the worst place to direct potential customers who are looking for information on a particular product or service. It has been proven that your conversion rates can be significantly improved by creating a landing page specific to your ad so that the potential customers are given exactly the information they are seeking. Having a landing page will also cut down on low-quality clicks and stretch out your advertising dollars. Make sure it is possible to purchase products directly from your landing page. Do not make your potential customer navigate through your site to discover how to buy your products.

- **Create a realistic budget** that you can live with but that also gives your campaign the ability to sustain your ads for a specified period of time. You likely will not see the results you want in the first month of advertising. Remember, the process is time consuming, and you must apply the techniques we have given you to optimize your account, which takes time to develop and implement. I recommend that you budget for a six-month to a one-year period.

- **Use the provided reports.** Just like Google™ AdWords and Yahoo!® Search Marketing, Microsoft® adCenter is packed with robust reporting and tracking. Use these to analyze your performance and tweak your ad setting to refine your campaign. If you are not achieving your desired click-through rates or conversion rates, use the tools to eliminate or modify under-performing ads, create new ads, refine keywords, or refine your demographic targeting settings.

- **Use the superior demographics targeting tool**s available in Microsoft® adCenter. The ability to target by customers by geographic location, gender, time of the day, and day of the week is powerful. However, you must invest the time required to define your target audience before you can use them effectively. Before you begin your campaign, define your target audience.

- **Monitor your click-through-rates, campaign effectiveness, and efficiency.** Use the statistics and reporting features to identify the deficiencies in your campaign to pinpoint where your problems may lie. Typically, the majority of problems occur because of:

  - poor keywords or key phrases

  - poor landing pages

  - no landing pages

  - insufficient budget

  - low daily/monthly budgets limit the time/days your ad is served

  - poorly written ads

  - ads which are misleading

- **Tweak your campaigns.** I have mentioned this numerous times throughout this book, and I cannot stress it enough. Put in the time, effort, and analysis to develop a continuous cycle of improvement within your PPC advertising campaign.

Microsoft® adCenter provides a whole new level of targeting not seen with Google™ AdWords or Yahoo!® Search Marketing, allowing you to select your target audience by age, gender, geographic location, day of the week, or time of the day to display ads. Using it highly refines your ads to the demographic groups and times that will be most effective in quality clicks and conversions, as well as affecting your budget by eliminating low quality clicks. adCenter implements the demographic profiles through the Web surfers MSN® Passport, Hotmail account, or Windows Live preferences. Demographic targeting on Google™ AdWords is only available on site-targeted campaigns and not on keyword-targeted campaigns, which are the most effective.

You should also be aware of an innovative pricing structure with Microsoft® adCenter. When you target specific demographic markets, you will choose an incremental pricing factor that is in addition to your basic cost per click when that demographic targeting feature is used when displaying your ad to Web site browsers. While the demographic targeting is highly innovative, it does come with a potential cost impact. However, as we indicated earlier, the cost will likely be offset by the elimination of low quality clicks that can consume your budget quickly.

The incremental price increase for demographic targeting is a percentage of your cost per click for your entire ad campaign. Therefore, if you pay $1 per click for the keyword phrase "restaurant consulting," and then activate demographics filtering tools limiting your ad to females during the hours of 8 a.m. to 1 p.m., you must agree to increase your bid by 20 percent to increase the likelihood that your ad will be displayed at a higher position during your specified period. You will pay $1.20 per click for clicks that you receive in that period. Incremental click cost increases are applied in 10 percent increments only.

Other PPC Advertising Programs and Providers

As PPC advertising has exploded in recent years, so has the number of service providers. Additional services have appeared to help advertisers simplify the management of different PPC ad programs. While Google™ AdWords and Yahoo!® Search Marketing are the most prominent, Microsoft® adCenter is sure to be a major player in the near future. There are numerous other PPC providers which you can research and choose additional ones that will work for your advertising plan. A great source of reviews on other services is www.payperclickanalyst. com. Under their PPCSE Reviews tab you will find reviews about the services we have already discussed as well as the following services:

- MIVA
- Lycos Insite Adbuyer
- Search123
- LookSmart.com

- Kanoodle.com
- ePilot.com
- Searchfeed.com

- Enhance.com
- goClick.com
- 7Search.com

Shopping Search Engines

Each of you has used Shopping Search Engines, and they have been increasing in popularity. The majority of shopping search engines operates on a PPC system with the exception of Froogle, which is completely free.

Froogle.com is a price engine Web site launched by Google™. Froogle allows Web surfers to type in a product search and it will return a list of who is selling the product searched as well as price information.

The best advice we can give is to start making plans now to submit your data to Froogle. Most major shopping carts can export your data into a Froogle data feed, including PDG Software's shopping cart **www.pdgsoft.com.** You should start positioning your products now to grab your share of the potential marketplace offered through Froogle. Froogle can already accept data feeds, even in beta or development mode, so you should take advantage of this extremely popular and growing service. You will need to use the Google™ Base (**base.Google™.com**) to upload products into the Froogle system.

Froogle helps you find and compare product prices both online and in nearby stores. You can even visit a store to see the item before you buy it. Google™ search technology helps you find everything from common products at the best price to the most obscure or unusual products. If you Fast Click on a product, you will either go right to the Web page where you can buy it from the selected company, or you will get the address of a nearby store where you can find it in your area. The best feature of Froogle for you, the advertiser, is that Google™ does not charge for product listings. Ranking is based on relevance to the Web surfer's search terms.

Froogle's power to help you find what you are looking for begins with search technology. After you do a search, Froogle helps you refine it to focus on the products you want. You can choose the "Preferences" link on the Froogle home page to customize your Froogle searches for language, search results per page, and so on. The Search by Store link in the left hand margin of any search results page is a list of online stores. Click one and you will get a new results page for your search terms showing only products sold by the store you chose. At the top of most search results pages is a list of related searches. Click one and you will get a new results page for your search terms showing only products sold in the category you chose. Froogle.com allows you to:

- Sort your search results by price, high to low or low to high.

- Search within a Price Range.

- "Compare prices" link in any search result to see prices for the same product at different online stores.

- Local Search to find products in your area.

- Map out nearby stores that sell the item you are looking for.

- Click to get directions to or from the store from any address you choose.

- Get lots of information about every product you find on Froogle — including the merchant who has it for sale.

Yahoo Product Submit is another application that will help you promote your products. You can find more information on this at **http://searchmarketing.yahoo.com/shopsb/index.php**.

Shopping.com has a merchant program as well. It charges anywhere from $0.15 to $1 per click, and it offers good exposure to product shoppers. Bizrate offers a variation on the fixed bidding scheme of the other shopping search engines by allowing merchants to bid on top rankings.

PPC Bid Management

If you invest heavily into PPC campaigns though Yahoo, Google™, or any other provider (or a combination of them), you may quickly discover it can be a time consuming to manage your bids, and you may consider an alternative method. These may have services the others do not offer you and it is definitely worth looking into them.

Here are a few PPC bid management programs:

- Atlas Search provides an all-in-one interface for managing PPC bids and they offer a free 14 day trial of their service that includes bid management and campaign optimization. See more information about Atlas Search at **http://www.atlassolutions.com/services_search.aspx**.

- BidRank is another useful automated PPC search-engine management tool that takes the pain out of PPC bid management. BidRank information can be found at **www.bidrank.com**.

- ClickTracks offers a PPC tracking and reporting feature for any PPC campaign. They also offer analysis of your site. For more information about ClickTracks, visit **www.clicktracks.com**.

Hiring a Professional Marketing Service Provider

By now you should realize that although a PPC campaign is manageable, it is certainly a time and money investment. Many companies that do not have the time or expertise to invest properly in their PPC campaigns have chosen to outsource the duty to reputable professional marketing service providers. These professionals will use their marketplace skill and mastery of Google™ AdWords, Microsoft® adCenter, and Yahoo!® Search Marketing to manage their campaigns. This is an excellent solution for some companies, but keep in mind it will affect your budget since the service is not free, and often not cheap. To point you in the right direction, I have listed some of our preferred service providers with their Web sites:

- SOHO Prospecting — **www.sohoprospecting.com**
- WPromote — **www.wpromote.com**
- NewGate Internet — **www.newgate.com**
- Spannerworks — **www.spannerworks.com**

How to Identify and Combat Fraud

I have provided you with all the skills, tools, and knowledge required to plan, design, implement, and manage a PPC campaign. PPC advertising can be extraordinarily profitable and, if managed correctly, will dramatically increase your customer base and potential revenue by driving targeted visitors to your site. Once you master the techniques of PPC advertising, your biggest challenge will be how to recognize and combat fraud.

Whenever I discuss PPC fraud with clients, they envision a competitor clicking on their ad every now and then just to drive up costs, or people who (for no reason) click on an ad again and again until they become bored and move on to some other unsuspecting advertiser. I am referring to an organized, targeted, technologically advanced, and highly destructive automated process of creating applications, scripts, robots (or even humans) that will continue to generate thousands of clicks using ingenious techniques to disguise their identity with IP spoofing (and many others) all designed to cost you thousands of dollars in fraudulent clicks while hiding behind a false identity.

You need to realize you will not sell a product with every click on your ad. If you have ten clicks today on your ad and sell two products as a direct result of those clicks, your conversion rate is 20 percent. Remember most PPC providers provide you with free tools to automate tracking of your conversions rates. Not everyone who clicks on your PPC ad will buy your products. Reasons may be that they were:

- Not interested in your products.

- Turned off by your Web page or Web Site.

- Not able to find enough information about your product on your site.

- Looking for a lower price.

- Looking for another brand.

- Too far away from you.

- Sold on your competition.

- Having technical problems (i.e., your shopping cart is not working).

What Is Fraud in Relation to PPC Marketing

Clickfraud.com reports that "click fraud is expected to reach $1.1 billion for 2005. By 2008, this is estimated to grow to $1.6 billion, an increase of over 45 percent" and that:

- In 2004, at least $500 million in PPC online advertising expenditure was wasted through click fraud.

- By 2008, the estimated cost of click fraud to online advertisers will be in excess of $1.6 billion.

- As much as 70 percent of annual online advertising spending is wasted because of click fraud.

- Corrupt affiliates of ad networks such as Google™ and Yahoo account for 85 percent of all click fraud.

Source: **www.clickfraud.com**

Clickfraud.com is one of a growing number of companies that can assist you in combating PPC fraud. See **www.clickfraud.com** for all the services Clickrisk offers.

PPC fraud is typically the result of

- Unscrupulous PPC traffic and content partners of PPC search engines) and directories. These companies gain financially, based upon the volume of referral traffic to their partner and may resort to fraudulent methods to obtain them.

- Competitors who attempt to break your budget by clicking away on your ad quickly consuming your budget with no sales conversion.

- WebBots, spiders, and crawlers designed to generate fraudulent clicks and consume your budget maliciously with no sales conversion.

You need to understand that the following are facts:

- Search-engine companies, PPC providers, and advertisers agree that click fraud exists.

- Search-engine companies and PPC providers agree that PPC advertisers should not be billed for fraudulent click activity.

- Search-engine companies have stated that they have effective "click fraud" protection built into major search engines.

Tips and Suggestions to Combat Fraud

Here are some tips and suggestions for combating click fraud without breaking your budget:

- Keep current with published anti-click fraud tips and suggestions.

- Do your research when selecting a PPC provider. While there are many reputable providers, review their policies and tools for combating fraud before you sign up.

- Do not sign up with PPC companies that allow "incentive sites." An incentive sight is typically one that offers free products, free competitions, or junk promotions. This really applies to AdSense type campaigns where you are allowing ads on your Web site.

- Monitor click-through rates.

- Review your Web site traffic reports.

- Place daily click limits in your campaign.

- Establish a daily budget to limit your total costs per day.

- Limit your ad to your target geographic audience. There is no need to display your ad in Russia if you do not do business there.

- Review your IP referral logs, usually provided by your Web site hosting company or the PPC provider. If you have multiple clicks from the same IP address, you are likely the victim of fraud.

- Report potential fraud to your PPC provider.

- Consider an advanced "fraud detection of tracking" tool.

A few articles I recommend for learning more about click fraud are:

- "Click Fraud: Six Things You Should Be Aware of before You Buy 'Guaranteed Traffic,'" by John Young, available at **http://www.articlealley.com/article_89257_3.html**

- "Google™'s Click Fraud Woes," by Peter Elmer, available at **http://www.articlealley.com/article_83210_7.html**

- "Google™ and Yahoo to Settle Click Fraud Cases," by Michael Goldstein, Esq, available at **http://www.articlealley.com/article_73826_18.html**.

Available Fraud Protection Options

This list of recommended fraud protection providers will help you in your fight against fraud and protect your financial investment in your PPC marketing campaign. Keep in mind all major PPC providers have active fraud protection measures in place. However, their degree of effectiveness is difficult for you to determine. If you want to provide an additional layer of protection for your investment, you may want to consider one of these companies:

- **AdWatcher — www.adwatcher.com**

- **ClickDetective — www.clickdetective.com.**

- **ClickForensics — www.clickforensics.com**

- **Clickfraud – www.clickfraud.com**

- **Clicklab — www.clicklab.com**

CLICKLAB

Clicklab was founded in 2001 as a Web analytics company that provided businesses with a smarter way to improve returns on their Web site and e-marketing investment. From their inception, they have focused on measuring and improving conversions and ROI for their clients, as opposed to counting Web site visitors. As a result, they have developed a unique blend of advanced technology and human expertise in click fraud detection and Web analytics to help online businesses succeed.

Clicklab is a privately held company with sales offices in the Washington, D.C., and San

ABOUT CLICKLAB

Web Address

www.clicklab.com

Mailing Address

Clicklab, LLC

1616 Anderson Road

McLean, Virginia 22102

Contact Sales

Toll free: 888-841-3342

E-mail: **sales@clicklab.com**

Francisco suburbs. The company's data center operations are located in Dulles, Virginia. Mr. Dmitri Eroshenko, a leading expert in Web analytics and click fraud, heads their management team. The rest of this chapter is taken from "How to Defend Your Website Against Click Fraud — White Paper," by Dmitri Eroshenko and Michael Bloch. It is reprinted with permission of **Clicklab.com** and Michael Bloch.

Clicklab Fraud Detection Technology

Clicklab Click Fraud Detection Service is the most advanced, enterprise-class click fraud detection technology on the market today. It is the result of more than two years of research and development work performed by mathematicians, programmers, and SEM and PPC specialists.

Clicklab monitors your Web site traffic for suspicious activity and applies more than 30 statistical tests to detect fraudulent click signatures. Each failed test is assigned a weighed penalty score. If cumulative score exceeds the threshold, Clicklab declares the visitor session as Potential Click Fraud (PCF) and flags it for analysis and further action.

Then PCF level is calculated for each PPC search engine and keyword, allowing you to adjust your bidding strategy and generate detailed actionable reports to negotiate a refund with PPC providers. Clicklab click fraud reports serve as a form of documentation from a third party service that has no vested interest in your PPC campaigns.

Click fraud is a problem that can seriously undermine your PPC advertising efforts. This white paper expands on what we know about click fraud and outlines the steps you can take to protect your investment:

- What you really need to know about PPC advertising.
- Who is behind the different types of click fraud.
- Using scoring algorithm to detect and document click fraud.
- Measuring your traffic quality with Click Inflation Index (CII).

PPC Advertising Briefly

PPC is a paid inclusion model used by some search-engine companies that usually requires you to bid on words (keywords) or phrases (keyphrases) that your target market might use when performing searches.

The highest bidder gets the top ranking in the search results, with the next highest bid below and so on. Each time a listing is clicked on, the bid amount is subtracted from the advertisers' deposits.

Some companies charge a flat rate per click, so there is no actual bidding. In this model, ranking is determined by the perceived quality of the page as calculated by a ranking algorithm. When this model is used, it then becomes particularly important to ensure that landing pages are optimized for search engines. In fact, regardless of the PPC model, considering the investment you are making, you should ensure your site is as close to perfect as possible in every aspect to achieve maximum conversions.

PPC is an excellent marketing strategy as it can send targeted clients to your site; but it can also be a budget black hole. Before you launch a PPC campaign, you will first need to perform some calculations for projected ROI (Return on Investment).

Calculating the Cost

You should first calculate your current visitors/sales ratio. If one Web site visitor out of 100 currently purchases your product, then bidding 10 cents per click will cost you an estimated $10 per sale. If your profit margin is $15 per sale, then it may be viable. If it is $9, it is just not worth it. This is just a rough guide.

Be Cautious of PPC Bidding Wars

Some PPC advertisers, through aggressive marketing strategies, ignorance or "auction fever," engage in bidding wars for the number one spot. Keep well clear of these scenarios. In very competitive markets, it is not unusual to see a difference of many dollars between the number one and number two ranked bids. Given that not everyone who clicks on a listing will purchase, it can become an extraordinarily expensive marketing exercise to be number one. Positions two through five may still perform well in terms of sending converting traffic to you.

Keyword Targeting

You may also find it more economical to bid on more targeted keywords and phrases that are not quite as popular. For example, a search on "freebsd Web hosting" on a leading PPC search engine showed that the top bidder only pays $.10 for each click, a difference of over $8.30 on the term "Web hosting." Using this strategy will cut down your advertising costs and the more refined targeting may generate improved conversion rates. Searchers who are clear on what they wish to buy tend to be specific in their search criteria. The novice searcher and "tire-kickers" tend to be more generalized in the search terms they use. If you bid on generic terms; you will be paying the bill while they are learning to refine their queries. Using a tool such as Clicklab will help you refine your keyword lists by identifying the words and phrases that actually result in conversions.

Choosing a PPC Search-Engine

Hundreds of PPC search engines have sprung up in recent years; but very few of them will actually deliver traffic, regardless of what their promotion states. A few companies, such as Overture and Google™, account for the vast majority of PPC traffic. PPC search engines extend network coverage by offering other site owners search boxes/feeds under a revenue share (affiliate) arrangement. The site owner is paid for each search carried out via their site, or for each click a search generates. The better PPC engines have networks consisting of thousands of good quality sites where your listings can appear. Things to look for in a PPC company are:

- **Tools:** Does the company offer keyword suggestion features and extensive reporting?

- **Coverage:** Who uses their data feeds?

- **Cost:** Are there setup fees or minimum balances? What is the minimum bid?

- **Support:** Try out their e-mail support. Ask a few questions before signing up. If they are slow in responding during the pre-sales process, you can practically guarantee that after-sales support will be shocking.

- **Click Fraud:** This costs advertisers millions of dollars each year. Ask what type of anti-click fraud strategies the company has implemented. Will the company investigate fraud aggressively and compensate you where click fraud is proven? It's also wise to invest in an external monitoring system such as Clicklab. Clicklab's advanced analytics engine will flag instances of click fraud that occur in your campaigns. There's no doubt that PPC advertising can be very profitable, but click fraud is probably the most ignored, yet potentially most expensive and damaging aspect of PPC that advertisers need to be very familiar with.

What Is Click Fraud?

Online advertising fraud has been around from the early days of the Internet. To justify the expensive rates and create additional inventory, shady publishers devised the means of artificial inflation of impressions and click-throughs to advertisers' Web sites. Today, click fraud refers to the premeditated practice of clicking on PPC ads without the intent to buy advertisers' products or services or take other actions. Essentially, click fraud is the practice of systematically clicking on links, or using software to do so, either to garner a profit for themselves through click commissions or to deplete the PPC funds of a competitor.

Who Engages In Click Fraud?

Click fraud can be as minor as an affiliate who clicks on an ad once a day to bump up his revenues, or a competitor who occasionally clicks on an ad out of spite. Major click fraud is very well organized, fleecing millions of dollars from advertisers each year. Some fraudsters create complex robots (software) to generate thousands of clicks, while spoofing IP addresses to avoid detection.

There are also ready-made software products, freely available on the market, for generating false clicks. For example, SwitchProxy, a third party extension for Mozilla Firefox browser, allows anyone to click on the same paid links repeatedly from a different IP address (that of a proxy server) without ever switching an Internet connection. Still too much work? There are commercial tools you can download, such as FakeZilla (**fakezilla.com**) and I-FAKER (**ifaker.com**), based in Bulgaria and Ireland.

Other fraudsters employ teams of people in developing countries to click on ads. This may sound a little extreme but with some click bids as high as $10 to $20 each, and if you only have to pay someone $5 a day to click on links, this strategy can be very profitable for the fraudster. In March of this year a 32-year-old California man was arrested and charged with extortion and wire fraud in connection with the software he developed called Google™ Clique. Google™ Clique was designed to click automatically on paid ads, while remaining virtually undetectable by the search engine.

Michael Anthony Bradley allegedly contacted Google™ and demanded a payoff, threatening to release it to the "top 100 spammers." Bradley claimed that Google™ Clique could defraud Google™ of $5 million in half a year's time. Bradley (or someone pretending to be him) posing under the nickname CountScubula, posted on alt.Internet.search-engines newsgroup. "Google™ even called me to their office. I flew up, met with them, and let's just say, they are scared and don't want this software to get out. Bottom line, I don't care anymore." Google™ wrote in its S-1 registration statement filed with the Security and Exchange Commission on April 29, 2004: "We are exposed to the risk of fraudulent clicks on our ads. We have regularly paid refunds related to fraudulent clicks and expect to do so in the future. If we are unable to stop this fraudulent activity, these refunds may increase. If we find new evidence of past fraudulent clicks we may have to issue refunds retroactively of amounts previously paid to our Google™ Network members."

On May 3, 2004, *The India Times* published a widely read article, "India's secret army of online ad clickers." An excerpt from that article: "A growing number of housewives, college graduates, and even working professionals across metropolitan cities are rushing to click paid Internet ads to make $100 to $200 per month."

Why Do People Steal?

"People shoplift to get something for nothing," said Terrence Shulman, an attorney, therapist, corporate consultant, book author, and founder of Cleptomaniacs And Shoplifters Anonymous (CASA), a self-help support group. Shulman estimates that the addictive-compulsive shoplifters represent 85 percent of total shoplifting population of 23 million (that is one in every 11 Americans!). "This group emotionally has a lot of repressed anger and often exhibits signs of other compulsive addictions, such as overeating, shopping, drug use, or gambling," said Shulman. "When caught and confronted, they will often break down and cry." The remaining 15 percent is shared between the professionals who steal for profit; impoverished stealing out of economic need; thrill seekers getting their fix; drug addicts; and kleptomaniacs, those who steal for no reason at all. Bradley "does not appear to be typical of most of the persons I have worked with," said Shulman. "His plotting and planning and brazen 'extortive' pressures on Google™ are different from the shy, passive-aggressive kinds of thefts I and most of my clients have engaged in."

Shulman hypothesizes that Bradley could have "rationalized that he was not hurting anybody—that Google™ is a rich company, not a particular person, and that they could afford it. There can also be a sense of inferiority in people who feel the need to outsmart others or 'beat the system'."

How Widespread Is The Problem?

Instances of advertisers who have had thousands of dollars drained from their accounts in just a few hours are not isolated. Over time, even on a small scale, click fraud can add up to significant amounts of money, dramatically affecting advertisers small and large. Click fraud can also inflate cost of each click for all advertisers as some PPC companies adjust the minimum price of each click based on the popularity of the category or keyword.

Some of Clicklab clients estimate that up to 50 percent of PPC traffic in certain competitive categories is illegitimate. While that figure may be somewhat of an exaggeration as a general average, it does occur in that range in some sectors, perhaps at even higher percentages. As PPC technology has evolved, so too have the inbuilt anti-fraud mechanisms that search companies implement.

The major companies recognize click fraud as a problem that seriously threatens their businesses. The situation is somewhat similar to the battle against viruses. As a "cure" for a virus is released, a new virus appears. Given the nature of the battlefield, it is of crucial importance that PPC advertisers have solid anti-fraud strategies in place and not to rely solely on the search company to provide protection.

Anti-Click Fraud Strategies

Fraud can be simple to minimize initially, only requiring you to choose a PPC company wisely and then monitor results on a daily basis. The increasing incidences of more organized fraudsters require you to use special tools to monitor activity. The following strategies will assist you in minimizing the amount you lose to click fraud.

Avoid PPC Networks That Allow Incentive Sites

Before opening an account, always ask the company if they allow incentivized sites into their network as feed partners or affiliates. An incentives site usually offers something to its visitors in exchange for clicking on links or performing some other action. Given this model, the clicks that you will receive from these sites will more than likely not convert as the focus of the click is not based on interest in your product. Incentive driven sites are not fraudulent, but it is important to gain this clarification.

FREQUENCY CAPS ON CLICKS

Ask the PPC company if they use frequency caps and what the cap is. A frequency cap is a method that will prevent duplicate clicks originating from the same IP from being deducted from your balance.

LIMIT DAILY SPEND

Start your campaign with a reasonably low daily spend limit, then increase it slowly while monitoring results regularly. As an example, let us say you set a limit of $50 a day and during the first week you average $40 worth of clicks for a 24 hour period. Then the following week, that $40 is chewed through in the first six hours without an appreciable increase in sales or leads. Click fraud could be involved. Using this strategy could have minimized your losses.

Country Filtering

What is your target market? Do you really need coverage, for example, in Romania? Keep in mind that the majority of all types of online fraud originates in Eastern Europe, Africa, and some Asian countries.

Server Log Analysis

Study your server logs daily and check for multiple clicks originating from the same IP or range of IPs.

Display Warning Message

For dealing with the rotten apples among your competition, have your programmers write a script that will display a nice warning message after several repeated clicks to your Web site from a paid listing on a PPC search engine:

> Greetings! Thank you for your interest in our product and services.
>
> We noticed that you visited our site more than once recently by following a paid link from one or more of the PPC search engines. Please bookmark our site for future reference so you can save a step and visit us directly. Enjoy your visit!
> IP address: 123.45.67.89

This technique can dramatically reduce your click fraud rate.

Use Specialized Click Fraud Tools

Manual fraud monitoring can be very laborious. Your valuable time is probably better spent in doing what you do best — marketing, following up on leads, refining products or developing new content. Modern third party analytical tools, unlike their predecessors, have become increasingly affordable, accurate, and easy to use. One such product is Clicklab managed click fraud detection service.

Statistical Scoring System to Combat PPC Click Fraud

Larger PPC networks have a working mechanism for detecting fraudulent clicks. Otherwise, we suspect that they would not be able to stay in business. Today's PPCs are likely to be able to weed out non-malicious bots and amateur perpetrators, but do these systems have the capacity to stop the professionals? We are not so certain. If the history of spam fighting is any indicator, the click inflation problem is here to stay.

DEFINE THEM. SCORE THEM. OWN THEM.

To remain undetected, professional inflators need to simulate real visitor behavior and visit parameters closely. They know the number of page views their clicks generate is among the first things to be evaluated. The good news is if you use statistical methods, you will be able to beat the perpetrators at their own game. Whether it is for your internal use or for negotiating a refund from a PPC provider, what is needed is a system for statistically defining and documenting fraudulent click activity. Enter the Click Inflation Index system. This system performs a variety of tests to detect fraudulent user session signatures, assigning penalty points to each offense. If the cumulative score — we call it Click Inflation Index (CII) 0- exceeds the threshold, the user's session is tagged as fraudulent.

This chapter explains the basic principles and tests you can use when developing your own Click Inflation Index algorithm. You will need a competent technical team armed with an adequate Web analytics solution. The process is fun and the results are well worth the effort.

Words of caution before you begin to implement a wide-scale click fraud fighting campaign: Make sure your keyword bidding strategy is up to date. Top expensive keywords remain a high-profile target for con artists. Unless your marketing strategy calls for you to engage in a bidding war—and provides the budget for it— it is a good idea to diversify and bid on the largest possible number of well-researched, lower-cost keywords.

The click-fraud detecting tests you can use include:

- **Test 1. Visit depth**. How many page views did this particular user session generate? If it is just one, it's a good reason to lift a red flag a notch or two — but not more. Keep in mind that there could be a variety of reasons behind the single-page visits. Perhaps your ad copy is not clear and misleads visitors, or maybe the network connection was too slow and the user decided not to wait for the other pages to load.

- **Test 2. Visitors per IP**. Because of the proxy servers and networks of users sharing one Internet connection, there will always be unique visitors with the same IP address. It is normal. You just need to calculate the "normal" for your Web site's unique mix of traffic sources. IP addresses whose visitor counts exceed the control group by a certain percentage go on the blacklist and trigger a penalty.

- **Test 2a. Paid clicks per IP**. Works the same way as Test 2, except counts only user sessions that resulted from clicking on one of your paid links. Typically, you will track these by the unique destination URLs used in PPC listings, such as your Web site. com/?source=Google.

- **Test 3. No cookie — no play**? Many marketers will tell you that because most bots and scripts are not capable of supporting the cookie mechanism, a user session without a cookie is a good cause for alarm. Others will say that it cannot be an accurate indicator because some privacy devotees do not accept cookies and thus look indistinguishable from bots. So, penalize or not? We think you should.

- **Test 3a. Page view frequency**. Most bots travel through your site and request pages from the server much faster than humans do. If a particular user session has generated a few page views in a matter of seconds, it is a good enough reason to penalize it. On the other hand, you have to be careful not to go overboard when defining your threshold. Humans can surf through your site fast, too!

- **Test 4. Anonymous proxy servers**. Click thieves know that IP address is the primary means for identifying the user session. Therefore, they need to launch their attacks from many different IP addresses. The more, the merrier.

  Fortunately, IP address spoofing is not a trivial task. For this reason, click inflators often channel their activity through anonymous proxy servers. Your solution is to develop and maintain an up-to-date list of anonymous proxy servers and penalize user sessions originating from them. Most legitimate visitors have no reason to use anonymous proxies.

- **Test 5. Geographic origin**. Now on to the politically incorrect part: you get to blacklist any country in the world you would like! Just think of the countries from which you never have and likely never will receive a viable lead.

Remember, you are not about to ban visitors from these countries to access your Web site. You are just going about your regular business of assigning points.

- **Test 6 and beyond. Finesse and customize**. You can devise your own triggers and assign points to them. For example, if 98 percent of your business activity occurs during normal business hours, you may want to penalize visitor sessions originated at all other times. Or you may track visits from a set of suspicious IP addresses for a period of time, and plot their activity versus time of the day. Does it follow your site's average activity patterns? It better!

Now you need to sit down with your technical, design, sales, and marketing teams. The agenda for the meeting is to: 1) decide on which tests to use, 2) come up with the scoring system for the selected tests, and 3) pick the right threshold.

To test and adjust your selections, run through the possible actions of a dozen or so hypothetical real user personas, and calculate their scores. They should not trip the alarm. Now do the same exercise using personas of click-inflating robots and humans. Visits made for the sole purpose of depleting your PPC account should trip the wire every time.

Remember, to make sure your scoring system works precisely as intended, always compare your results against a control group of unbiased traffic sources, such as Google™'s and other major engines' organic search results. Click fraud is a contact sport with no rules. Click Inflation Index is a defense system you can use to protect yourself and fight back.

ABOUT CLICKLAB CLICK FRAUD DETECTION SERVICE

Clicklab Click Fraud Detection Service is the most advanced advertiser-side click fraud detection technology on the market today. It is the result of more than two years of research and development work performed by mathematicians, programmers, and SEM and PPC specialists.

Clicklab Click Fraud Detection Service monitors your Web site traffic for suspicious activity and applies a series of statistical tests to detect fraudulent click signatures. Each failed test is assigned a weighed penalty score. If cumulative score exceeds the threshold, Clicklab declares the visitor session fraudulent and flags it for analysis and further action.

Click Inflation Index (CII) is then calculated for each PPC search engine and keyword, allowing you to adjust your bidding strategy and generate detailed actionable reports to negotiate a refund with PPC providers. Clicklab click fraud reports serve as a form of documentation from a third party service that has no vested interest in your PPC campaigns.

Dmitri Eroshenko founded Clicklab (**www.clicklab.com**) in 2001 as the first web analytics firm to focus on marketing ROI and conversions. He continues to oversee the company's rapid growth.

Prior to Clicklab, Mr. Eroshenko founded several successful e-commerce related ventures. In 1996, he created Ad Juggler (**www.adjuggler.com**), one of the first online advertising management solutions. That software continues to help companies in both B2B and B2C markets manage their ads and increase profitability. In 1998, Mr. Eroshenko co-founded ISPcheck (**www.ispcheck.com**), another trail-blazing service that has allowed thousands of ISPs and web hosting services to expand their business using PPC advertising. It was this experience that alerted him to the problem of click fraud and inspired him to develop strategies to combat it. Mr. Eroshenko co-founded Web Hosting Magazine in 2000, where he served as editor and publisher. In 2001, he launched the very successful Web Hosting Expo, a trade show and conference in Washington, DC. Mr. Eroshenko is known as a leading ecommerce efficiency expert who has written extensively on subjects such as PPC advertising, web metrics, click fraud, and how to improve ROI. His articles have appeared in many respected marketing publications such as PayPerClickAnalyst, Search Engine News, and WebProNews. Mr. Eroshenko received his MS in Physics and Engineering from the Moscow Institute of Physics and Technology in 1990.

Michael Bloch is a marketing and development consultant with various qualifications in business, training and assessment that complement his broad information technology, ecommerce and web marketing experience gained since the mid 1990's. Michael's main site, Taming the Beast.net (**http://www.tamingthebeast.net**), receives millions of visitors a year and contains a wide variety of online business tools, tutorials and resources.

Increase Profits
With Google™ AdSense

Throughout this book we have concentrated on learning the elements of constructing and managing a cost-effective and profitable PPC advertising campaign. Throughout the rest of the book, we will look at alternative methods to increase revenue, and one of the most popular and effective is Google™'s AdSense. I will be honest with you — there are dozens of books out there you can read on Google™ AdSense, and most claim if you implement AdSense correctly you can just sit back and watch the profits roll in. I am not convinced that this was ever the case, and recently Google™ has changed the terms and conditions of AdSense placing stricter limitations on the revenue potential. That said, it is a proven alternative income stream that can be used in conjunction with, or independent of PPC or other marketing techniques.

Google™ states, "Google™ AdSense is the program that can give you advertising revenue from each page on your Web site — with a minimal investment in time and no additional resources. AdSense delivers relevant text and image ads that are precisely targeted to your site and your site content. And when you add a Google™ search box to your site, AdSense delivers relevant text ads that are targeted to the Google™ search results pages generated by your visitors' search request." (Source: **http://www.Google.com/services/adsense_tour/index.html**).

To take Google™'s AdSense virtual tour, visit **http://www.Google.com/services/adsense_tour/index.html**. At the end you can also apply right online.

How to Set up your Google™ AdSense Campaign

The first step is to complete the simple application form, which is available at **https://www. Google.com/adsense/g-app-single-1**. It is critical that you carefully review the terms of service. In particular, you must comply with agree that you will:

- Not click on the Google™ ads you are serving through AdSense.

- Not place ads on sites that include incentives to click on ads.

In other words, you cannot click on your ads, nor have others click on your ads, or place text on your Web site asking anyone to click on your ads. The reason for this is simple — you cannot click on (or have anyone else) click on your own ads to generate revenue.

Screenshots © Google™ Inc. and are reproduced with permission.

When your Web site is reviewed, and your account is approved, you will receive an e-mail from Google™ outlining what to do next.:

Google™ AdSense Program Policies

A successful Google™ AdSense campaign must comply with all the program policies. These policies can be located at**https://www. Google™.com/adsense/support/bin/answer.py?answer=48182&so urceid=aso&subid=ww-ww-et-asui&medium=link&hl=en_US**. Be sure you review these very carefully when beginning your AdSense campaign.

Setting up Google™ AdSense on Your Web Site

When you first sign up in your account, you will see the "Today's Earning" text, along with any action notices, such as on the one in the screen shot to release payment. In addition, you can navigate to your AdSense setup and My Account. To set up your initial AdSense account, click on the "My Account" tab. Be aware that because you will be paid by

Screenshots © Google™ Inc. and are reproduced with permission.

Google™, you will be required to complete several steps before your account is activated, such as provide W-9 tax data and choose your form of payment (electronic transfer or check payment). You may review edit all of your account settings including payment options, and review payment history data from the "My Account" tab.

Click on the "Account Setup" to begin setting up your ads. The screen below will be displayed:

Screenshots © Google™ Inc. and are reproduced with permission.

Choose which product you would like to add to your Web site. You may choose ether AdSense for Content, AdSense for Search, or Referrals. We will set up a Google™ AdSense for content ad on our Web site. You will now choose your Ad Type. You may choose Ad Unit (use the drop down menu to choose: text and image ads, text only, or image only ads). Ad Unit with Text and Images is the default (and recommended) setting, or you may choose a Link Unit (which displays a list of topics relevant to your Web page). Click on Ad unit to continue.

Screenshots © Google™ Inc. and are reproduced with permission.

You will be presented with several options to choose from including unit format, colors, and other options. Choose your desired options using the drop down menus (*note*: this is not the actual ad that will be displayed on your Web site, but merely a sample of how it may appear).

Screenshots © Google™ Inc. and are reproduced with permission.

You may use the "more options" to enable Custom Channels or elect to alternate ads or colors, including the option to show public service ads if there is no ad ready to be displayed on your Web site. For more information on these Channels visit **https://www.Google.com/adsense/support/bin/answer.py?answer=32614**.

After choosing your selections, you will be provided with HTML code that simply needs to be placed in the HTML code on your Web site. You are free to place the code on one or many Web pages within your Web site.

AdSense for Content

Choose Ad Type > Choose Ad Format and Colors > **Get Ad Code**

Wizard | Single page

Click anywhere in this box to select all code.

You may paste this code into any web page or website that complies with our program policies.

For more help with implementing the AdSense code, please see our Code Implementation Guide. For tips on placing ads to maximize earnings, see our Optimization Tips.

Your AdSense code:

```
<script type="text/javascript"><!--
google_ad_client = "pub-2693250782343896";
google_ad_width = 120;
google_ad_height = 240;
google_ad_format = "120x240_as";
google_ad_type = "text_image";
google_ad_channel ="";
//--></script>
<script type="text/javascript"
  src="http://pagead2.googlesyndication.com/pagead/show_ads.js">
</script>
```

Screenshots © Google™ Inc. and are reproduced with permission.

When you insert the HTML code into your Web site, your campaign is activated and ads are immediately served to your site. Remember: Do NOT click on your ad at any time, even to "test" them. Google™ provides a preview mode for testing.

A few articles to read over for more information on this program are:

- "Five Ways to Improve Your AdSense Earnings," by Jimbo Qwerty, available at **http://www.articlealley.com/article_92505_17.html**

- "Google™ AdSense Profit; Three Steps to Triple Your AdSense Earnings," by Shannon Baker, available at **http://www. articlealley.com/article_77899_3.html**

How to Set up your Google™ Referrals

Google™ AdSense program policies allow you to place one referral per product for a total of up to four referrals on any page. All you have to do is click on the referral link to choose your referrals as shown to the right. For more information about referrals visit **https://www. Google.com/adsense/static/en_US/ Referrals.html**.

Choose the product you'd like to refer.

Google referrals

○ **Google AdSense**
Ad revenue for web publishers

○ **Google AdWords**
Targeted online advertising

○ **Firefox plus Google Toolbar**
Improved web browsing

◉ **Google Pack**
Collection of essential software

○ **Picasa**
Photo organization software

Screenshots © Google™ Inc. and are reproduced with permission.

Google™ AdSense will even generate the HTML code for your Web site. After the code is placed on your Web pages, your Referral will be activated and displayed on your Web site as shown below. You have a variety of options in size, color, and wording to choose from and are free to change your Referral ads at any time:

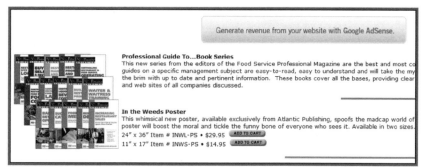

Screenshots © Google™ Inc. and are reproduced with permission.

Google™ AdSense is simple to implement, non-intrusive to your Web site and allows you to open channels to earning potential revenue for your business.

Hints and Tips for Maximizing Google™ AdSense on your Web Site

Google™ AdSense is an outstanding way to generate Web site traffic, attract advertisers, and create a revenue stream for your business. Use these hints and tips to maximize your earning potential:

- Always follow the Google™ AdSense Guidelines.

- Do not modify or change the Google™ AdSense HTML code you place on your Web site.

- Do not use colored backgrounds on the Google™ AdSense ads. If you have a Web site with a colored background, modify the ad to match your background.

- Place your ads so they are visible. If someone needs to scroll down to see your ads, you will likely not get any clicks on them. Play with the placement to maximize visibility.

- Do not include incentives for anyone to click on your ads (i.e., click here or click on my ads). This is also a violation of the Google™ AdSense guidelines. Do not have friends, family, or co-workers click on the ads.

- Do not click on your own ads. Do not reload your browser and click on your ads; do not test your ads out by clicking on them.

- Do not place ads in pop-up windows.

- Do not buy an "AdSense Template Website," which is readily available on eBay and other online marketplaces. These get-rich type "click" campaigns are against Google™'s policies and do not make money.

- Text ads typically do better than Image ads. If you insist on image ads, keep them reasonable. I recommend only using the 300 X 250 medium rectangle.

- You can modify the URL link color in the ad through the Google™ AdSense account panel; this makes it stand out among your ads and attracts the eye of the site visitor.

- If you have a blog, use it to have others place ads in it. You will need to get Google™ approval for your blog, and when you do, this is a successful area to insert ads.

- If your Web site has articles on it that you wish to imbed an ad in, use these guidelines: short articles — place the ad above the articles; long articles — imbed them within the content of the article.

- Wider format ads are more successful. The paying ad format is the "large rectangle."

- Distribute ads on each Web page. Combine ads with referrals and search boxes so your Web site does not look like a giant billboard;

- Put the Google™ Search box near the top right hand corner of your Web page.

- If your ads are based on content, the first lines of the Web page determine your site content for ad serving purposes.

- Set the Google™ AdSense search box results window so that it opens in a new window. Doing so will keep your browser open and visitors will not navigate away from your Web site.

How To Increase Sales
With Affiliate Marketing

The beauty of affiliate programs is that they are simple to establish, and literally expand your Web presence through hundreds and potentially thousands of Web sites increasing the visibility of your products well beyond your own Web site. Once you have established your Web site, completed search-engine optimization, implemented e-commerce, and established your PPC marketing campaigns, implementing an affiliate program may be the right option to extend your online presence.

Definition of Affiliate Programs

Affiliate programs have been around for a long time because of the success that they have achieved for thriving online businesses. Another name for an affiliate program is an "associate program." An affiliate program means that an individual or company promotes products and/or services provided by a merchant in return for a commission. The concept is simple. You have your Web site with your products for sale on it. You allow someone to become an "affiliate" of yours, and that person can then promote your products on their Web site. When a site visitor attempts to buy one of the products, they click on the link and are actually taken back to your Web site to complete the transaction. By using an affiliate program, this "click-through" is tracked, and the affiliate is given "credit" for the sale. Typically, an affiliate earns 8–15 percent of the total sale—for doing nothing more than allowing the merchant's products to be sold on their Web site. In some cases, the merchant pays commission to their affiliates for these product sales, sales leads, or some other defined sales-related activity that is of value to a merchant; but typically, commissions are only based on sales. One of the largest affiliate programs that is in place on the Internet is with **Amazon.com**, who have over 1,000,000 affiliate Web sites in place at this time on the Internet since selling products as an affiliate of Amazon costs nothing and you can earn a monthly income at no cost with little effort! While becoming an affiliate of others may increase revenue, your goal should be to establish an affiliate program so that others will become affiliates of your Web site.

In most cases the arrangement between affiliate Web sites is based on:

- The total number of Web visitors that they send to your site,

- The number and total dollar value of sales that you get from the people sent to your site, or

- The number of clicks you get back to your site.

When you use affiliates to send Web visitors to your site, you are taking advantage of a marketing technique that is extremely effective, while at the same time very affordable for even the smallest business Web sites.

When an affiliate program agreement is put into place, there are three separate entities that are involved with each of the actions that take place:

- The Web site of the affiliate.

- Your business Web site.

- The Web visitor, or customer, whom you are trying to attract to your Web site. Often, there is a middle-tier layer, which is an Affiliate Link application or server that actually records the "click-through" transaction.

Who Uses Affiliate Programs?

You may be wondering just what types of Web sites and businesses use an affiliate program. The answer is that almost any business can use this type of advertising program, although some plans place restrictions on language or Web content they consider offensive. Usually, the Web site is called a "merchant Web site," but this does not mean that a Web site needs to sell anything to use an affiliate program. There are many Web sites that have a high traffic volume on the Internet that make their money simply by the number of advertisers to which they sell space or through an effective affiliate program.

Once you do some research, you will find that there are all sorts of affiliate Web sites on the Internet, which include some high quality, popular Web sites all the way to the personal Web page of some unknown person. Even small Web sites can make money when they become an affiliate for another Web site.

Affiliate Payment Process

Affiliate programs use different ways to determine payment. Each can be successful in its own way, but there are slight differences between each. The three most common methods of payment are as follows.

- **PPC.** If you enter into this type of payment agreement, you will be paying your affiliates a total price that is determined by the number of Web visitors that click on a link on the affiliate Web page to arrive at your business Web site. These Web visitors are not required to buy anything; all they have to do is visit your Web site.

- **Pay-per-lead.** If you are using this type of payment method, you will be paying your affiliates an amount that is determined by the number of Web visitors who leave information at your Web site. All the Web visitor needs to do is to fill out a form on your business Web site, which you can then use as a lead to further sales and communication with the Web visitor. Your goal is to make a sale and obtain the Web visitor as a repeat customer so that you can increase your client database.

- **Pay-per-sale.** (The most common and my recommended method.) If you have this payment agreement with your affiliates, you pay a total (or percentage of the sales total) that is determined by the number of sales you make from Web visitors who are sent to your business Web site via the Web site of the affiliate. The amount you pay is based on either (a) a predetermined amount that is fixed ahead of time for each sale or (b) a certain percentage of each sale. **Amazon.com**'s affiliate program is an example of a pay-per-sale program. In this case, **Amazon.com** pays their affiliate when the affiliate sends them a customer who purchases something.

You will find that there are types of payment agreements between you, the online merchant, and the affiliate as well. No matter what arrangement you come up with, you will be paying your affiliates a certain amount of money each month that is based on the specified actions of the Web visitor. Two methods of affiliate payment that are becoming more popular are (1) residual payment programs and (2) two-tier payment programs.

Residual Payment Program

With this type of affiliate payment program your affiliates will be making a profit from the Web visitors that they send to your business Web site when these visitors continue to purchase your products or services. This is a great affiliate program if you are getting a constant and reliable payment from customers each month since your affiliates know that they can count on your payment.

Two-Tier Affiliate Payment Programs

These affiliate programs have a structure similar to multilevel marketing organizations such as Amway or Avon, which profit through commission sales and sales recruitment. In addition to receiving commissions based on sales, clicks, or leads stemming from their own site, affiliates in these programs also receive a commission based on the activity of affiliate sites they refer to the merchant site.

You may also run across some affiliate payment agreements that use the page view, or "pay-per-page-view (impression)," payment method. With this method, you will be paying your affiliates a total that is determined by the number of Web visitors that actually look at your banner ad. This type of payment agreement is really just an advertising technique that is linked to the use of your banner ads. There is one big difference between an affiliate program and an advertising program such as banner ad network programs: In an affiliate program, you only pay your affiliates when the action is completed such as a sale, a click, or a page view.

How Affiliate Programs Work

You will find that affiliate programs work quite easily once they are correctly set up; however, there are many processes that run in the background that you should be aware of and that are necessary for the smooth operation of these programs. You will need to keep a log of the actions that determine how your affiliates are paid. This means keeping track of the number of sales that you generate from your affiliates to the number of page views that occur after Web visitors have linked to your business site via your affiliate. Most reputable affiliate software packages automate this task and simplify the process by keeping track of all affiliate sales, affiliate earnings, affiliate payments, and other critical information. Here is a list of some of the items that need to be tracked:

- The total number of Web visitors who arrive at your business site after clicking on your link on your affiliate's Web site.

- The total number of Web visitors who notice your banner ad on your affiliate's Web site.

- The total number of Web visitors who generate an actual sale after arriving at your Web site via your affiliate.

You need to keep accurate numbers of the above actions so that your affiliates are paid accordingly. Although it may seem to be much effort and time for you to administer your affiliate program closely by yourself, you will find that the advantages outweigh the disadvantages. When you have complete control over your affiliate program, you will be able to decide which affiliates are most beneficial for you.

Affiliate Program Networks

If you do not want to do all the administrative work yourself for your affiliate program, you can join what are called affiliate program networks, or "affiliate brokers." Affiliate networks act as the go-between for you and your affiliates. These network programs will keep track of all the activity that occurs on your Web site and your affiliate's Web site that has to do with the payment agreement that you've set up. Affiliate networks will (1) take care of all the payment agreements and methods, (2) keep a log of all the actions that take place between your

Web site and the affiliate's Web site, (3) manage and maintain all of the links and banner ads that need to be set up on your affiliate's Web site, and (4) keep a list of your affiliate program within their network directory. An alternative to affiliate program networks is purchasing a stand-alone affiliate program by utilizing an application server (hosted elsewhere) and requiring you to install some portion of HTML code on your website. I highly recommend Affiliate Link (**http://www. affiliatetracking.com**) as one of the most effective, simple to use, yet highly customizable web-based affiliate programs on the market. Their newest product is ROIAdvantage, which incorporates TrackingSoft's state-of-the-art tracking solution for affiliate program and advertising campaign management. Information about ROIAdvantage is available at **http://www.trackingsoft.com**).

One of the advantages of using an affiliate program network is that you'll have access to a number of different types of affiliate programs at one time so that you can mix and match your payment agreements. You'll be able to find just the right affiliate program that works best for you and your business. Of course, you'll have to pay a commission fee when you join an affiliate program network. Usually, the cost of hiring an affiliate network is about 15 to 25 percent of each transaction that occurs.

Becoming Part of an Affiliate Program

Becoming part of an affiliate program is a way that you can increase the success and profits of your Web site. Before you take part in an affiliate program you need to decide what role you want to play in the process: the affiliate, the merchant Web site that offers affiliate memberships, or a combination of both. If you have an online business Web site, you'll most likely want to have affiliates that are going to send potential customers to your site and increase the success and profits of your online or brick and mortar business. Those people who have a small Web site that offers content rather than sales may want to be an affiliate for a few business Web sites. The bottom line is that you need to decide how your business will best benefit from an affiliate program.

The steps you need to take to be an affiliate for other Web sites are easy to implement. All you need to do is find an affiliate program network site on the Internet and join by filling out a simple application form that gathers the following information: (1) information that is personal, such as your name, address, and the type of payment plan that you prefer, including payment address and (2) information about your Web site, such as your Web address (URL), the name of your Web site, and a description of your Web site. Once you have filled out the information form, you will be asked to sign what is called a "service agreement" so that both you and the affiliate network are clear about the terms and conditions. You won't have to pay any money to become an affiliate since most networks have no charge for you to become an affiliate.

You may have to wait a few days to find out if your application to become an affiliate has been approved, at which time you can choose the type of affiliate programs that appeal to you the most and in which you would like to take part (most merchants have only one option). After you have chosen a few affiliate programs it will be time for the "merchants" to view your Web site to see if they want to use you as an affiliate. Once you have been approved, the affiliate program network will help you in hosting the links and banner ads on your Web site that correspond with your chosen affiliate program. At this time you may be asked to work out the finer details of the payment side of things, such as which action you are going to be paid for and how much, such as pay-per-click, pay-per-lead, or pay-per-sale; however, this is typically set in advance. Most affiliate programs will only pay you once a certain minimum amount of earnings has been reached per month (typically $50), because the profit that you make as an affiliate does not amount to thousands. This is so that the affiliate network does not send out small amounts of money on a monthly basis. Additionally, most affiliates do not honor sales for purchases which you make through your own affiliate link. After you have been set up as an affiliate and understand for which actions you're being paid, and how much, you can concentrate on the content and purpose of your Web site.

If you want to have affiliates who are going to advertise your products, you will need to start your own affiliate program, and as I mentioned earlier, I highly recommend Affiliate Link (**http://www.affiliatetracking. com**) as one of the most effective, simple to use, yet highly customizable web-based affiliate programs on the market. Most affiliate software packages (including Affiliate Link) offer free installation and setup.

When you first contact the affiliate network, you will be asked to fill out an application form that defines your Web site and gives a general description of what products or services it promotes and/or sells. At this time you'll also sign an agreement for the conditions and terms of the program such as for which actions you want to pay (pay-per-click, pay-per-lead, or pay-per-sale). You will also have to make a few deposits and pay a fee to become a member of the affiliate program. Many affiliate networks will charge you a one-time fee to join as well as a fee that you pay each year so that you can use the services that they provide.

The cost of joining an affiliate network will be anywhere from $500 to $6,000, depending on how successful the network is, which is a major factor in joining the network or in initiating your own affiliate program. Keep in mind that you will also be paying each of your affiliates, and in addition, a portion of each payout will go back to the affiliate network.

Most affiliate program networks will give you the choice to choose your affiliates, or you can also choose to use any and all Web sites that are interested in linking to your Web site, which is a very common choice.

Joining an affiliate program network means that you won't have to do all the hard work necessary to running a successful affiliate program. When you run the show yourself, you need to find the right affiliates, buy software that is going to keep track of the affiliate actions so that you can pay accordingly, show your affiliates how to post your links and banner ads on their Web sites, manage all the accounting for your affiliate program, and be available at all times to help your affiliates and answer any questions that they have.

How Affiliates Link to Your Web Site

You need to understand how your affiliates are going to link back to your Web site. There are several ways that this can be accomplished, depending on which method works best for you and your Web site. Here is a list of some of the more common methods of having your affiliate's link to your Web site:

- **Banner ad links.** Banner ads use a combination of text and graphics to catch the attention of Web visitors so that they click on the link and end up on your Web site.

- **Text and content links.** Text links on your affiliate Web site are mixed in with the content of each Web page and usually appear as blue text so that Web visitors can click on the text and link to your Web site. Text links are a great form of advertising because they are less intrusive to the eye of a Web visitor than other advertisements that many Web visitors are trying to avoid. Using text links in the content of Web pages is becoming more popular as advertisers search for ways to make advertising on the Internet more subtle.

- **Links from a search box.** When Web visitors search through databases online, they can follow links back to your Web site. This method of advertising has yet to catch on in a big way when it comes to Internet advertising.

When Web visitors use the links that they find on Web sites there are different ways that they can end up linking back to your Web site. The most common link is a jump to the home page of your Web site. When they arrive at your home page, Web visitors can find out general information about you and your business in a natural way without being forced to immediately look at the products or services that you are selling.

The second way that Web visitors can link to your Web site is by linking from an affiliate's Web site directly to a specific product or service that you're selling. Web visitors can easily find the products that you offer without searching through your Web site for the right Web page. This type of link is known as a "product-specific" link. Most affiliate packages (including Affiliate Link) simplify the entire process by automating the creation of links so you can create entrance pages, product specific pages and many other options giving your potential affiliates a wide variety of highly customizable and simple options. We will discuss Affiliate Link in depth later in this chapter.

Another way that people can link back your Web site is through the use of storefronts. The storefront is a great way to let visitors to your Web site see a variety of the products or services that you're selling. You will have the ability to change the way your storefront looks and the products that you're featuring whenever you want to try something new.

The fourth method of letting Web site visitors link back to your Web site is called "co-branding." With this method, your affiliates can have their own separate identity on the Internet, while at the same time having visitors to their Web site link to your business Web site. Your

Web site will handle all of the sales for your business, but you'll have some appearance on your Web site of your affiliate so that many times, Web visitors won't even know that they have been on two different Web sites.

The final way that Web visitors can link back to your Web site is by clicking a link and ending up on a registration page on your Web page. Using the registration link method, people need to register before they can browse through your Web pages. This is the least preferred method as many site visitors will go elsewhere when presented with yet another request for information or personal data.

The Success of Affiliate Programs

Just what makes an affiliate program a successful and profitable choice? The main reason is that when you use an affiliate program, you have the ability to use links to encourage people to visit your Web site, browse your content, browse through your products and services, and potentially become customers in your database.

Essentially, by using an affiliate program, you are replicating your Web site and/or products to hundreds or thousands of other Web sites throughout the world, dramatically increasing the exposure and potential sales for your profits—all at little or no cost.

For the most part, affiliate programs work best when the affiliate, the merchant, and the links all have something in common with the product or service that is being sold. When you, as a merchant, make wise choices about which affiliates you want to host your Web links, you have a better chance of catching the interest of customers and potential customers. You come out ahead because you get those customers that you might not otherwise get, while at the same time your affiliates come out ahead because they can be linked to products that have something to do with their Web site without ever having to run an e-commerce Web site of their own. If you are using an affiliate network program, the network also comes out ahead because they earn a profit by bringing you and your affiliate together and taking care of the finer details of managing the affiliate program for you.

Setting Up an Affiliate Program

Atlantic Publishing Company established a highly successful (and profitable) Affiliate program by implementing the Affiliate Link System (available at **http://www.affiliatetracking.com/**). Atlantic Publishing Company's Affiliate program is available at: **http://atlantic-pub.com/ affiliate.htm.** One of the first things you will need to establish is an introduction page which will entice potential affiliate to sign up. Of course, one of the main reasons to join an affiliate is to generate income, and Atlantic Publishing offers "an amazing 20 percent commission on ALL ELIGIBLE SALES!!." The reason you should consider establishing an affiliate program is you can potentially increase your total sales exponentially as your affiliates grow throughout the web. Below is the text from Atlantic Publishing Company's affiliate Web page:

Atlantic Publishing Company Sample Web Text

Earn an Amazing 20 percent Commission on all eligible sales! The highest commission rate in the Industry!

Atlantic Publishing Company is now accepting affiliates into their brand new Affiliate Program. This program pays a minimum of 20 percent commission to all affiliates, with the potential to earn even more.

If you have a Web site, you can earn money by selling books and other Professional Food Service Industry products by linking with Atlantic Publishing Companies Affiliate Network or selling our products on your Web site. We have greatly expanded our product lines to include:

- Food Service and Hospitality
- Entrepreneurial
- Human Resources
- Internet/Web
- Professional Books
- HACCP
- Food Service Encyclopedias
- Real Estate
- Personal Finance
- Hospitality
- Spanish Products
- Training
- And Much More!

Atlantic Publishing Company Sample Web Text

When you join our Affiliate Program, you will have multiple options to customize your affiliate link options. These include linking to our site, linking to a pre-set "entrance" page so you can target the product lines you wish to sell, linking directly to any of our individual products, and even putting the products directly onto your Web site through our "custom" landing pages.

We also offer banner ads for your Web site if you prefer to use banner advertising. All you have to do is set up links on your site by following the simple instructions we will provide. We take care of everything else.

You can earn fantastic revenues by simply participating in the Affiliate Program, earning 20 percent of the total eligible purchase! Our Web-based Affiliate Management Program allows you to track sales and commissions online through our advanced reporting interface. The program is simple to join and easy to implement on your Web site. Technical support is available to help you maximize your affiliate setup and marketing campaign.

We feature an online Affiliate Program Application which allows you to adjust your preferences; choose different banners, entrance pages, and landing pages; as well as monitor your affiliate statistics (click-through and sales) — All for free! Plus, you will receive e-mail notification after an Affiliate Sale is processed through your account, notifying you of the total purchase, and your commission amount.

Please note: "Affiliate Eligible" products are those produced or published by Atlantic Publishing Company. A complete list of products is available by clicking HERE. Although all products sold on our site are not eligible for affiliate-based commissions, our system will recognize which items are eligible (even if someone orders a mix of eligible and non-eligible products on the same order) and provide you with an accurate accountability of your actual earnings through your notification e-mails, and online reporting tools. If you have additional questions, please review our Affiliate Frequently Asked Questions Web Page."

Atlantic Publishing Company also created a "frequently asked questions" page to address any potential questions or concerns surrounding their program.

When you click the "Join Us" button on Atlantic Publishing Company's Web Site, you get the Affiliate Link sign up screen, which has been customized for Atlantic Publishing. See the screen shot to the right.

Once your affiliate setup is approved, you will need to have it installed and customized. Many providers will do this for free or for a minimal one-time charge, leaving all the hard work up to them. You do nothing other than customize your application after it is properly installed and tested. Affiliate Link Network charges a small, one time fee for installation, and I have found their technical support to be above average. Affiliate Link Network will set the components on your web site—you literarily do nothing more than sign up your business to create an affiliate account. Once established, you will have a web-based administration control panel to manage all areas of your affiliate program, view sales data, approve payments, e-mail affiliates, and establish entrance pages, banners, and manage affiliate accounts.

The following information is taken from www.affiliatetracking.com and reprinted with permission.

Affiliate Link

Affiliate Link is my choice for an affiliate program. As I also mentioned earlier, you may want to take a close look at ROIAdvantage, which is TrackingSoft's state-of-the-art tracking solution for affiliate program and advertising campaign management. ROIAdvantage includes all the features of Affiliate Link, and combines them with full featured advertising campaign management.

Affiliate Link, will help you to:

- Increase traffic and sales
- Save time and money
- Pay only for what your affiliates sell

It is also Feature Rich. It offers:

- Direct Linking Capability
- Cookieless Tracking Capability
- Multiple Site Support
- Recurring Commission Support for Select Processors
- Unlimited Affiliates Supported

Features of Affiliate Link (ROIAdvantage) Network

BRANDING

Whether your focus is on affiliate marketing, e-mail marketing, search engine marketing, media buys and/or offline advertising efforts, branding is a key element of any advertising and marketing formula. **AffiliateTracking.com** caters to this elemental need in providing the option to brand the look and feel of the software as well as the links used to promote your affiliate program and/or in house advertising campaigns.

DIRECT LINKING SUPPORT

In a Direct Linking model, traffic flows uninterrupted from a partner's Web site to your domain. By choosing direct linking, you are maximizing the benefit your partnership program brings to your business. Not only do your affiliates refer you traffic, which increases your sales, but you also gain the advantage of all those additional links from sites with related content pointing directly to your site, which increases your search engine ranking and drives even more traffic to your site!

CLEAN LINKING

Build your brand, instill confidence in your customers, and make your affiliates' job easier with Clean Linking support. Clean Linking allows your affiliates to register their web domain with your program once, and then records all traffic originating from that site and arriving at yours. Affiliates can link to any page in your domain from any page in theirs, without any additional parameters in the URL.

MULTIPLE CAMPAIGN MANAGEMENT

ROIA software is completely scalable to your affiliate program's exact needs, including the ability to manage multiple offers on multiple sites.

FULL ADMINISTRATIVE ORDER CONTROL

Mistakes, returns, credits, and chargebacks do occur no matter what you may be selling or what channel it is sold through. You decide if orders coming in are accepted automatically or on a pending basis for your manual approval. You can also edit order details (before or after approving the order) in the event the order amount was discounted, commission raised or lowered, or to manually give your affiliate credit for a referred order that was placed offline, for example. Original order details are kept in the system as a fraud prevention/cross check feature.

FLEXIBLE COMMISSION MANAGEMENT TO ACCOMMODATE ANY INDUSTRY

Do you have a subscription-based service and would like to offer a flat rate and percentage per subscription, a pay per click program or a simple product-based program offering a small percentage? You can set, change, and manage these commission models easily from the web based admin panel.

MULTI-TIER CAPABILITY

AffiliateTracking.com does not participate in or support Multilevel Marketing schemes, but they do provide two tiers of tracking to their clients in an effort to grow their affiliate databases via affiliate referral incentives.

GIVES YOUR PROGRAM AN ADDED ELEMENT OF INTEGRITY

It is a well known fact that some seasoned affiliates are weary of partnering with new sites or programs. In addition to using their well established domain for your affiliate links, the AffiliateTracking name will instill confidence in your prospective affiliates: confidence in their technical solutions, in the accuracy of their reported earnings, and in the legitimacy of your affiliate program.

Detailed Affiliate Program Reporting

With web-based access for both the admin and the affiliate, neither will be in the dark about how well the program is doing. Admins will be able to see the number of impressions, clicks, sales, leads, sales by site, sales by member, sub-affiliate sign ups, sub-affiliate clicks, sub-affiliate sales and commissions, and more for each affiliate. In addition, affiliates will be able to see the same statistics for their personal efforts

Wizard-Based Interface for Ease of Use

Regardless of whether you have been in affiliate marketing for a day or a decade, ROIAdvantage is a user-friendly solution that fits your needs. Beyond step-by-step wizards to guide you through every process in the system, our client services department will provide you with one-on-one online training time following your purchase, to ensure that you are up to speed and ready to earn with your affiliate program.

Affiliate Payout Made Easy

RegaAffiliates are rightfully concerned with the speed and accuracy of affiliate payouts in any program they consider joining. With this in mind, they have implemented a powerful affiliate payment management function that allows you to track, process, and record commission payments, and export the files to Excel or CSV format for import into your accounting software of choice.

Affiliate Management Control

You can choose to defer affiliate applications for review and manual approval to ensure they meet your standards. If you choose to accept submissions automatically, you can also review the affiliates' details, as you receive a notification each time someone joins your program.

Use the Email Capability to Maintain Affiliate Contact and More

Affiliate Tracking and ROIAdvantage allow you to e-mail one, some, or all of your affiliates using convenient filters such as affiliate id, category and country. The e-mail capability can also be used to manage customer and subscriber lists.

BANNER PUBLISHING, LANDING PAGES, CREATIVES AND CUSTOM TEMPLATES

We have all heard tales of affiliates misrepresenting (either purposely or mistakenly) the merchant's offering, resulting in angry customers that descend upon the merchant with a flood of returns and ill will. This can easily be avoided by educating your affiliates about your product or service, and providing them with the materials necessary to pre-sell your offer successfully. Their affiliate software has individual management areas for adding links, banners, creative documents (such as HTML pages or custom e-mailers) that automatically replace all URLs with affiliate coded links, custom templates for newsletters, promotions, and a files area where you can post any information you need to get to your affiliates. All items entered into your administration panel appear instantly in the affiliate's panel, pre-coded with their affiliate id for quick copy-and-paste inclusion into the promotional medium of their choice.

BANNER ROTATION ENGINE

Instantly circulate new banner ads without waiting for publishers to take any action. ROIAdvantage allows you to configure priorities for individual banner ads of a given size. Your partners can then generate placement codes for a size instead of placing individual banners. Create a new banner of a given size, and all affiliates displaying placements that match that size will immediately begin displaying the new ad! With banner rotation, you can similarly stop circulation of an outdated or poorly performing ad.

TRACK PERFORMANCE OF INDIVIDUAL LINKS AND BANNERS

Use the powerful ROIA reporting features to see detailed performance information about specific links and banners in your program. You can easily remove any poorly performing creatives from your program, or encourage affiliates to place those that convert well.

FRAUD PROTECTION

Regardless of the affiliate program model you use, ROIA possesses a control to ensure your program is not defrauded. In addition to our behind-the-scenes fraud prevention measures, you can apply additional filters like blocking duplicate emails or duplicate orders.

COOKIELESS TRACKING CAPABILITY

Due to a recent study just released from Jupiter Research that states as many as 39 percent of internet users delete cookies on a monthly basis. There have been a number of affiliates and affiliate marketers concerned that traditional cookie based tracking systems are no longer sufficient. While we feel this metric is skewed, ROIA has had the ability to track without relying on cookies for some time.

ROIAdvantage is TrackingSoft's state-of-the-art tracking solution for affiliate program and advertising campaign management. ROIA represents the culmination of their seven-plus year experience in the affiliate tracking and web advertising market by incorporating technological advances, client feedback, and innovation. The result is a comprehensive solution, which provides not only tracking of traffic and conversions, but also an advanced interface, multi-level drill-down reporting, publisher management, support for multiple ad campaigns, advanced website analytics, and very, very much more. Full details about ROIAdvantage can be found at **http://www.trackingsoft.com**, and a demo of feature and functionality can also be found at **http://affiliatetracking.com/demo/roia_demo.shtml.**

Conclusion

Affiliate programs offer you the potential to increase your sales with minimal investment in both time and money. There are few other business ventures which offer minimal investment while offering such an extraordinary potential increase in sales. The next step after implementing your pay-per-click marketing campaign should be to establish an effective affiliate program. While I highly recommend you install an affiliate program on your web site to promote your products, you may choose to avoid this and join others affiliate networks (essentially selling their products on your Webs ites – earning a commission for each sale). If you want to join someone else's affiliate program, I recommend you only join established and professional affiliate programs such as **Amazon.com** or Atlantic Publishing Company (**www.atlantic-pub.com/affiliate.htm**).

Increase Profits
With an eBay Store Front

You should consider establishing an eBay Store Front as an additional strategy of your marketing campaign. Do not make the mistake of overlooking the potential of eBay sales and how they can dramatically improve the visibility and sales of your products. There are many advantages to advertising and selling products on eBay, and the low cost is one of the main reasons. When you open and operate an eBay Store Front (or eBay store), you can connect with millions of people every day who shop on eBay.

By opening an eBay store, you can promote your products online through eBay. To assist you with the process, eBay provides you with an array of tools and wizards. You can typically have your Store Front operating in less than an hour. eBay provides you with a wide range of management tools, and most importantly provides you with the eBay turbo loader software, which manages your inventory, controls pricing, and allows you to list any or all products on eBay with just few simple mouse clicks. An eBay Store Front is the final component to be used in conjunction with a well-established e-commerce Web site, a highly effective PPC marketing campaign and a robust affiliate program.

eBay stores are a part of eBay where individual sellers can show you all of their current listings and tell you more about their business through their own customized pages. Most eBay stores include store inventory items, additional fixed price (Buy It Now) items not available in regular search results, and categories on eBay. This means that shoppers have access to millions of additional items when you search or browse in eBay Stores. It costs very little to open an eBay Store. For as little as $15.95 per month, you can start to boost your Internet presence, increase your sales, and add to your customer database. When you start an eBay Store, you will have these tools at your disposal:

- An online Store Front that is completely yours to develop and create to fit your business needs.

- Easy tools to manage your eBay Store.

- Tracking methods and a way to analyze how your business is doing within the eBay community.

- Tools at hand for marketing and merchandising your product.

When you open an eBay Store Front, you will find many benefits to your business. An eBay Store Front gives you the opportunity to reach thousands of people each day and increase the exposure that you need to obtain more customers. One of the big benefits of having an eBay Store Front is that it gives you an additional professionally designed outlet establishing the credibility that you need to reach customers who are looking for a particular product or service on the Internet. It takes only a few minutes to start your eBay store, which means that you will be up and running in no time, and ready for customers to find you. Many businesses that already have their own Web site still use eBay Store Fronts as a tool to reach even more sales customers on a daily basis.

You are able to customize your Store Front to the exact design that you feel best stylizes the products that you are selling. There are more than 20 different design categories that you can choose from when you sign up with eBay Store Front or you can simply design your own (even based on your current Web site design). One of the most overlooked benefits, aside from the increased visibility and generated Web sales, is that when you operate an eBay Store Front you are given a unique Web site address or URL (Uniform Resource Locator) on the Internet for your Store Front. It lets customers find you fast and easily, bookmarking your Store Front Web site so that they can return later for repeat sales and to find out what is new in your Store. Of even more significance is the fact that this Web site URL can be submitted to all search engines, dramatically increasing your sales visibility within them and on the World Wide Web.

Each month you will have access to a variety of reports that will let you know exactly how your product sales are doing. Some of the data that you will receive each month includes

1. a traffic report so that you know how many Web visitors are stopping by your eBay Store Front

2. sales reports, to let you know how many sales your Store Front has generated, and

3. accounting information that you can use to export your PayPal and eBay sales transactions into accounting software programs such as QuickBooks or your own Excel spreadsheet.

When it comes to the promotion of your eBay Store Front you will not be left in the cold, since eBay will give you all the help that you need to bring customers to your eBay Store. eBay will list your Store Front on all the appropriate listings within their Web site pages and will send out marketing correspondence to your customers.

When you sign up with eBay Store Front you will have a search engine in the content of your Store. This means that your customers will be able to use this search tool to find the products or services that you are selling. You will save time using the eBay Store Front to sell your products and spend more time concentrating on your business and other marketing strategies. When you sign up with eBay Store Front, you will see a definite increase in your sales and profits, as well as watch your customer database grow and turn into repeat sales. You should consider linking your main Web site to your eBay Store Front offering the opportunity for customers to shop in the "auction" style Store Front setting of eBay as an alternative to fixed prices.

eBay Tips, Tricks, and Secrets to Generate Sales

- **Start your listings at a low price to encourage interest and bids.** eBay sales are predominantly auction based; therefore the more bids you receive, the more likely your product will sell at a higher price. Products with multiple bids tend to sell more frequently, and at a higher cost than similar items with a high initial listing price.

- **It is all about feedback.** This is what your customers say about their shopping experience with you. Feedback can be given on any transaction, and savvy eBay shoppers check the feedback quality of the prospective seller before they bid. It is simple to attain 100 percent positive feedback. Just follow through with the sale, quickly package, and ship the products and you will always have satisfied customers. As your number of positive feedback grows, so does your status as a reputable seller within the eBay community.

To create listings from your eBay Store Front, here are some simple rules to follow. Again, we recommend you use one of the eBay templates, or use Microsoft® FrontPage (**www.Microsoft®.com**) to develop your HTML code.

- **Do not use ALL CAPITAL LETTERS.**

- **Be descriptive and provide lots of detail on your products**. You can expand to include much more than just the product details. This is a great opportunity to tell the prospective bidder the benefits of having the product.

- **Always include one or more digital images.** You get one free with eBay, but we recommend more for certain products where multiple angle views may enhance the sale.

- **Use HTML code to create your descriptions.** If you just type into the eBay description block, your paragraphs will not be broken up properly and will be difficult to read. Create your description in Microsoft® Front Page, go to the HTML view, cut and paste the HTML code into the description block in eBay. Although this is not readable, when displayed in the browser the HTML code is interpreted and displayed with proper formatting, coloring, and tables. Keep your coding simple and classy. Do not overdo it with flashing icons, images, and text that distract the viewer. A clean, simple interface is best to sell your products. We also recommend you only use white backgrounds for any descriptions or Web pages.

- **Include Shipping Costs and Methods** (First Class, Media, Priority). We recommend you ONLY include flat rate shipping (which covers your costs for the packaging and shipping). You can also pay for shipping and print USPS shipping labels directly from PayPal after the completion of the sale. Shipping estimates or unknown shipping costs will lose potential bidders who are wary of unknown shipping costs. You should figure high for shipping costs, but be reasonable. Twenty dollars to ship a one-pound book is not reasonable. However, $5 may be reasonable. As a side bonus, you can ship books media mail for under $3 making a profit off the excess shipping costs. This is a great way to offset the costs for your eBay and PayPal fees. You should also give some thought to packing materials, which can be expensive. By using USPS Priority mail services, you can get free boxes and packing tape. Do not forget about USPS Flat Rate boxes and envelopes, which are also free packing material, plus the benefit of flat fee shipping costs, regardless of the envelope or box weight.

- **Ensure your description and title are relevant** to what the user will be searching for.

- **If you have multiple items to sell, space them out over time**; do not list one after the other. Turbo lister from eBay simplifies this process, and you can use delayed listings to specific auction listing start times.

- **Highlight the unique features of your products in the title.** Instead of just listing your brand new product as ASUS K8N-E Deluxe Socket 754 Athlon 64 Motherboard, list it as ASUS K8N-E Deluxe Socket 754 Athlon 64 Motherboard **BRAND NEW** to emphasize the fact that it is a brand new product.

- **You can list items for three, five, seven, or ten days.** (You do pay a ten-cent premium per listing for ten-day listings). There is much debate about how long to list items for, and when the best time/day is to start a listing. Seven-day auctions are the standard, and this is what we recommend unless you must sell products quickly and opt for the three- or five-day options. As an experienced eBay seller, you will soon discover the last 60 seconds of all auctions are when the most bidding action takes place.

- **Auctions should start at the lowest amount possible.** Bidders are looking for bargains, and starting bids of a few dollars or less are more likely to attract more interest than bids that start at or near full retail value. In most cases, bids for low starting prices produce significantly more interest (and thus more bids), and typically sell above the expected final bid amount.

- **As discussed earlier, the flat shipping fee should cover your shipping costs including packaging** and potentially some of your eBay and/or PayPal fees. Under no circumstances should you ever allow shipping charges to be lower than the actual shipping costs.

- **Do not use a reserve price.** The main reason is that people are looking for a deal, and they know if you have a reserve price, you are not willing to part with the item at a lower price and let them get a great deal. Most bidders will ignore anyone who puts a reserve price, and you should never put a reserve on your products. You do take a risk that they may sell for less than your desired profit.

- **Make sure you follow up with bidder via e-mail.** Typically, there is no reason to use the telephone, as all eBay communication is Web/e-mail based. eBay accounts should be checked daily at a minimum, and more often for Store Fronts. You should review the "My Messages" folder for any questions or comments from sellers. We highly recommend your store create template e-mails that are generated by eBay when an item you are selling has been won. These e-mails validate the sale, confirm payment information, act as an invoice, tell the auction winner that you value and appreciate his or her business, and ensure they are satisfied with the transaction.

- **You should also send out a template e-mail when an auction is paid for.** This confirms that payment was received, the order will be processed, and you can tell them how the item will ship.

- **I highly recommend using Paypal to generate shipping labels for all your products.** In addition to being very simple, it also includes free delivery confirmation from the U.S. Postal Service and also automatically notifies the winner that their item has been shipped and provides the date and delivery tracking information via e-mail.

An excellent article about selling on eBay is "Why Your Company Should Be Selling on eBay," by Daniel Buys, available at **http://www. articlealley.com/article_85721_3.html**.

An eBay Store Front offers you the potential to increase market share significantly and potential sales with minimal investment in both time and money.

Summary

Remember the number one question I am asked by my clients that we discussed in the introduction; "Will my Web site will be number one in all major search engines, such as Google™, Yahoo, and MSN®." We hope you realize the answer is POSSIBLY — if you design your Web site properly, implement a solid Search-engine Optimization plan, engage a variety of marketing campaigns, balancing all major online marketing and sales techniques including PPC, affiliates, and some of the other techniques I have discussed at length in this book. As I stated in the introduction; "Obtaining high search-engine rankings is a combination of many factors, starting with Web site design and culminating with an effective Web site marketing strategy that maximizes your potential for high rankings and ultimately increased revenues or Web site traffic, while balancing the constraints of often limited resources and budget." To this end I have armed you with all of the tools you need to ensure your Web site is successful, and your PPC and other online marketing campaigns are highly effectively and PROFITABLE!

The advantage of an e-commerce business is that you can easily change marketing techniques and implement multiple campaigns through a variety of techniques simultaneously without significant investment of either time or money — returning significant increase in Web site traffic and generating enormous revenue.

I recommend that you build a library of reference material to assist you with your Web site design, creation, search-engine optimization, online marketing programs, PPC marketing campaigns, affiliate programs and other hints, tips and techniques I have provided. Create a checklist of items to complete, and work your way through them so you have an organized, well-thought out approach to your e-commerce venture. This checklist may quickly grow and seem to be a daunting and overwhelming task. However, you do not have to do everything at once, and you can implement various techniques and monitor how they perform for you, as you implement others and modify existing techniques.

Top Eight Reasons to Follow the Guidelines in this Book

1.) PPC advertising is a moneymaker if done correctly. You have the potential to increase your Web site traffic and sales performance exponentially.

2.) You can quickly — almost instantly — reach millions of potential customers every day.

3.) PPC marketing is highly cost-effective. You only pay when someone is interested enough to visit your Web site.

4.) As your business becomes more prominent and established, you gain enormous credibility in the eyes of competitors and most importantly potential customers by turning those "potential" customers into "repeat" customers.

5.) PPC advertising and all of the techniques in this book are significantly less costly than a traditional marketing campaign and more effective.

6.) If you feel your PPC campaign is not effective or your ads are not exactly the way you want them, you can change them — instantly and at no cost. Try doing that with a print marketing campaign.

7.) The Internet is becoming more and more expandable when it comes to the types and methods of advertising that can take place on the Web.

8.) Geographical targeting allows you to direct your PPC campaigns to the geographical area, or even demographical groups, where you will be most effective.

Take the time to follow the guidelines we have provided on search-engine optimization, Web site design, e-commerce integration, Web site automation, branding, and online business promotion to keep your site on the competitive edge. No business should miss the nearly unlimited free or no-cost advertising, marketing, and promotional potential of the Internet. No guarantees exist about achieving top ranking across the major search engines, but the techniques we have provided, along with hard work, determination, and self-promotion will put you well on your way to achieving top ranking — with the satisfaction that you did it on your own, without hiring "experts," and saving countless thousands of dollars along the way!

PPC Marketing
and SEO Case Studies

Onvia Software was facing a challenge in its search marketing: It was working too well. As a provider of Web-based research and bid notification services for companies looking to bid on all types of government contracts, Seattle-based Onvia had started using PPC search marketing two years ago to generate sales leads. The company quickly saw its initial harvest of a couple thousand clicks a month grow into more than a million—with a search marketing budget to match. The program, managed through search marketing firm Point It! was undoubtedly bringing in many leads for the Onvia sales team to pursue.

But last year, company-mandated marketing cuts forced Onvia to take a closer look at those online leads. "Our organization sets different priority tasks every six months or every quarter, and one of our tasks was to reduce the cost of lead acquisition," said Jennifer Day, Onvia's director of marketing communications. "Search-engine marketing is our primary way of driving leads, so we knew we needed to test to understand whether we could lower the cost without giving up the quality."

Working with Point It! Onvia started by segmenting the leads its PPC ads were already bringing in, sorting them into three categories according to the prospect's readiness to buy. Onvia's in-house sales department was to follow up every SEM lead that came in within 24 hours, to evaluate how close they were to a purchase.

In addition, there were many near-purchase leads in the net. "Compared to many B-to-B providers, our service is not a high-consideration item," said Day. The leads Onvia generates through search usually wind up being those with buying authority at their companies; and the relatively low price of Onvia's services—about $2,500 for an annual subscription—means the sales cycle can be as short as several days or as long as several months. Day estimates that Onvia's average sales cycle takes about 30 days from first contact to sale.

However, Onvia found it was also digging up leads that would require more handling to convert, such as a live consultation or online demo of services. And some of the leads generated were at the very beginning of the purchase funnel and could not be expected to convert without much more information, including some very basic instruction in how government bidding works.

Such newbies to government contracting were not really the sweet spot Onvia was aiming for, said Lisa Sanner, client manager at Point It! Rather, Onvia wanted to work with experienced bidders of all sizes who already had some contracts under their belts and who could benefit most from the efficiencies built into its service. These represented the best prospects for service renewals and long-term business relationships.

After segmenting the leads they were receiving, Onvia and Point It! cross-referenced the segments to the keywords that brought them in and found a positive correlation: certain keywords had a stronger draw among the ready-to-buy, while others seemed to attract mostly the early-stage researchers.

The pair then tested specific landing pages that targeted the groups most likely to be captured by a given keyword. Research-only leads were delivered to a microsite that offered basic information about government contracting. Mid-stage leads got landing pages tailored to help them over whatever their remaining hurdles might be: online demos of the services, sample guides, live consultations, market assessments, and the like.

In addition, Onvia segmented its leads into 10 industry verticals, doing A/B tests of landing pages for each segment using generic pages versus pages that featured the name of the vertical in the headline and throughout the copy. The aim was to examine the effect of optimized landing pages on the response and conversion rates within those key verticals. Other elements were tested too, including different offer wordings and the inclusion of professional awards Onvia has won.

"Onvia uses a promo code to bucket the leads from those landing pages," Sanner said. "Then someone at Onvia works with the sales department to track actual conversions for each of those promo codes."

As those conversion results came in, Onvia started going back to see which campaigns were underperforming in producing the hottest leads and began cutting those from its search marketing budget.

The results so far have been a 50 percent decrease in monthly clicks from the level reached last January and a two-thirds reduction in the cost of acquiring leads, thanks to the elimination of those less-qualified clicks. Day said the company went from paying around $20 a lead at the beginning of the year to about $7 now.

"We're now refining the program even further," Day said. "We're still spending too much time talking with those people who are just looking into doing business with the government. Where before we thought we wanted to talk to them, now we're really interested in engaging with the audience who have already made the decision to do this kind of [contracting] work." Onvia has optimized its "Government 101" microsite for organic search, to keep its name in front of those early researchers. However, it is still trying to keep them out of the reach of its sales force until they are serious and ready to be contacted.

The verticals have also narrowed down to a key half-dozen industries, although several different landing pages may be deployed within those verticals depending on the ad keywords. For example, Sanner said the construction group can see as many as 15 uniquely optimized landing pages, particularly during the cold-weather months when most entrepreneurs are in their planning and bid submission mode.

In addition, Point It!'s management of Onvia's SEM is still aimed at helping the company's sales force make the most efficient use of its resources. "We periodically get 'pause' notices from Onvia to put a hold on their search marketing efforts for a week, to allow their sales force to catch up with the backlog of leads," Sanner said. "But that's a good problem to have."

Case Study: NetReflector

NetReflector provides full service online survey solutions for enterprise level organizations. Their value proposition includes superior customer service. The company had tried a variety of advertising methods, including e-mail, banners, trade shows, and cold calling.

Each had failed miserably and the sales team was suffering from poor morale. They needed to be in front of prospects when they had a survey project in mind.

Search Marketing Challenge

The goal of the campaign was to generate leads, which meant that people completed lead forms. The online survey field is very crowded and the keywords that convert tend to be generic; which were resulting in unqualified leads.

Solution

Point It! developed a multi faceted strategy of combining generic keywords with very qualified phrases. Ad copy was tweaked to "filter out" unqualified visitors. Point It! also worked with NetReflector to bucket visitors by service type and develop specialized landing pages. Finally, Point It! consulted on Web site design and conversion optimization to remove unnecessary barriers to conversion.

Results

Point It! PPC management boosted Web site activity immediately. The sales team received qualified prospects, boosting morale. An $82,000 investment in search-engine PPC advertising resulted in more than $250,000 in sales. This translated to an average ROI of over 300 percent. Also during this time, NetReflector was recognized as one of the fastest growing companies in Washington.

About Point It! (www.pointit.com)

Point It!, a Seattle-based search-engine marketing firm, has built a solid foundation of local and national clients over its four-year history. Launched in the middle of the dotcom implosion, it provides value by building and implementing targeted PPC lead generation campaigns with tools to track the ROI of the campaign components directly. The combination of market expertise, hard work, and dedicated client focus has led to significant corporate growth.

Case Study: NetReflector

Point It! specializes in managing PPC search-engine programs that generate interest from your target audience and deliver leads directly to your Web site. Focused on your goals and objectives, Point Its search experts offer programs with measurable ROI that integrate with your existing lead generation initiatives.

Case Study: REA Increased Qualified Traffic300 percent with Google™ AdWords

Launched in 1997, realestate.com.au (REA), is Australia's largest source of real estate listings and information. It is recognized locally and internationally as Australia's largest property Web site with more than 75 percent of all Australian real estate agents plus numerous developers.

Together they market more than 360,000 properties for sale or rent on the site every month.

Launched in 1997, **realestate.com.au** (REA), is Australia's largest source of real estate listings and information. It is recognized locally and internationally as Australia's largest property Web site with more than 75 percent of all Australian real estate agents plus numerous developers.

According to Nielsen//NetRatings, in August 2005 REA attracted more than 2.3 million unique visitors consisting of 2.1 million Australians and 250,000 others. Traffic to REA has doubled since July 2004, resulting in a lead of more than 75 percent over the nearest competitor.

Approach

To drive high volumes of quality traffic to realestate.com.au for the company's real estate agents, REA uses a broad marketing mix that includes print, television, outdoor, and radio ads. Online marketing vehicles e-mail, display ads, search-engine based PPC campaigns such as Google™ AdWords and content distribution are also pivotal to the company's sales efforts. In May 2004, REA conducted a test to evaluate the impact of PPC campaigns, putting all of its PPC advertising, including AdWords, on hold. "Surprisingly, net traffic from all search engines only fell marginally, so we initially concluded that PPC was not a very cost-effective way to generate traffic," explains Tania Taylor, Online Marketing Manager for REA.

Case Study: REA Increased Qualified Traffic300 percent with Google™ AdWords

Results

This initial assumption proved to be wrong. REA began to experiment with AdWords by investing in more keywords. While some keywords were more expensive, the increase in traffic volume reduced cost-per-click by 25 percent, making AdWords a more attractive option. "One of the most valuable attributes of AdWords is the ability to measure results quickly and make adjustments to achieve higher return on investment," said Taylor. Then online marketing firm Found Agency was contracted in October 2004 to assist in REA's online media efforts and help fine-tune the company's AdWords campaigns further by carefully researching and expanding the keyword list considerably and providing a more proactive and strategic approach to bid management.

"With further enhancements to our AdWords campaigns, results skyrocketed," said Taylor. "We gained a 300 percent increase in PPC traffic for no additional expense. The key measure for our business is unique browsers, not clicks, so these results are even more impressive. Achieving results like this with the same budget firmly entrenched AdWords into our marketing budget as a cornerstone of cost effective, high quality traffic generation." In addition to driving qualified traffic for its real estate agents, AdWords has also become a valuable tool in driving brand awareness. Taylor notes that click-through rates (CTRs) are typically significantly higher for search-based advertising campaigns such as AdWords when compared with display advertising campaigns, commonly charged on a cost-per-impressions (CPM) basis. "Even if an AdWords campaign had a 0 percent CTR, it may still be more cost-effective in driving brand awareness than an average performing display ad, given the high CPM of display ads relative to the PPC model that only charges per click," Taylor explains. REA continues to invest in a mix of offline and online media, including search based advertising especially AdWords because of its excellent accountability and results.

"Even if an AdWords campaign had a 0 percent CTR, it may still be more cost-effective in driving brand awareness than an average performing display ad, given the high CPM of display ads relative to the PPC model that only charges per click,"

Tania Taylor, Online Marketing Manager

Case Study: Wotif Shares Success

Matthew Varley said search marketing has been an essential element in Wotif.com's growth.

"From the very beginning, Wotif.com's board and management recognized that search marketing was an essential cost for our business. It has been the major consistent marketing cost for which Wotif.com has budgeted," Varley said, adding that "a large portion" of marketing expense is concentrated on search alone.

Varley values search's ability to acquire new customers and its ability to track the return on investment directly for each dollar spent.

"It allows us to acquire customers at a lower cost than most of the traditional marketing mediums and, importantly for Wotif.com, it operates in the same medium as our business, i.e., potential customers are already online, actively searching for our product, and search marketing ensures that they find it with us instead of our competitors," Varley said.

Wotif.com worked with The Found Agency to review its natural SEO strategy as well as providing input on maximizing its rankings within the search engines.

"Natural SEO is a major part of the business going forward, and in the short time since the changes earlier this year, we've seen a large and rapid increase in growth in natural SEO traffic," Varley said.

It has also been running PPC campaigns since 2001 and is constantly looking at new ways to improve the effectiveness of this medium, he said.

It seems to be working. According to Hitwise's weekly rankings for the week ending May 13, Wotif.com was the number one ranked site by visits in the "travel destinations and accommodation" category with 5.4 percent of market share. And four of the top 10 search terms driving traffic to travel destinations and accommodation Web sites contained the search 'wotif.'

An in-house team runs Wotif.com's entire search marketing activity, as the Brisbane-based business believes keeping this knowledge within the company is "extremely important. Our search team is intimately aware of the business objectives and is therefore able to use this knowledge to create search campaigns that are aligned with these goals.

"However, in extreme cases such as the revamping of the natural SEO strategy, we are not averse to requesting specialist external advice,"

Case Study: Wotif Shares Success

Varley adds. With competition in the travel category intense, the team has to stay vigilant.

"There are more than 150 sponsored advertisers bidding on Google™ just for the term 'Sydney hotels.' This compares to other industries such as real estate, which I have worked in previously, where there are as few as 35 companies in the running for the most vital of terms to that industry," Varley said.

"Every week there seems to be a new travel competitor bidding on keywords within the search engines, so I do anticipate the competition to increase. However, people are falling out of the race at the same time. Many people seem to enter into the online travel industry but not all of them will survive on search marketing alone," he said.

While search marketing is the main focus of the business' online marketing activity, Varley said it has a team that is dedicated to setting up "affiliate and strategic relationships both on and off line" to ensure its success continues.

With the company soon to float, its visibility both online and off looks set only to accelerate.

About The Found Agency (www.foundagency.com.au)

The Found Agency is an Australian interactive firm specializing solely in search-engine marketing. Although our background includes traditional marketing, advertising, and Web design, we are now 100 percent focused on performance-based Paid Search and Web optimization aimed at high visibility in search engines.

We are young, energetic, and pride ourselves on results. We already have experience advising and implementing our unique SEM strategies for several of Australia's top 100 Web sites. We have a proven record of accomplishment as a market leader in results-based search advertising and optimization, and we are keen to add your business to our list of successes in online promotion.

Fundamentally, we live for this stuff. We are driven by a passion to help our clients maximize their SEM returns, and we have the skills and expertise in Internet marketing to get the best results. If your business follows our recommendations and you do not gain a healthy return on our SEM initiatives, we would rather break our relationship with you than your trust in us.

www.bandt.com • www.foundagency.com

Case Study: Advanced Micro Controls Inc. (AMCI)

Advanced Micro Controls Inc. (AMCI) has been a leader in the design, manufacturing, and sales of Industrial Control Solutions for 20 years. Offering a wide selection of products, ranging from rotary sensors to automation controllers, they serve the packaging, METAI stamping, and factory automation industries.

With eight different product families being marketed to multiple industries, it was difficult for AMCI to know if their advertising dollars were properly distributed for the best results. Tradeshows and trade journals were becoming increasingly specialized, increasingly expensive, and measuring ROI through these channels was very difficult. AMCI's sales team was eager to find more effective methods of promoting their industrial automation controls.

In pursuit of measurable marketing, AMCI recognized the Internet's capacity as sales tool and launched their first Web site in 1999. In the years following, (www.amci.com) produced increased sales on existing product lines and reduced tech support phone calls. At the same time, a trend analysis of AMCI's Web site results revealed that newer product lines were not enjoying the same volume of visitor traffic as their seasoned counterparts.

> *"Today's buyers are an impatient bunch. They want to get product information as quickly and conveniently as possible, and their tool of choice is the Internet. In fact, 91 percent of buyers go to a supplier's Web site before picking up the phone. And if they do not find the information they need, 80 percent choose another supplier, according to a recent B to B Magazine article."*
>
> ### Katrina C. Arabe, ThomasNet News

AMCI needed to boost their Web site's exposure on major search engines, penetrate aggressive markets, and synchronize their advertising spend with real-time marketing reports.

They explored their goals and needs with IndustrialClicks.com who helped them develop a new marketing strategy that included PPC advertising. The company's sales team explained that **www.amci.com** ranked well on the major search engines for various keywords/keyword phrases. However, in the more competitive markets, their online visibility was low.

Case Study: Advanced Micro Controls Inc. (AMCI)

"A strategic PPC campaign, featuring paid placement on a search engine's results page, can drive leads and sales while generating brand and product awareness."

Jim Grinney, BtoBonline.com

IndustrialClicks.com reviewed AMCI's Web site, becoming familiar with their products, the industries they serviced and identified their customer base. (Who buys their industrial controls and how do they define value?) Once this preliminary research was done, IndustrialClicks.com began compiling keywords/keyword phrases that were associated with company's competitive product lines. Using a search term valuator, IndustrialClicks.com identified which keywords would ultimately serve as "triggers" for the delivery of AMCI's PPC ads.

With this collection of viable keywords in hand, IndustrialClicks.com began designing advertising copy that was compelling and "click-friendly." Additionally, it was important that all ad copy demonstrate high degrees of relevancy, focusing closely on the target product. Generic ad copy runs the risk of driving poorly qualified prospects to the AMCI Web site, reducing the likelihood of a conversion (sales contact, request for quote, or order), increasing marketing cost, and lowering the company's return on investment.

In summary, by leveraging their years of industrial Internet marketing experience, IndustrialClicks.com developed PPC ad copy that spoke to AMCI's industrial audience, marketing the features, benefits, and value of their products. Using proprietary formatting strategies, IndustricalClicks.com enhanced AMCI's advertising click-thru-rates, while keeping their bid-costs low.

Within the first three months of 2005, IndustrialClicks.com drove more than 16,000 qualified prospects to various landing pages on AMCI's Web site, at an average cost of $.10 per visitor. Calculating the quick math, AMCI spent $1,660.81 to promote their products to an audience of 16,176 engineers, technicians, and purchasing agents who had searched on keywords/ keyword phrases closely tied to their industrial controls.

Case Study: Advanced Micro Controls Inc. (AMCI)

"Search-engine traffic is highly targeted. That is because potential buyers who find your B 2 B offerings through search engines are looking for your products and services on their own; as a result, they are predisposed to hear your marketing message. You cannot find a more qualified prospect than that."

Paul J. Bruemmer, Marketingprofs.com

Since IndustrialClicks.com provides in-depth reporting on all of their PPC advertising, it was easy for AMCI to zero in on key metrics. Data, such as their average actual cost-per-click, the number of times their ads were shown, and how many times users clicked on their ads, were accessed through user-friendly spreadsheets and e-mailed, weekly, to the Sales team. This quantifiable information made it very easy to for AMCI to compare PPC advertising to their other marketing programs.

In review, AMCI leverages several different marketing channels: tradeshows, trade journal ads, and direct mailings.

AMCI was leveraging multiple marketing channels, tradeshows, trade journal ads, and direct mailings, in support of their goals. During the 1980s and 1990s tradeshows were effective for AMCI, but dwindling attendance, escalating costs, and fewer definitive leads forced them to re-evaluate their marketing strategy. The company's tradeshow attendance was approaching an average cost of $4,000 to $6,000, and Sales was finding it increasingly difficult to justify their return on investment. While AMCI continued to participate in tradeshows nationally, they began scaling back their presence in this arena, dedicating more resources to their PPC-Advertising online marketing efforts.

Trade journal advertising has driven industrial marketing for many years. AMCI regularly advertised in several trade publications and focused on industries such as packaging controls, electric motors, and sensors. Sales could never adequately gauge their marketing exposure, and measuring performance was very difficult. Split-testing (A versus B testing) print ads was a slow and laborious process, requiring several months and producing questionable results at best. Additionally, promoting various products to different industries required advertising space in multiple trade publications, raising marketing costs and creating more work for AMCI.

In contrast, IndustrialClicks.com used PPC marketing to promote each of AMCI's eight different product lines simultaneously with pinpoint accuracy. The team developed more than 200 segmented PPC ads, each selling a

Case Study: Advanced Micro Controls Inc. (AMCI)

different product with unique applications, at no additional cost to AMCI. Further, all of AMCI's PPC ads are actively split tested (A versus B testing) and analyzed. Data such as click-through-rate performance, ad position, and average cost-per-click drove ongoing revisions and helped deliver a robust ROI. This type of aggressive marketing was simply not possible with printed trade journal advertising.

> *"Not only did Internet advertising grow faster than B-to-B magazine advertising in 2004, Internet ad revenue was bigger than B-to-B magazine ad revenue last year, $7.4 billion versus $5.2 billion, according to TNS."*
>
> **Sean Callahan, BtoBOnline.com**

AMCI enjoyed reasonable success with direct mail, realizing a moderate return on investment. Unlike other forms of marketing communications, such as print ads, direct mail delivered their message straight to the buyer. At the same time, direct mail suffered the same shortcomings as trade journal ads inflexibility, no performance reporting, and higher flat costs.

Promoting several different products simultaneously required AMCI to either sacrifice marketing focus by placing multiple products on a single ad, or design and pay for several unique direct mail pieces a costly and time consuming plan. From a return on investment standpoint, PPC marketing is not the "all or nothing" proposition that defines direct mail. Instead, AMCI can distribute their advertising dollars across all product lines, regulating ad exposure and marketing expenses on a real-time basis.

Today, IndustrialClicks.com continues development on AMCI's PPC advertising, empowering their Sales team with expanded market reach and real-time campaign performance reporting. Moreover, IndustrialClicks.com has recently synchronized PPC campaign development with AMCI's new product releases, creating instant market awareness of the company's newest automation controllers and sensors on the Internet.

About IndustrialClicks.com • www.industrialclicks.com

IndustrialClicks.com combines PPC expertise with a strong knowledge of the industrial marketplace; positioning AMCI's product marketing where today's business to business buyers shop – the Internet. Now, AMCI is reaping the benefits of Internet technology, enabling them to focus on their core strengths engineering industrial innovations.

Case Study: Advanced Micro Controls Inc. (AMCI)

IndustrialClicks.com is a specialty industrial marketing company that works exclusively in the Industrial/Business-to-Business/Manufacturing sector. We develop PPC Internet advertising services that bring immediate, quantifiable results for our clients. Our expertise, in combination with this powerful sales tool, helps deliver your marketing message with pinpoint accuracy to targeted individuals. Your success will be measured by the collective number of "clicks" your campaigns receive and, more importantly, the increase in your B 2 B sales orders and inquiries.

IndustrialClicks.com specializes in PPC advertising. Our goal is to deliver exceptional return on investment to industrial clients by increasing their requests for quotes and product sales. By specializing in PPC advertising, we are able to apply our in-depth knowledge of the industry and optimize use of this dynamic marketing channel with every client.

Basic marketing principles are the foundation of IndustricalClicks.com's advertising services. Our marketing strategy is driven by research and knowledge of the target audience. We bring more than five years of Industrial marketing experience to our clients; promoting products and services to a variety of industries including Packaging, Press, and Factory Automation.

IndustrialClicks.com will work with you and your technical development group to determine the most effective keywords for your product line(s). We then handle the bidding process, continually manage your keyword(s) for effectiveness, identify and re-bid new keywords/changes, monitor your competition, and run and distribute reports. Following development and implementation, the growth and quality of your PPC traffic is our highest priority.

Case Study: Expert Building Maintenance

You do not think about the carpets at work. They are just something you walk on to get to your cubicle or head for the restroom. Nevertheless, carpets, restrooms, and windows do not stay clean forever, and that is where Expert Building Maintenance comes in. This Simi Valley firm cleans and maintains those places you never consider.

Robert Pedder and Alberto Duarte were maintaining buildings for another company when they decided to start their own janitorial cleaning firm. Expert Building Maintenance began as a home-based business with two clients.

Today, Pedder and Duarte have more than 300. They include car dealers, churches, and building managers with several business tenants. Most came to them through word-of-mouth referrals from other satisfied clients.

But they wanted Web site management services focusing on PPC campaign management to find clients who were actively searching for services like theirs. Expert Building Maintenance's Marketing Manager Carolyn Moreno went looking for some outside help to find them.

"I called a business acquaintance at yellowpages.com, somebody I knew here who had moved to Los Vegas. But I felt like it was too broad — we wanted to focus on Ventura County and Los Angeles County. We did not want to go nationwide."

After a bad experience with another Web marketing company that took her money and did not deliver anything, Moreno got a professional-looking brochure in the mail from SOHO Prospecting.

"We contacted them, and they came the next day. They sat down with me and covered everything." Expert Building Maintenance chose PPC marketing, since it allowed a tight geographic focus.

With PPC bid management and Web site traffic promotion, you pick keywords that trigger your ad on a PPC service. Some PPC campaign management services target regional traffic, and others target nationally, so you can choose your reach. When a visitor searches for those keywords or similar ones, your ad appears at the right of the search listings. Moreno filled out a form to help discover the right keywords. SOHO tested for the ones that pulled best. Then they recommended PPC services for the local markets Moreno wanted.

When Expert Building Maintenance started getting PPC inquiries from prospects in San Diego, SOHO revised the campaign to draw only the local clients Moreno wanted.

Twice a month, Moreno gets reports showing how many visitors clicked her ads from the PPC campaign management efforts, how many saw them without clicking, or impressions, and the total cost. The reports are easy to figure out. But they are also easy for her boss. "College taught me about

Case Study: Expert Building Maintenance

computers and marketing, but the way SOHO laid it out was helpful for me to explain to my boss — impressions, click-throughs were really easy to follow. The reports were very detailed. It helped to have actual charts showing growth and how many people were hitting the site."

SOHO went beyond reports and location tracking. "When they saw someone clicking who might be a great client, they would always be sure I was notified."

Moreno has been very pleased with the PPC bid management results and the Web site management services campaign, many of them in Los Angeles County, outside their usual business area. "We have gotten good clients from it — record companies in Santa Monica, a car dealer in Glendale, and many more. It was definitely worthwhile."

Carolyn Moreno
info@thebuildingexperts.com • www.thebuildingexperts.com

Case Study: Solar Electrical Systems

In 1978, when Solar Electrical Systems began designing and installing photovoltaic panels for homeowners and businesses who wanted to get off the grid, the Web did not exist. So president and founder Greg Johansen attracted customers with direct mail. Customers were picky – they wanted solar power providers with a good reputation for finishing the installation, and systems that kept working. SES gained recognition for its accurate solar performance figures before the sale, and reliable systems that have been working for over 20 years. The company won the "2001 Best Photovoltaic Installer" rating from the California Energy Commission. SES is the longest-running success story in the solar power industry.

But there was one catch—each new customer was costing Johansen about $70 with direct mail. Even with high energy costs, rebates, and tax incentives driving heavy interest in solar power, Johansen wanted better sales numbers. Direct mail was not reaching enough customers.

Case Study: Solar Electrical Systems

So Johansen went to the World Wide Web. "Web intricacies need an expert, almost on a daily basis, and we did not have that kind of support for maintenance and vigilance. We went to three or four different people first. None of them put all the pieces together."

A contact in one of his business networks referred Johansen to SOHO Prospecting. "Web design and enhancement – it is how that page interacts with the whole Web – it is much more dynamic than most people think. Most other Web designers do not offer SOHO's expertise and diversity – they guaranteed performance and they delivered."

The SES Web site did not develop overnight. " SOHO evolved with the Web site. They changed keywords and METAfiles, to attract Google™ crawlers – that is stuff you typically do not find on the street. To most people it is a foreign language."

Johansen's cost per sales lead dropped to $7 with SOHO's search-engine optimization. Solar Electrical Systems won a $40,000 order in their first month as a SOHO client. And Johansen's Web site results? "They're excellent. We went from 400 to 1,400 unique hits in a month." Five weeks after the latest round of SEO improvements from SOHO, Solar Electrical Systems' Web site traffic had increased 200 percent.

SOHO President Dale DeHart directed business growth at several high tech companies before he founded SOHO Prospecting. His goal is providing marketing that works at a cost smaller and medium-sized companies like Solar Electrical Systems can afford. "Our greatest gratification comes from helping our clients build their businesses."

Greg Johansen
sales@solarelectricalsystems.com
www.solarelectricalsystems.com

Case Study: J.C. Palomar

Environmental remediation is front-page news around the world. After toxic spills threatened drinking water in the Songhua and Bei Rivers, China's environmental protection agency ordered cleanups at 11 heavily polluting factories.

Closer to home, remediation experts J.C. Palomar recently finished a system to remove arsenic and rust from groundwater before it entered the water supply. The Orange County, California, environmental construction firm has worked for Edwards Air Force Base, General Electric, Federal Express, and Exxon/Mobil. Along the way, they have tackled everything from heavy METAl extraction from a former factory site to removing and replacing underground storage tanks for diesel fuel.

Most of J.C. Palomar's clients came through word of mouth and cold-calling. Engineer Chris Bason needed a Web site with affordable SEO Web site promotion to pull more of them and give them information about his company. And he needed a professional image for a brochure with corporate Internet branding on it. "When I was looking for Web developers, everybody's design work was lacking. I wanted a technical look, but professional more impressive, a clean look." His online search led him to SOHO Prospecting for his SEO Web site needs.

SOHO gave him personal attention and professional results. The first challenge was J.C. Palomar's logo and corporate Internet branding. "SOHO's account manager called regularly to get my ideas, and I'd fill in what I wanted when they came back with a suggestion. We'd bounce ideas back and forth. I talked to three or four people there, but mainly her."

SOHO had three different ideas for the J.C. Palomar logo. "About halfway through one idea, I found another company's logo and said, 'This is cool. Can you do something like that?' And they did."

Bason got the professional logo he wanted. His brand-new Web site was next.

In the Web's early days, putting up a site and waiting for visitors was enough – the few sites out there got traffic from sheer novelty. In addition to compelling content and simple navigation, today's sites need to be optimized for the keywords visitors use to search for them. SOHO Prospecting builds Web sites with easy-to-find content to satisfy visitors. Then SOHO's search-engine optimization specialist uses the best legitimate techniques to help search engines – and visitors find clients' sites.

Case Study: J.C. Palomar

Bason knew he needed SOHO's affordable SEO Web site promotion help. "I had no clue about the Web. They optimized for the search engines, how to get it higher on the rankings list. After the site was up, they got the words that worked best."

Bason was pleasantly surprised by the results from the search-engine optimization specialist. "There was actually more traffic than I expected. They sent me a little program where I can see breakdown per hour. I was surprised how many people were looking. There were 95 visits this week, five today, a lot in our business."

SOHO designed Bason's brochure to follow the Web site's theme for a unified look. SOHO handled the whole job here, too. "It was a couple proof checks, then off to the printers, then the business cards. They did everything fast – logo two weeks, SEO Web site four weeks. It was a total of two months for all of it. They arranged printers for me and did everything. It has been really smooth – no problems."

J.C. Palomar's best result from their new Web site? "I got a call from MCI. We're working on a master service agreement with them." Chris Bason was very pleased.

SOHO's traffic software lets Bason check his site's performance whenever he wants. SOHO also takes an active role. "My account manager comes in with leads once in awhile. If she comes across something that looks like what we do, she throws it my way. I talk to her once a month."

About SOHO Prospecting • www.sohoprospecting.com

SOHO Prospecting was founded by Dale DeHart after over 25 years in industry, having served at the Vice Presidential level of several private and publicly traded companies, and seven years as a management consultant.

His experience with the difficulty of working fast and furious for his current clients and trying to focus simultaneously on marketing his services to his next clients convinced him of the need for the types of services that SOHO provides. In fact, nearly all the small businesses with whom he associated agreed that they needed a part-time marketing effort at a part-time cost. At the same time, the growth of the Internet as a marketing media was apparent and search engines were the best means of gaining visibility, hence the name SOHO (Search-Optimized, High Output) to designate that all SOHO products and services are aimed at Internet compatibility.

Case Study: J.C. Palomar

Since then SOHO has provided just that for its clients, assuring them that their services were being promoted to their target markets. We started in 2001 as a home-based business and in 2002 moved to our offices on Mobil Avenue. We are soon to move again to accommodate our dramatic growth and acceptance by our clients. We expand our facilities and services when necessary and currently have eight staff members and several subcontractors to serve the needs of our clients.

Our clients do not need to hire and train staff. SOHO 's people are professionally trained in marketing and sales by industry professionals such as Customer Centric Systems. Our clients do not need to provide space and capital equipment. SOHO's offices in Camarillo, CA, have all the resources required to conduct an effective marketing campaign. Our clients do not need to commit to long-term investments in infrastructure. With SOHO's marketing services you pay for what you use.

SOHO Prospecting provides marketing services to primarily B 2 B businesses. We are dedicated to enabling your success by helping buyers recognize your capabilities and visualize how those capabilities can solve their problems.

Chris Bason
info@jcpalomar.com • www.jcpalomar.com

Case Study: Sony Style

Wpromote Solution: Leverage the powerful brand name of Sony and official nature of the Sony online store through optimized ad creatives.

Wpromote created a search-engine campaign encompassing the entire Sony online catalog.

The goal was to match search-engine users seeking specific Sony products with ads tailored to those products and deliver the user to individual product pages on the online store. Additionally, we wanted the search-engine campaign to leverage the Sony brand effectively, creating a coherent link from offline advertising to online sales. The combination of these tactics resulted in vastly improved conversion ratios, lowering cost per click by 60 percent, doubling the click-through ratio, and increasing average revenue per click by 200 percent.

Case Study: Sony Style

"As an established e-commerce player, we looked to Wpromote to expand the online reach of the Sony Style store and actively drive customers to the site. They launched a comprehensive campaign producing immediate results, and through constant tracking and analysis, have optimized and expanded the campaign. The results have exceeded our expectations, and the campaign built by Wpromote has averaged month-over-month sales growth of over 30 percent. Wpromote's support and accessibility is second-to-none. They have grown to be one of our top partners and we look forward to a long and rewarding relationship."

**Danielle Hayman, Associate Manager, Direct Marketing
Sony Electronics Inc. e-Solutions Company LLC**

About Wpromote • www.wpromote.com

Wpromote has been a leader in the field of search-engine marketing since its inception in 1999, working with thousands of clients from more than 60 countries. One of the original firms specializing in search-engine submission, Wpromote established its place online based on its superior, proprietary software, unmatched customer support and honest approach. We have helped our clients gain visibility, gather leads and ultimately build successful businesses with more powerful online presences. From the beginning, our goal has been to seek out creative, efficient, and effective strategies to help our clients achieve their objectives online.

To help our current and future clients realize greater success through online marketing and to reflect the changing landscape of search-engine marketing Wpromote provides a full-service PPC advertising management service.

Through PPC advertising, our clients develop a more comprehensive online presence and are able to reach highly targeted clients more effectively than ever. Using our proprietary bid management and keyword analysis software and team of seasoned marketing and advertising specialists, Wpromote provides measurable results and helps our clients maximize their advertising return on investment.

Wpromote is a privately held firm that is able to adapt quickly to a rapidly changing marketplace and effectively employ strategies and technological solutions for clients who were previously available only to the largest online advertisers; this is the Wpromote Advantage.

Case Study: Sony Style

Founded in 1999, Wpromote is one of the world's leading search-engine marketing firms. Wpromote has helped more than 10,000 clients in over 50 countries achieve their online marketing goals using proprietary, cutting edge technology and superior personalized service. Wpromote provides expert PPC management, search-engine submission and pay-for-performance marketing services.

Michael Mothner, CEO, Wpromote, Inc.
Toll-Free 1-866-WPROMOTE • Direct: 1-310-421-4844
www.wpromote.com • sales@wpromote.com
1650 Pacific Coast Highway, Suite 310
Redondo Beach, CA 90277

Case Study: The Hitchin Post

The Hitchin Post **www.thehitchinpost.com** makes deerskin products, including moccasins, handbags, and wallets. In November 2004, we incorporated a Yahoo!® Marketing PPC campaign into their marketing plan.

Below is a chart showing what The Hitchin' Post spent on Yahoo for click-through charges (the number of people that visited their site) compared to the amount of sales that month. You will see that their spending went up, but their sales went up as well, at a higher rate.

Month	Spent on Overture	Amount of Sales
September	$0	$128.40
October	$0	$610.70
November	$550	$2,375.55
December	$885	$4,131.59

We used very specific terms with the campaign such as deerskin moccasins, deerskin wallets, and deerskin handbags. We wanted to make sure the people going to the site were looking for deerskin items and were more likely to buy. The PPC campaign was the only change we made to their marketing and definitely made a difference.

Case Study: The Hitchin Post

Bio for Tammy Schultz

Tammy Schultz is president of Virtualtech Web Site Design and Promotion, Inc. She started Virtualtech in January of 1997 when she saw that small to medium size companies did not know how to market their products and services on the Web.

Tammy has been instrumental in establishing Virtualtech as a rising star because she looks at her clients' Web sites from the visitor's point of view. Her ability to explain all that is involved in creating and marketing a Web site in terms that people understand has been another driving force to Virtualtech's success.

Tammy is a professional speaker and author who has hosted a number of cable television and radio shows. Her four-step program, Elements of an Effective Website, explains the steps in creating and marketing a Web site, has been featured on the SCORE and Business Professional Women's Web sites, and for several seminars for Chambers of Commerce, SCORE, Wisconsin Women's Business Initiative Corporation (WWBIC), Concordia University, and others.

Tammy currently serves on the local boards for Women Entrepreneurs of Wisconsin and Executive Women's Golf Association, is a member of the Fox Cities and Heart of the Valley Chambers, is a counselor with SCORE, and supports numerous non-profit organizations through Web site development services.

You can learn more about Virtualtech Web Site Design and Promotion at <http://www.virtualtech.com> or contact Tammy directly at 920-954-1923 or tammy@virtualtech.com.

Case Study: CorpRat

CorpRat Pty Ltd is a fast growing business publishing and training organization. The company publishes products, programs, and training courses targeted to business and coaching/consultancy sectors. The main areas of specialization include business development, lead generation, marketing, performance coaching, balanced scorecard, and profit improvement tools.

Case Study: CorpRat

Search-Engine Optimization increases the Web site traffic by 2000 percent

After three months implementing CorpRat's search-engine optimization campaign, Apex Pacific has achieved several top ten positions for the site across the world's most important search engines and directories.

CorpRat's Web site now attracts 200 quality visitors per day, an increase of 2000 percent, and they have reduced their PPC spending to $500 per month.

"With the continuing search-engine optimization support from Apex, we will achieve more top rankings for our targeted keywords. We will stop our PPC campaign within three months when more visitors are coming to our Web site from the free search ranking results," Peter said.

Can Apex Pacific's offer support and expertise on running a Successful SEO Campaign?

Of course! Our experienced consulting team will be happy to develop an effective strategy, to help give your business a competitive advantage over your competition. Please contact us now.

About Apex Pacific Pty Ltd • www.apexpacific.com

Apex Pacific Pty Ltd has been in the Internet marketing industry for over eight years and have developed world renowned software to support search-engine marketing strategies. Our SEOSuite encapsulates the essential steps to optimizing your Web site and getting it higher-ranking positions. Our PPC Bid Maximizer software is a bid management tool to monitor and manage a PPC campaign with less time and cost. Finally, we also provide an excellent e-mail marketing tool to help any business run e-mail campaigns efficiently and track the results. For more information regarding the software tools available, refer to **www.apexpacific.com/ products.html**.

Apex is also an Internet marketing service provider. We offer both SEO and PPC Management service to a variety of companies who desire result driven performance. Using our industry knowledge and experience, we have step-up service procedures that will get the desired results. Below is a case study by one of our SEO service clients who has succeeded in the business through the use of online marketing. For more information about the services offered by our company, refer to **www.apexreach.com/ search-engine-marketing-services.html**.

Case Study: CorpRat

Finally, Apex also offers business the opportunity to enter into the booming Internet marketplace. We provide a variety of Internet marketing courses tailored so that each business can establish a successful Internet marketing strategy or profit from adding value to their existing business through this industry. For more information, please refer to **www.apexreach.com/ Internet-marketing-college.html.**

Case Study: 800florals.com

The Flowers, Greetings, and Specialty gifts category was ranked among the top 15 online retail categories based on an average order size of $51.61. Two out of the top ten online retailers, based on high sales conversion rates, were FTD.com and proflowers.com1.

What do these numbers mean to those in the floral industry? For one, statistics like these mean that more advertisers in the floral industry, like Phillip's 1-800-Florals, are turning to PPC to keep an edge on the competition.

Methods of Advertising

"Our other advertising methods have included print, outdoor, radio, direct mail, e-mail, and affiliate program, but PPC advertising gives us greater control over driving qualified search traffic to our site based on highly targeted keywords. We control the search terms, listings, and cost in real time, adjusting for performance, seasonality, and budgeting needs," said Baxter W. Phillip of Phillip's 1-800-Florals.

Starting a Campaign

Searchfeed.com allows for simple campaign setup. Phillip was able to set up a campaign for the 1-800-Florals Web site by filling out a three-step online form and then submitting keywords and listings related to his business.

"We've worked with many PPC sites and think Searchfeed.com is among the most user-friendly. Setting up an account, entering keywords, and launching a campaign are a snap," Phillip said.

Case Study: 800florals.com

Online Tools and Reports

"We use Searchfeed's reporting tools religiously, to monitor results, improve bid management, and drive more sales. We also like Searchfeed's Keyword File Uploader, but the most important thing is that all the advertiser tools are easy to use and easy to understand," said Phillip.

Sales Conversions

PPC advertising allows florists to change their advertising campaign based on the season or holiday, making a difference for online sales conversions.

"The cost per conversion with Searchfeed.com is as good as or better than any other PPC search engine out there today," said Phillip.

Cost of Running a Campaign

With a minimum deposit of $25 and minimum bid of $.01, it is no surprise that advertisers find that running a campaign with Searchfeed.com is very cost-effective.

"Searchfeed.com seems to have done a better job than others in maintaining qualified traffic over the years, and it also remains one of the more economical online advertising opportunities today," said Phillip.

Overall Results

By advertising with Searchfeed.com Phillip's 1-800-Florals was able to have their ads on sites related to their industry, resulting in targeted sales leads. For example, ads for the floral business are displayed on wedding-centric Web sites, such as AllAboutWeddings.com, because this is good place for consumers to type in a search related products like wedding flowers or wedding bouquet, resulting in high sales conversions for a minimum campaign cost.

Case Study: UnitedDiamonds.com

United Diamonds distributes bridal and custom jewelry over the Internet. To attract targeted sales leads they have used many forms of advertising, and turned to PPC, specifically Searchfeed.com, to boost their advertising efforts.

Case Study: UnitedDiamonds.com

Methods of Advertising

"In the past, we have advertised on some comparison shopping networks and have done some minimal banner advertising that ended with poor results. In the end, PPC has been the best for us," Bruce Larsen of UnitedDiamonds.com comments on why he turned to PPC advertising.

Business Solutions

Two of the main business solutions that many advertisers have derived from their online advertising efforts are an increase in targeted traffic to their site, and, as a result high conversion rates. United Diamonds.com comments below on their campaign results.

Traffic Quality

"We have highly sophisticated Web analytics software tied into our Web server that analyzes traffic from various advertising sources. The numbers speak for themselves. Searchfeed.com has delivered phenomenally high quality traffic compared to some of the alleged big PPC advertising companies," said Larsen.

"Searchfeed.com's Keyword File Uploader has been the most useful tool for us. It allows us to create thousands of targeted keyword ads with ease. The reporting tools provided by Searchfeed.com show us, at a glance, which keywords are receiving the most clicks, and how much this is costing us," he said.

Sales Conversions

Searchfeed.com works with many niche sites to provide advertisers with quality traffic that converts into targeted sales leads for their specific industry. For example, UnitedDiamonds.com receives traffic from sites related to the bridal jewelry industry.

"Searchfeed.com traffic can be broken down into three categories: Conversions, Conversions, and Conversions. In our experience, we have some of the best conversions from Searchfeed.com visitors," he said.

Overall Results

Larsen sums up the results of his campaign simply, "50 percent of our advertising budget is committed to PPC for one simple reason-it works!"

Case Study: TargetedVisitors.info

CLASSIFIED CASE STUDIES ™ *directly from the experts*

Approach

Methods of Advertising: TargetedVisitors.info is an Internet advertising service. The company's marketing professional, Daniel Grossman, discusses past advertising techniques in comparison with his current search-engine marketing strategies and his PPC campaign with Searchfeed.com.

"I used to spend a lot of time on traditional Internet marketing. Most of my advertising budget went to banner ads, forum sponsorships, contest sponsorships, and newsletter ads. They still play an important part in my month-to-month advertising, but PPC advertising has become the dominant method, and for good reason," he said.

"Many advertisers find that search-engine marketing, using PCC technology is a cost-effective way to generate targeted sales leads. By providing a unique form of online advertising, Searchfeed.com offers any size business a way to reach their target audience via the Web.

"Search advertising is incredibly effective. Because the Web surfer is actively seeking out my type of service, I can target these people specifically and show them that what I am offering is what they are looking for. PPC advertising has benefits other mediums cannot provide. It enables me to control my message, my reach, and my cost on a day-to-day basis," he said.

Online Tools and Reports—Searchfeed.com offers advertisers a wide variety of self-management tools and real-time reports that help to monitor the success of each campaign from every angle. Many advertisers find Searchfeed.com's suite of online tools helpful, especially the Campaign Cost Estimate tool, which helps advertisers assess campaign costs based on up to 5,000 campaign keywords.

"I can fine-tune campaigns or test new copy without an expensive commitment, and readily measure and compare the ROI from each campaign. If an ad is not drawing clicks or isn't converting, I can stop and figure out why," stated Grossman.

An important feature that keeps advertisers informed is the use of Searchfeed.com's real-time reports that enable advertisers to check immediately how their account is performing and offers virtually instantaneous feedback about account information.

Case Study: TargetedVisitors.info

"Overall, the reports are quickly generated, comprehensive and quickly show me where I'm spending my money and what searches are sending me the most visitors. Detailed payment history reports make recording expenses easy," he said.

Advertisers have access to many useful campaign tools through their advertiser interface login screen. Through Searchfeed.com's auto bid management tool multiple keyword bids can be changed simultaneously to help ensure the best ranking. Searchfeed.com's position maintenance tool ensures top position for campaign listings and helps to eliminate bid gaps.

"Searchfeed.com's advertiser interface is very straightforward and easy to use. Editing listings, changing bids, and generating reports are all a single click from sign-in, and the individual pages are intuitively easy to understand and use. Searchfeed.com's mass "change bids" tool has been very useful and is a great time-saver, allowing me to raise listings to number one, two, or three in search results without spending more per click than I am ready to. This makes my Searchfeed.com results very easy to maintain."

Solutions

Searchfeed.com provided TargetedVisitors.info with an additional form of advertising that works with their current campaign by presenting an affordable way to advertise online.

"The great thing about PPC advertising compared to banner, e-mail and other advertising methods is that you pay for performance. With other forms of advertising, I have to commit to long campaigns that may not bring a good return. Searchfeed.com allows me to control my day-to-day spending, and since conversion rates can be accurately predicted after some time on a Searchfeed.com campaign, I know how many sales to expect for each dollar I spend. Compared to banner ad campaigns, the cost to acquire new customers through Searchfeed.com is lower and more predictable. Compared to other PPC search engines, Searchfeed.com has a lower average cost per click while still having enough reach to deliver lots of high-quality traffic to my site," states Grossman.

Solutions   To start a PPC campaign with Searchfeed.com, advertisers simply fill out an online form with one listing, including a title, description and keywords. Advertisers can bid on search terms that are relevant to their site content. An account can be up and running in no time, as most search terms are reviewed within 24 to 48 hours and a confirmation regarding submitted search terms is provided.

Case Study: TargetedVisitors.info

In January of 2004, TargetedVisitors.info started an advertiser account with Searchfeed.com. Grossman commented about the ease of beginning a campaign. "Searchfeed.com's advertiser area is very easy to use. Becoming an advertiser was a quick and easy process. I entered my search listing, chose keywords, and funded my account with a credit card. I do not have to worry about my advertising ending prematurely thanks to automatic deposits whenever my account starts to run low."

Increased ROI When evaluating the cost of running an online campaign with Searchfeed.com, he stated," All of the details I need for determining ROI of my ads are a click away from sign-in through Searchfeed.com's reports area."

Customer Relations Searchfeed.com is dedicated to developing strong customer relations and is committed to satisfying advertiser needs through the highest levels of customer service. An advertiser relations specialist addresses all advertiser needs with a personal touch.

When asked about customer service, Grossman answered, "Searchfeed. com's support team has been quick to answer my questions and to offer suggestions for improving my campaign."

Overall Results Searchfeed.com offers advertisers the ability to reach their target audience through a simple, cost-effective method of online advertising. By providing quality traffic from thousands of leading Internet portals and industry-specific Web sites, advertisers experience high conversions and a greater return on investment (ROI).

"My conversion rate with Searchfeed.com is often greater than 10 percent. It is the single most effective advertising I've ever done."

About SearchFeed • www.searchfeed.com

Searchfeed.com provides online advertisers with a cost-effective, easily tracked method of generating sales leads while offering Web publishers a better way to monetize Internet traffic. With a primary goal of maintaining its leadership position as an innovator in the PPC industry, it is Searchfeed. com's belief that Web surfers must easily gain access to relevant search results, advertisers must be able to identify a clear Return on Investment (ROI), and publishers must add revenue to their bottom line.

Case Study: TargetedVisitors.info

As PPC search-engine advertising has become popular over the years, so has the success of Searchfeed.com's network, which was established in November of 2000. Through search-engine advertising, Searchfeed.com has built a cost-effective model for online advertisers to track the success of a campaign easily.

Similarly, Searchfeed.com's network offers Web publishers an excellent way to earn revenue from existing traffic without disrupting their core business model."

During the past four years, ongoing software improvements and advancements in click monitoring software have allowed for Searchfeed.com's continued growth. With an increasing acceptance in search-engine advertising and PPC programs, Searchfeed.com has grown from a smaller "in-house" model into a large network of industry-specific Web sites, regional Internet service providers, and other emerging Web sites.

Just as strategic partnerships are established with leading Web properties, Searchfeed.com continues to increase search volumes through its Private Label Feed (PLF) program and alternative integration of sponsored search results. Business growth is a direct result of Searchfeed.com's ability to engage in long-term relationships and establish industry benchmarks. A transformation can be seen throughout the business model, primarily with advancements in traffic monitoring and enhanced reporting tools that deliver greater comfort to both advertisers and Web publishers alike.

With the growth of its distribution network, Searchfeed.com has continued to preserve the principles by which the company was founded. The ability to produce high converting traffic for advertisers is ensured through the use of TrafficAnalystSM, a patent-pending traffic ranking system. Additionally, ongoing personal review of each Web publisher helps boost profitability for many leading portals while ensuring conformance to usage guidelines. Special online tools and a responsive client care team allow for easier content integration while maintaining a Web publisher's site brand.

Case Study: Admiral

Background and Objectives

Admiral specializes in car insurance for younger drivers, people living in cities and those driving performance cars. Admiral had three clear objectives.

1. To increase the volume of inquiries to its call center.

2. To raise brand awareness among consumers actively interested in car insurance.

3. To promote MultiCar, a new Admiral car insurance policy, which offers customers the opportunity to get lower premiums if they insure two or more cars on the same policy.

Strategy

Through its media agency, Steak Media, Admiral booked the "motor insurance" Ad Group for a two week campaign.

As an "Own Ad Group" campaign, Admiral was able to deliver separate TXT//AD executions when consumers requested:

1. Admiral's own number: an execution introducing the new MultiCar policy was developed, providing a powerful mechanic for up selling to consumers already looking to engage with the Admiral brand.

2. Numbers of other companies in the motor insurance Ad Group: an execution with a specific call to action and free phone number was developed to help drive inquiries to the call center and raise brand awareness. During the second week of the campaign, a price discount was added to this execution.

To enable accurate campaign tracking and evaluation, Admiral used a separate free phone number throughout the two-week campaign.

Results

- 9,290 Admiral TXT//ADs were delivered over the 2 week campaign.

- 3.9 percent of consumers receiving the TXT//AD execution which included a call to action went on to phone Admiral.

- The number of consumers going from call to final quote increased by 50 percent when Admiral added a price discount to the execution.

- Call volumes were consistent throughout the two week campaign; however, the highest volumes were generated on Mondays and Thursdays.

Case Study: Admiral

Client Comment

TXT // AD provided a new tool to help increase the volume of enquiries into our call center. The availability of Ad Groups enabled us to develop highly targeted executions that reached active purchasers at a key stage in the buying process."

About MIVA • www.miva.com

MIVA (NASDAQ:MIVA) is a leading independent online advertising network, dedicated exclusively to helping businesses grow. MIVA has relationships with 100,000 businesses. MIVA Media is a leading PPC network born out of the merger of FindWhat.com in the United States and Espotting.com in Europe.

MIVA is not a destination site but a network of partner Web sites and portals. MIVA distributes advertiser's PPC ads across thousands of partner Web sites, in particular Web publishers and industry-specific sites.

MIVA has three advertising products:

MIVA PPC Ads—Powering more than two billion queries a month, MIVA runs PPC networks in the United States, the United Kingdom, France, Germany, Spain, and Italy. MIVA operates a completely transparent bid for position auction. Advertisers can see the actual bid price. In Europe, MIVA displays advertisers' brand logos as part of their PPC Ads.

MIVA Pay-Per-Call Ads—MIVA was first-to-market with pay-per-call ads. Like PPC, advertisers bid for position in an auction and only pay when an Internet user calls their business. The key difference in this MIVA offering is that an advertiser only needs a phone to advertise online. Thus MIVA allows companies with or without a Web presence to connect with targeted Internet users.

MIVA Pay-Per-Text Ads—In 2006, MIVA was first to launch pay-per-text ads providing advertisers with a way to connect with consumers via SMS through a deal with Britain's leading directory assistance.

Web Publisher Products

To view product demos of MIVAs partner products just visit www.miva. com/us/content/partners/partner_product_suite.asp. MIVA was also the first to offer private label solutions to large publishing partners looking to offer a performance advertising solution under their own brand. MIVA's private label partners include Verizon Superpages.com and Eniro, the largest directory company in Scandinavia. The company operates across three continents: North America, Europe, and Asia.

Hints, Tips, and Advice From the Experts Who Do It Every Day

Keyword Bid Optimization

By James S. Lee, President/CEO, www.varazo.com

Keyword bid management is one of most important activities of paid search advertising. It is probably the most time consuming and difficult task if you do not rely on the tool. That is why most advertisers with a decent budget use it. To understand the challenge of the task, here is a list of the issues at hand.

1. **Google™ does not offer guidelines on keyword bid prices on search ranking the way Yahoo does.** The result is customers end up bidding higher than necessary. We did a study on average Google™ keyword prices on a three-keyword combination and four-keyword combination. The result is four-keyword combinations were slightly more expensive than three keywords. It caught us by surprise, since the common belief is low search volume keyword is cheaper than high search volume keyword. However, in Google™'s case, since advertisers bid on keywords without a clear price guideline, they tend to overbid for low search volume keywords.

2. **Finding optimum keyword prices and updating them daily is impossible to do manually.** When you have hundreds of keywords and need to study keyword price to keep up with keyword bidding strategy, it is beyond your capacity. That is why most advertisers, who do not use the tool, set the maximum CPC for all keywords in the same ad group uniform, believing that search vendors do not overcharge them. However, with this strategy, customers end up bidding more than necessary for some keywords or unconsciously promote a bidding war.

3. **There are not enough budgets to place all campaign keywords in a desirable ranking.** Every year, keyword price goes up and many keywords already are out of reach for many advertisers. It means even if you have a tool that guides your bid price for your target ranking, you have to give up on some keywords if you want to generate any significant visitor count. Unfortunately, most keyword bid management tools are based on search ranking, and that means you have to bid for low ranking to generate more clicks. However, this is not a good strategy, since you do not have to sacrifice ranking if keyword price is low.

4. **Keyword bid optimization is more than searching for keyword bid price to maximize click count. It involves improving conversion count.** Eventually, optimization is to generate most conversion actions on a given budget. Thus, once keyword bid price is optimized for the most economical clicks, the next step is to adjust keyword spending to promote more conversion. It includes awarding high performance keywords and penalizing low performance keywords with keyword price. It also includes not spending more than ROI break point.

Varazo develops a tool called "ClickSweeper" to address these issues. This is a tool to generate the most economical clicks by not bidding more than necessary to spend daily budget. It also optimizes keyword bidding to maximize conversion action and the return on advertising. It supports both Google™ and Yahoo paid advertising in one screen.

Varazo is an Internet marketing company. The service includes PPC management and optimization service, search engine optimization service, Web site analytics and Internet marketing consulting. The product Varazo offers is a pay per click bid management tool called ClickSweeper. You can read their Web blog at **www.varazo.com/blog.htm**.

Search Engine Optimization

By Tammy Schultz, President, www.virtualtech.com

To achieve good results using search engines, including natural and PPC, you need to start at the beginning—the beginning of your Web site design that is. If a Web site is not designed with search engines in mind, you will have a much harder time, and it will be a more expensive endeavor to get your site listed well.

The first thing you need to do is view your site as a marketing tool. Before you put anything onto your Web site, you should ask yourself, "How will this help make a sale?" Of course, you need to define what a "sale" is. It could be a phone call, subscription to your newsletter, someone stopping in, or an actual sale. When you define "sale," you can track the effectiveness of your site.

Another thing to keep in mind is that just increasing the number of visitors to your site does not guarantee more sales. My philosophy has always been this: I would rather have 100 people visit my site and have 95 buy than have 1,000 people visit my site and still only have 95 buy. Rather then focus on the number of visitors your site gets, focus on getting quality visitors to your site.

I like to have my clients select their search terms before we start designing. It is much easier to create a site around search terms rather then plug them in later. Here are some general guidelines to follow.

- **Use terms that your potential visitors are using, not what you would use.** Bodacious Basketry **www.bodaciousbasketry. com** makes custom-made reed baskets and marketed their site using "reed" in their search terms. The problem was that people used "wicker" when searching for baskets, not "reed." Though technically the baskets are made of reed, people were not searching that way. Once the change was made, traffic to the site increased. If you do not know which search terms your clients are using, ask them, "If you were looking for our type of product, what would you search on?" The results may be very surprising.

- **Narrow your search terms as much as possible.** Cross and Oberlie **www.promotesigns.com** is a sign manufacturer specializing in advertising yard signs. At first, you might think that "signs" would be a relevant search term. However, if you search for "signs," you find everything from signs of pregnancy, zodiac signs, and signs of the times, none of which has anything to do with their business and is not the market they are trying to reach. We instead narrowed the terms to include "corrugated plastic signs," "job site signs," and "construction site signs." Doing so may lower the number of visitors to the site, but it will increase the return on investment.

- **Your Web site will be seen world wide, but if you can only support clients in a limited area, add the area to your search terms.** Hotel Stebbins located in Algoma, Wisconsin, wants to appear when someone is looking for hotel accommodations in that area. Therefore, instead of using search terms such as "lodging" or "restaurant," we used "Restaurant in Algoma" and "Lodging in Algoma."

- Page Specific Search Terms: If your site offers many product or service choices that cannot be categorized into two or three search terms, you may need to create individual pages for maximum search engine listing. All-Lift Systems is a manufacturer's representative for several companies including Coffing Hoist, Duff Norton, and CM Hoists. Because of the different products, individual pages were created to accommodate each search term and each page was submitted to the search engines individually.

- After you have determined your search terms, you will need to create META tags. META tags are found in the source code of a Web site between the <head> and </head> tags. Search engines focus on two of these META tags when listing a site "title" and "description."

The "title" is the most important META tag and should contain your two most important search terms. The "title" appears in three main places 1) in the upper left hand corner of your browser (Internet Explorer), 2) on a printed page of your Web site, and 3) in the link in most search engines. In creating your title, keep it to no more then ten words and include your two most important search terms. Avoid using unsearchable words such as "and," "that," and "Inc." In most cases, you will not use your company name in the "title." Unless it is one of your top search terms, keep it for the "description."

A "title" example shown in HTML format
<title> Decorative Art and Mural Painting in Connecticut </title>

The "description" is what I refer to as the "classified ad." It appears on search engines below the title and is what most people read to determine whether they would visit the site. This should include search terms from your "title" and be kept to no more than 25 words.

Site content is important because search engines want to give searchers a list of sites that will answer their questions. When people first started to market Web sites, the "keyword" META tag was most important. However, what happened was that people would just list the search terms that people were searching for even if they had nothing to do with the Web site. This resulted in search results that had nothing to do with the search. The situation has gotten better, and it is because search engines now use site content when listing sites. The search terms in your META tags need to appear in the text of your Web page.

Along with site content, search engines like to see text links and if you can create those links with your search terms, it is even better. For example, your Web site sells household cleaners. Rather then saying "Click Here for more information" and having that be the link, use "Learn more about our kitchen cleaners" and have "kitchen cleaners" link to your page about kitchen cleaners. If that page is named kitchen-cleaners.htm that makes it even better.

Keyword relevancy is used to determine the quality of your site. To determine keyword relevancy, search engines pick search terms from your META "title" and "description" and count the number of times those terms appear on a Web page. The search engine will then count the total number of words on that page and figure the keyword relevancy.

For example, a search term appears 10 times on a page that has 100 words. The keyword relevancy rate is 10 percent. This is one of the reasons I like to use bulleted lists on a Web site. It gives the needed information with few words, increasing the keyword relevancy rate.

Search engines also use "link popularity," specifically Google™, when listing sites. A search engine will count the number of RELEVANT links to and from your site. For example, if Donna's Bridal wants to increase her "link popularity," she would contact florists, caterers, and limousine services to link to her site. However, a link to Bob's Bait and Tackle would not be a relevant link. Once people discovered the importance of links, they started linking to everyone, creating a whole page of links. This strategy will backfire if you have too many nonrelevant links as search engines will figure out that you are trying to trick them and will not index your site. In addition, why would you give a visitor a reason to leave your site after you have worked so hard to get the person there?

PPC Campaigns

Many people I talk to say they tried PPC but found it cost them too much money with little response. I believe the number one reason for this idea is that they tried to go after the most generic term they could. Not only do they tend to be very expensive, but also the visitors are not interested in buying your products.

You want to think about and research the terms you want to use. You also need to know what your monthly budget will be. Once you know that, you can decide whether you want to go after one or two of the generic terms in your industry or focus more on many terms that are less popular or more targeted.

For example, you manufacture wheelchair lift ramps. Your first thought might be to bid on "wheelchair" which at 124,714 searches done in August 2006 with a bid amount of $1.60 for the number one spot. This word would generate traffic but would also cost quite a bit of money. Instead, look to terms that include the words "ramp" or "lift" such as "wheelchair lift ramp" that had 16,741 searches done in August 2006 and is currently going for a bid amount of $2. Sure, it costs more per click, but those 1,674 searches were for what you sell. Using this method, in theory, will increase the number of sales, increasing your return on investment.

Do not forget about local searches. If you do business in a certain location, use the local searches that are offered. Both Yahoo and Google™ offer you the ability to have people within a certain mile radius see your ad when they search for something. For example, you are selling a fitness franchise but only want to sell to people looking to start a business in the Chicago area. You would then create an account, have "fitness franchise" as one of your search terms, and select a 50 mile radius around an address in Chicago. The other way to do a local search is to add the area to your search term. For example, you are a carpet cleaner in Rochester, New York. One of your terms might be "carpet cleaner Rochester."

After you have your search terms and your budget figured out, it is now time to write the ads. I find that by focusing each ad specifically to that search terms I get a better result. I like to have the title match the search term exactly, and then the description repeats. The description should read like a classified ad and generate excitement. Make searchers want to click on your link and not your competitors'.

Unless your objective is to brand, do not focus on getting the most traffic to your site, focus on getting quality traffic to your site.

SEO and PPC TIPS

By Eric Gillette , Managing Director, www.gsolutionsonline.net

- **Tracking is everything.** Make sure that for your standard marketing campaigns (free search) and for your PPC campaign search campaigns, you track everything you do, as this is critical to your success with PPC campaigning and/or standard search engine optimization marketing. In fact, tracking is critical to ANY kind of marketing but more so for Internet based marketing since everything can be tracked easily. Tracking will help you determine which keywords are profitable for you and which ones are not, as well as which pages on your site convert better. It will help you to understand your target market better, and will help you to determine the best ways to deliver what they require.

- **Split-testing is another vitally important thing for you to do for any PPC campaign** and standard search engine optimization marketing as well. Split testing will allow you to determine if Page "A" delivers better than Page "B" and vice versa. It is literally a human split-test. You should also split-test your actual PPC ads. Try ad "A" against ad "B," and see what happens. Keep the ones that deliver and watch your conversion rates increase!

- **Keep in mind that there is no "silver bullet" to high conversion rates and high revenue producing Web sites.** It takes elbow grease or in the case of Internet marketing, due diligence. Testing and tracking are the way to determine what works best for your site and your target market.

- **Never underestimate the value of a good hosting company!** Hosting companies are widespread, and sometimes it is difficult to choose a good one, but keep in mind that with most hosting companies you get what you pay for. It is essential to your campaign success to have a good host. What good is all the traffic you are going to be driving to your Web site if your Web site is down all the time? Choose wisely. Try hosts like iPowerWeb **www.ipowerweb.com**, or DreamHost **www.dreamhostweb.com**, as they are reliable, and have 99 percent uptime guarantees, which is what you are looking for.

- **Survey your visitor base!** Ask them what they like/dislike about your site. Your visitors are usually brutally honest about where your site is performing well or under-performing. Doing this will help you improve your Web site and retain more visitors. You will have to offer your visitors a freebie to get them to take your survey, since most will want some kind of incentive.

FINAL TIP

Make it as easy as possible for your visitors to pay you. Accept as many methods of payment as possible, and do yourself a favor—ship internationally, if possible. Most people choose not to do this because of higher shipping costs, but they do not realize that most foreign buyers are aware of those shipping costs and are willing to pay them to get a product! You do not want to create a situation where you eliminate a certain demographic of your potential customer base because you do not accept credit cards, or perhaps you do not ship to Australia where your product may be heavily in demand!

WEBSITE DESIGN TIPS

- **Never create a full flash Web site,** as search engines will not be able to index it, and in turn, you will lose standard search engine traffic aside from the PPC traffic you are paying for.

- **Never use music on your Web site,** or if you do, do not make the music play as soon as a visitor enters your site. Keep in mind that your visitors may be at work or in a place where music on a Web site may be inappropriate. If you do use music, provide a way for visitors to disable it quickly and easily in the event they do not want to hear it. Just because you like it does not mean your visitors will.

- **Too much, too soon.** Do not try to cram everything on your home page. Your home page should be light and lean. It should load quickly and give your visitors just enough information to entice them to click further into your site. Nothing is a bigger deal killer than clicking on a PPC ad, only to have to wait for the Web site to load! Visitors will leave your site before they see your offering. It should load in under 15 seconds, as this is the attention-span that most of your visitors will have when waiting for your site to load. If it takes longer than that, you will lose visitors by the hundreds for every second past 15 that your site takes to load.

- **Never use a third-party hit counter that is visible on your Web site.** Although it is nice to buy from small businesses, they can also portray an unprofessional image for you, since your visitors will know exactly how many people have visited your site besides them. No one wants to be the first to buy your product. They want to see that other people are okay buying it. If you ditch the visible hit counter, for an invisible one, those visitors will never know if they are the first to buy your product, and they will not feel awkward if they are the first, because they will not know it!

- **The biggest mistake most Web site owners make is that they design their Web site according to their own likes and tastes.** You should be designing your site with your user in mind. You may think pink lettering looks nice on your site, but if your target market is senior citizens, pink can be rough on their eyes, meaning fewer sales. Keep your target market in mind!

FINAL TIP

Make life easy for your visitors. Reduce the number of steps required between your home page and the page where you have your product's or service's call-to-action, the page that says: "Buy this now," or "Do this now." The more steps there are in the process, the less likely your visitors are going to take the action you want them to take. If you are offering a single product or service, you might set up a sales-letter type Web site. On the other hand, someone with many products or services may consider a "contact us" page or a simple shopping cart that allows their visitors to purchase products quickly and easily.

"GSolutions Online is a full-scale, search engine marketing and optimized Web site design firm dedicated to helping small businesses realize revenue goals and conversion rates that are usually more typical of larger businesses. Through the productive use of intelligent search engine marketing techniques, creative PPC marketing strategies, and the intuitive use of our proprietary GSOL Web Tools, we help small businesses realize goals that would be out of their reach in most cases."

Services Provided:

- PPC Campaign Management
- Search engine Optimization and Marketing
- PHP/MySQL Custom Web Development Programming
- Website Design and Logo Development
- Business Card, Stationery, Postcard, and Brochure Design and Printing
- Inexpensive Website Hosting

Save Money by Getting to Know Your Competition

By Chris Hickman, E-mail: chris@silverscopepromotion.com
Silver Scope Promotion, www.silverscopepromotion.com

What I am about to tell you is the most important thing you can do to make money on the Internet.

Like it or not, your competition is going to play a huge role in the success or failure of your PPC campaign, so make sure you KNOW THEM BETTER THAN YOU KNOW YOURSELF. Your potential customer will compare you to your competition, and you do not want to lose in that comparison. Many people get a Web site and just throw their ads on the Internet without paying any attention to anything else out there.

Here is the magic question: if 100 people were to come to my site and then those same 100 people went to my competitor's site, am I confident they would buy from me? If I am not sure that the answer is "yes," then I am not ready to start advertising. Do not spend your hard-earned money on any advertising until you are 100 percent positive you have the best product or service.

It is very easy for Internet users to shop around. All they have to do is move their hand an inch and click in the next site they see. You and I know that people will shop around. You just have to be prepared for it.

Compare putting your ads up on the Internet with playing a sport. Pretend that you are a boxer and another boxer has challenged you, and the winner of the fight gets $10,000. Do you just say, "OK. Sounds good. I will see you in the ring," or do you get to know your competition for his strengths and weaknesses before you meet him in the ring? I know what I would do.

Now do the same thing for your PPC ads. Perform a search for the products or services that you sell and see what you are going up against. You need to know your competition's strengths and weaknesses. Here are a couple of examples. If you see a competitor offering the same product you sell at half the price you sell it for, you are not going to be very successful. You are not in a good position to make some money. In another instance, if you see that your competition gives away a free shirt with each purchase, you give away two free shirts.

Just make sure you are one better than everyone else. Give people reasons to buy from you rather than the competition. If you do not give them reasons to buy from you, guess what? They probably will not. Keep this advice in mind as a simple and free way to determine whether you are ready to start advertising in PPC or any other medium.

Chris Hickman is a writer, speaker, and founder of Silver Scope Promotion, LLC, a full service marketing company specializing in PPC Advertising on Yahoo and Google™, Website Analytics and Split Testing. Visit **www.SilverScopePromotion.com** or e-mail him at chris@silverscopepromotion.com.

Hire Someone or Do It Yourself?

By Chris Hickman, E-mail: chris@silverscopepromotion.com
Silver Scope Promotion, www.silverscopepromotion.com

I am going to give you some information you can use to decide whether you want to hire someone to manage your PPC campaign or if you want to do it yourself. The bottom line is that the biggest factor is YOU. I am just going to tell you what is on the other side of the hill, so you do not have to climb up to the top to see for yourself. In the process, I can save you some money, too.

If you want to manage your own PPC campaign, here are a few things you should take into consideration:

1. **Time** — How much time do you have? How much are you willing to give up? Managing a PPC campaign can be very time consuming, depending on the industry.

2. **Experience** — How much do you already know about the PPC industry? Most of the bigger companies have someone with at least four years of PPC experience. If you do not have much experience, there are a few ways to get it. One way is to read the marketing and PPC forums. This way is free. Second, just go ahead and open your own PPC accounts and dive in head first. This is what I did, and it was very expensive. Nevertheless, both are good ways to gain experience, and either can put you on track to make a profit.

3. **Competitiveness** — How many other advertisers are there? How much are the bids going for in the top three to eight positions of the ads shown on the first page of results for a specific keyword.

4. **Keywords** — How many keywords will you be managing? Do you know how to find all the relevant keywords for your business? Keep in mind that if you are in a competitive industry, you will probably be going up against other advertisers who are using expensive bid management software.

5. **Descriptions** — Do you know if you can write good PPC descriptions? I am not talking about normal ad descriptions, but relevant PPC descriptions. The difference can be the deciding

factor between your site's making a profit or taking a loss, a lesson I learned first-hand.

6. **Budget** — How much do you have to spend? If you are new to PPC and plan on spending more than $500 per month, I recommend you start by hiring someone to manage your PPC ads or to act as a consultant. It will be well worth the money if you shop around for the right person or company to help.

7. **Learning new techniques and strategies** — The PPC market is constantly evolving. You have to stay up to date with everything, because you can be certain your competition is up to the minute. Staying up to date involves reading newsletters and forums regularly, consistently, and carefully.

If you are going to hire someone to manage your PPC campaign, here are a few things you should take into consideration:

1. **Experience** — What type of experience do they have? How long have they been in business? Do their current clients recommend them unconditionally?

2. **Price** — Shop around. You can always find a good deal on the Internet. Just watch out for the ones that are TOO good. (Remember that if it sounds too good to be true, it probably is.) Talk to at least three different companies and compare them carefully before making your choice.

3. **Bid monitoring** — How many times per week do they check your bid positioning?

4. **Friendliness** — You are going to be communicating (via e-mail or phone) with the person running your PPC ads. You should enjoy talking with them.

5. **Response time** — How quickly will your calls or e-mails be returned?

6 **Support** — Do they offer phone support or just e-mail support?

7. **ROI tracking** — Is it offered? It is not necessary to have ROI tracking, but in today's market, it drastically increases your chances of having a profitable PPC ad.

If you are still on the fence and do not know which side you want to land on, I have another option for you: consulting. Hire someone to help you take off your training wheels and give you a push.

Chris Hickman is a writer, speaker, and founder of Silver Scope Promotion, LLC, a full service marketing company specializing in PPC Advertising on Yahoo and Google™, Website Analytics and Split Testing. Visit **http://www.SilverScopePromotion.com** or e-mail him at **chris@silverscopepromotion.com.**

When First Might Be the Worst

By Chris Hickman, E-mail: chris@silverscopepromotion.com
Silver Scope Promotion, www.silverscopepromotion.com

Most people think that having their Web site in the first PPC position means they will get more clicks and sales. After you read what I have to say, you may think twice about putting your ad in the first position, especially for competitive keywords.

With highly competitive keywords, I normally recommend the second through eighth position. Just make sure you are on the first page. I will tell you why I normally, but not always, try to stay away from the first position. I have found this strategy to be very effective, and it can definitely save you some money.

This is how MOST people CASUALLY search on the Internet. MOST= Not all people. CASUALLY = Searching for information on a favorite TV show or looking to buy something for entertainment online.

1. Sam goes to his favorite search engine (Yahoo!®, Google™, AOL) and types in what he is looking for.

2. Sam glances at the first PPC ad to see if his search term is in the ad's description. This assures him that the ad will have some information on what he is looking for.

3. If Sam is in a hurry, he may not even read the description before clicking on the ad.

The first ad people see on the PPC listing is like an "auto click" ad. Most people will automatically click on the first thing they see. Even I do it. In reality, however, the first three ads get the same exposure. The only difference is the order they appear on the search engine results page.

This is why. If the ad Sam clicks on gives him good information/prices, he will probably click on the next one to see if the information/prices are better. This cycle will be repeated until the time he is spending far outweighs what he will save by continuing this search.

If the ad Sam clicks on gives him bad or irrelevant information/prices, he will probably go back and pay more attention to what the ads say and/or consider typing in a more specific search term. It is faster and easier just to click on the first ad you see, but you do not always get the desired results.

Most of the time, people realize if they need to narrow down their search term or just be more selective on which PPC ads they choose after they click on the first ad. Consequently, the first ad could be considered the test Web site for the user to see how accurate and useful the search results are.

If you have the budget, you want your ad to be no lower than the third position. The top three PPC ads get the most exposure. If you do not have the budget, just make sure you are on the first page of the search results for your keyword(s). You must at least be on the first page, or there is really no point in putting your ad up. When was the last time you, the reader, looked at PPC ads on the second or third page of search results?

When you are deciding what position to put your ad in, you need to ask yourself if you can afford and/or want to have your ad in the first position. Just keep in mind that if you are in the first spot, your site will be the test site for the user to determine if the search results are what he expected, and you risk depleting your financial investment because of the "auto click" reaction.

If you can afford to experiment, try it out and see for yourself if you get a better ROI by NOT being the first PPC ad listed and let me know the results — good or bad.

Chris Hickman is a writer, speaker, and founder of Silver Scope Promotion, LLC, a full service marketing company specializing in PPC Advertising on Yahoo and Google™, Website Analytics and Split Testing. Visit **http://www.SilverScopePromotion.com** or e-mail him at **chris@silverscopepromotion.com**.

Lower Advertising Costs and Increased ROI with Conversion Tracking

By Chris Hickman, E-mail: chris@silverscopepromotion.com
Silver Scope Promotion, www.silverscopepromotion.com
Do you know where your sales are coming from? If not, you should. In my opinion, tracking your ad's performance, or conversion tracking, is one of the most important aspects of all types of advertising, not just PPC. Here are two analogies to help understand conversion tracking.

EXAMPLE 1:

Pretend that one of the windows in your house is poorly insulated, and it is costing you money to keep your house heated. There are two ways to fix the problem. One way is to replace all the windows because you do not know which window is the poorly insulted one. The second way is to walk around inside your house and feel every window to see which one is letting in cold air.

The first option of replacing all the windows is wasting money because you only need to replace one window. The same may be true with your PPC ads. You may have only one or two ads that are costing you a lot of money with no ROI. Instead of calling it quits because you are losing money, you can track which ads work and remove the ads that are not converting visitors into customers.

EXAMPLE 2:

Company ZZ puts ads on 15 different PPC search engines. They make a 200 percent ROI but do not know the performance of the individual ads. What if the ads on Google™ made a 600 percent ROI while the ads from smaller search engines did not make a profit at all?

When it comes time to renew the advertising contracts, which ones should company ZZ renew and which ones should they cancel? If they cannot track their ads, they will have no idea which ads to renew and which ones to cancel.

Now that you understand the situation, here are some questions you should be able to answer about your site that will help you make more money by tracking how many visitors are converted into customers:

1. **Where do our visitors come from?** You need to know where your traffic is originating, especially if you are paying for it via PPC or another paid method. This is vital in determining profitability for specific ads and also to help you decide to renew or stop specific advertising.

2. **Where are your paying customers coming from?** Just as vital is the need to know where your paying customers are coming from, so you can attract more of them to your site.

3. **Which search engines, keywords, or campaigns are most effective?** You may have multiple PPC ads on many different search engines. In some cases, there will be one or two well-performing ads bringing a profit and the rest may be losing money, but if you are not tracking your results, there is no way you can differentiate between the profitable ads and the ads that just cost you money.

4. **What are the dominant monitor resolution and the color depth of our visitors?** You should also track how people are viewing your site and, if necessary, make changes to it or to your ad design to accommodate your target audience.

5. **What percentage of visitors leave right after entering the Web site?** If people are leaving as soon as they arrive at your site, they did not immediately find something of interest. You have about 10 seconds to grab their attention. If you do not, your competition probably will and you just lost a sale. If people are not spending time on your Web site, you need to make changes to the ads that brought them there, to your target audience, or to your Web site.

6. **How do visitors navigate through the site?** You should have a start to finish (sale) path planned out. Most people do not go into a Web site and make an immediate purchase. If you hold them for those 10 seconds, they are going to navigate though your site to find more information. Knowing where they go and where they do not go can be very useful when deciding what changes to make to your site to increase ROI.

So what is the next step if you want to use conversion tracking? An easy way is to go to your favorite search engine and type in "web stats," "web analytics" or "conversion tracking." Other terms could be used, but try these and compare what you see for service and price for products that track conversion.

If you have time, you can analyze your own Web site to save money, but if you need to hire it out, shop around and be very picky. You can get a good deal. You just have to find it among all the rest of the services that are either ineffective or over-priced.

Make sure the conversion tracking service you choose will be able to give you answers to all six questions above. Check out user forums for advice, reviews, and actual experiences others have had with the companies you are considering.

Affiliate Programs

Dom Pizzuto, E-mail: dom@affiliatetracking.com
Tracking Soft LLC, affiliatetracking.com

Planning and correctly implementing an affiliate program is crucial to its success. The most powerful technical solutions available cannot possibly help a poorly implemented affiliate program. In our experience, the most important thing you, as an affiliate program manager, can do is consider affiliates as partners. Provide them with promotional tools beyond a standard supply of banners and carefully consider any feedback they provide you. Remember that affiliates may have a new market for your product or service, but they still need quality creative materials to send those new customers on through to your site. When running promotions, mobilize your affiliate program by supplying updated links, banners, or even a co-branded page for display on their site.

After implementing your plan for an affiliate program, providing affiliates with complete, accurate information is vital to their continued success. Giving affiliates the capability to track their performance and commissions enables them to determine what is working. This, in turn, may result in feedback you can integrate into your program to ensure its continued growth and success.

It is worth considering allowing your affiliates to market key search terms related to your product. Allowing affiliates to bid on your terms can broaden your exposure to potential consumers. Those affiliates who seize this opportunity may become your top earners, both for you and for themselves.

On the subject of top earning affiliates, consider a program where you can provide incentives to those who are most productive. Customized commissions or specialized support for these affiliates can do nothing but improve your bottom line.

Search Engine Optimization (SEO)—Ethical Strategies

Oliver Moran, Internet Marketing Manager
Apex Pacific Pty Ltd, www.apexpacific.com

The search engine has become a fundamental means for people to find what they are looking for. Research confirms that 80 percent of Internet users go to search engines and directories to find products, services, and information [Jupiter Research Study, 2006]. The number of people using the Internet and search engines gives any business the potential to earn thousands of dollars through one advertising medium. Hence, search engines bring more visitors to Web sites than any other method of advertising.

Research also clearly demonstrates that your Web site needs to show up within the first 20 search results (first two pages) for people to find your Web site. How often have you trawled past the first couple of pages looking for your information in the search engines? Research has proven:

> *Ninety percent of all search engines users click results within the first three pages. Sixty two percent of these users click only on the first few results. Most users perceive that the top ranked Web sites are market leaders.*
> — *Jupiter Research Study, 2006*

Why has search engine optimization (SEO) become one of the classic methods of developing Internet marketing strategies? The point of this technique is to increase your Web ranking positions in the search results so that your customers can find you and your products or services. Simply said, the process of optimization involves choosing keywords that are directly related to your Web site and placing them meaningfully within your pages to build your Web site link popularity. However, as easy as this sounds, an average Web marketer usually finds SEO a daunting task without any guarantee of success. For this reason, if you want a marketing strategy that drives immediate results, PPC will be the best solution. However, the long-term cost benefits of running an effective SEO campaign are substantial, and this is the reason that it is still a popular choice for people who want the competitive edge on the Internet.

Take a better look into the processes of search engine optimization. SEO actually consists of two techniques that work together to achieve optimal results. One technique is called "on-page optimization" (also known as Web-page optimization) and the other is "off-page optimization" (also known as link building). The combination of these two techniques gives a Web site a better chance for successful results. However, many a time Web marketers do not use both methods effectively.

On-Page Optimization

This technique focuses on the optimization of the Web site content. There are various user and search engine friendly SEO techniques that can make a site easier to spider to maximize its chances for obtaining top natural/organic search engine listings, while enhancing the user experience:

- analyzing key phrases thoroughly
- ensuring Web site design that favors indexing
- improving HTML coding and HTML code validation
- using external style sheets
- using external Java script files
- improving the layout and/or design of your site
- improving your site's architecture and navigation
- implementing inter—linking techniques throughout the site
- META tags optimization
- optimizing other elements such as headings, images, links, and anchor text
- rewriting and editing content, and copywriting additional pages if necessary
- using a site map to provide alternate links for users and search spiders

- using bread crumbs and alternate footer text link menus for better user experience and search engine indexation

All or a combination of these elements mentioned above will help your Web site be recognized by the search engine for the search terms relevant to your industry. Adding keyword enriched content and META tags to your Web site will help improve your Web ranking positions and Web traffic. There is also a set of off-page techniques that will further improve your rankings and drive solid long-term results to your Web site.

OFF-PAGE OPTIMIZATION

Every major search engine uses link popularity to some extent as a part of its ranking algorithm. As such, an effective off-page optimization or link building strategy plays a critical role in improving Web site rankings. "Link popularity" measures the quantity and quality of sites that link back to a Web site. For example, Google™ uses its ranking algorithm called "PageRank" to determine the relevancy of each Web site. Naturally, the higher the relevancy of the Web site, the better is its listing in the Google™ results.

Search engines are using link popularity more, but they have become wiser and rank Web sites based more on their importance and relevancy. A Web site can establish itself as important if:

1. It has a large number of quality links.

2. It has a few links from pages that are highly important (high Page Rank).

There are a few techniques within link building that will help the link popularity and reputation of your Web site grow. Building high quality incoming links is one of the most challenging aspects of search engine optimization. However, it is one of the most effective strategies to achieve high-ranking positions on search engine results. We are not talking about getting thousands of any links quickly. We are talking about getting high quality links from popular, respected Web sites because that is what search engines will recognize, and these links will bring high quality traffic to your Web site — your ultimate goal.

Some of the ways to get high quality incoming links are through link exchange with reputable Web sites. This is commonly known as reciprocal links. However, in this instance we recommend that you exchange links with relevant Web sites instead of with link farms! Another strategy to acquire natural incoming links is through becoming a "content provider." This means writing relevant articles, testimonials, and informative advice on forums and blogs related to your industry. The links from these sites will be classified as reputable and help improve your page rank and position.

Search engine optimization in effect helps promote your Web site most cost-effectively on the organic search results than any other marketing medium. This strategy can get a Web site solid long term results based on how well it is optimized. By using ethical techniques, you can get the search engine to recognize your importance to your industry and place you higher in their search results. Ultimately, this strategy will generate quality Web traffic, leading to more conversions.

SEARCH ENGINE OPTIMIZATION TOOLS

There are many search engine optimization tools in the market that can help you manage your SEO work quickly and easily. We would recommend the SEO Suite at **http://www.apexpacific.com/seosuite. html.** This tool is extremely comprehensive and allows you to submit your site to more than 1,000 different search engines at the click of a button, as well as generate META tags, check your Web sites ranking, and also check all of your backlinks within one simple interface.

Oliver Moran is an Internet Marketing Manager at Apex Pacific Pty Ltd, pioneers of Internet marketing solutions to help companies boost online sales and profitability. If you would like to learn more about Paid Search Advertising, visit Apex Pacific at **(www.apexpacific.com)** *or e-mail Oliver at* **oliver@apexpacific.com.**

Paid Search Advertising that Delivers the Maximum ROI

Poorani Prithiviraj, Internet Marketing Manager
Apex Pacific Pty Ltd, www.apexpacific.com

Paid Search Advertising, also known as Pay Per Click, (PPC), has gained a significant influence in the search engine industry. While traditional search engine optimization remains the number one online marketing strategy, more e-marketers are discovering the potential of online advertising campaigns. Properly designed and managed, PPC campaigns can deliver highly qualified visitors to an "online shop."

PPC SUMMARY

PPC Advertising is built on a principle similar to auctions. The difference is that you bid on search terms (keywords) that people use when they are searching for information or products on the search engines.

The concept of PPC bidding is rather simple: buy (bid on) keywords that relate to your product. The highest bidder gets placed at the top of the search results; the second highest bidder gets the next listing, and so on. Every time someone clicks through to your Web site, you pay the amount you bid on for that particular search term. Generally, the more popular the keyword, the more it will cost to bid for the top position. You can start your bid from one cent per click and finish paying five dollars (or more) for very competitive keywords.

The well-known and most popular PPC Search Engines are Google™ AdWords, **www.Google™.com/ads,** and Yahoo!® Search Marketing (previously Overture), **www.overture.com**. Advertising with these two industry leaders will get your Web site the greatest exposure and traffic. Furthermore, statistics show that the top three listings in Google™ AdWords and Yahoo Search Marketing appear on an extensive network of sites (including Yahoo!®, MSN®, AltaVista, Excite, and many others), so you can reach up to 80 percent of all active Internet users. However, be prepared to pay quite a bit.

THREE KEY ADVANTAGES WITH PPC ADVERTISING

1. **Attract Highly Targeted Traffic**. Bidding on keywords that are related to your product or services will actually pre-qualify the type of visitors you wish to attract. You can determine how much you are willing to pay (bid) for the click and only pay when someone clicks on your ad. This implies that the PPC marketing strategy can direct qualified visitors to your Web site cost-effectively.

2. **Fast Exposure, Immediate Results**. Traditional search engines, such as Google™, usually take a few weeks (even months) to list your Web site in their organic search results. If you are having problems getting your Web site indexed by search engines or if you would like to get a result immediately, PPC advertising is the best strategy. Most of PPC search engines will list your Web site within a couple of hours (maximum few days) under their "sponsored search" section. This approach will provide immediate Web site traffic and conversions.

3. **Guaranteed Top Position**. Unlike the search engine optimization strategy, PPC advertising will guarantee high rankings on the search results. Often, by spending just a few cents per click, your Web site can get to the top three positions within 24 hours! If your business relies on immediate results and guaranteed positions, PPC is the best solution.

DESIGNING A SUCCESSFUL PPC CAMPAIGN

The golden rule of PPC bidding is "Attract highly qualified buyers and keep the bids as low as possible." Since you are paying for each visitor entering your Web site, you would obviously want to maximize the effectiveness of your PPC campaign. Look at some basic guidelines to help you optimize your campaign and ensure a greater return on investment:

1. **Determine your bid cost**. The calculation of the bid cost, also known as cost per click, requires a rather complicated formula. Here is an example using a baseline that will help determine how much you can afford to bid:

   Step 1: Find out the conversion rate of your Web site. This means the number of unique visitors who will convert to a sale. For example, if you need 50 visitors (50 clicks) to make one sale, the conversion rate is 2 percent.

   Step 2: Find out the profit margin. If your profit margin is high enough to justify the cost, you can consider increasing the bid and getting a higher position for your ad. By doing this, you may increase the number of clicks through your Web site and acquire more sales.

Step 3: Calculating your conversion cost. If your bid is ten cents per click, one sale costs five dollars in bids. Also, calculate whether the extra sales justify the extra cost and adjust the bid accordingly.

2. **Focus on highly targeted keywords.** To take advantage of PPC advertising, it is important to choose keywords wisely. The key is to be specific. For example, instead of bidding on "skin care" you can consider bidding on "anti-aging herbal treatments." More targeted keywords attract buyers who are more qualified. It is easier to convert them into paying customers because they found exactly what they were looking for. This strategy is also a big money saver: more specific keywords tend to be less expensive than the generic keywords.

3. **Customize compelling ads.** You will attract more attention from qualified buyers by writing creative ads specifically for each of the keywords you bid on. Advertise directly to the type of visitor you want to serve. For example, instead of writing an ad for "pies" you can write "home made meat pies."

   When tailoring your ads to a specific audience, be sure that you direct your visitors to a page on your Web site where it is easy for them to buy these items rather than to your site's homepage.

4. **Use less popular PPC search engines.** Google™ AdWords and Yahoo!® Search Marketing are clearly the PPC market leaders. However, you can still benefit from using PPC search engines that are less popular as a means of customer visibility:

   • MIVA, previously known as FindWhat **www.findwhat.com**

   • Espotting **www.espotting.com**, (biggest PPC engine in UK and European market)

   • 7search.com **www.7search.com**

   • Kanoodle.com **www.kanoodle.com**

   • Enhance Interactive **www.enhance.com**

   Bids on these less popular PPC search engines are much cheaper and you can purchase your listings for as little as one cent per visitor. Even though you may not get the same exposure as you would get with Google™ and Yahoo, you can still generate a decent amount of traffic. In addition, while you pay only for actual clicks to your Web site, you never waste your money.

5. **Choose the best position for your ad.** It is not always a smart move to be listed first on the search results. It certainly helps to attract many visitors, but may cost you money at the same time. People usually visit the five top listings before making a final decision about their purchase. Therefore, it is more profitable to have lower ranking for highly competitive keywords. Generally targeting positions three to six will still get your Web site sufficient traffic, while keeping within a restricted bid cost.

6. **Managing PPC Advertising Campaign**. You have designed a killer of an ad creative, chosen highly targeted keywords, calculated the maximum you can afford to bid on each of search terms, and determined which spot on the search results you wish to secure. However, there is no guarantee that you will be displayed at all times or be displayed in your desired position for the same bid cost just by doing all of the above only once.

This is where PPC management is critical for a successful campaign. The key to maintaining the desired position is to adjust your bids correctly in accordance to the PPC market conditions. It is like monitoring shares on the share market: to get the best deal, you need to watch prices constantly and react immediately to any change.

The main factor influencing the price of the bids and your position is primarily your competitors. Take a few examples of bidding strategies you can consider in your PPC campaign, assuming that your maximum cost per click is one dollar and your goal is to secure position number three at the most effective cost.

- **Maintain Target Position.** In this scenario, your aim is position number three; however, your ad appears at position number one. Knowing that the current holder of position number three pays 51 cents per click, you can improve your position and take over his place by bidding 52 cents. This strategy sometimes tends to drive up the keyword prices; therefore, watch that you do not cross the limit of spending one dollar per click.

- **Remove Bid Gaps**. Yahoo Search Marketing (Overture) defines the bid gap as "the difference between the amount you are currently paying for a click and the minimum you could be paying to remain above your next highest competitor in the search results." For example: If you pay 70 cents per click and your next highest competitor pays 60 cents per click, you need only pay 61 cents per click to remain above your competitor. By closing this bid gap, you save nine cents per click, which in 1,000 clicks is $90!

- **Control your Maximum Cost per Click.** The calculation of your maximum bid cost (cost per click) requires you to collect a list of statistics about your Web site. Based on our assumption, you are willing to pay a maximum of one dollar per click; you should not pursue any positions where the bids are over your one dollar limit. Wait until the price falls under one dollar to prevent any possible losses.

You should consider an automated bid management software product to get the most accurate bidding results without having to watch your advertising campaign continually. These tools consistently monitor your bids and adjust them accordingly to maintain your desired position so that you do not have to be alert 24/7. We would recommend the product Bid Maximizer that can be found at **www.apexpacific.com/bidmax.html** because it is one of the most comprehensive and most affordable bid management software tools on the market.

Below I have listed the main features you should be looking for when choosing bid management software for your campaign:

- The ability to create and identify targeted keywords and phrases that convert leads in sales.

- The ability to set the maximum amount you want to bid.

- The ability to fix bid gaps so you do not pay more money than is necessary

- The ability to set your desired position.

- The ability to compile comprehensive reports on your keywords, bidding cost, bid position, and current bid for each keywords.

- The ability to monitor competitors' activity by checking competitors ranking and current bids.

Apex Pacific offers an automated bid management tool that meets the criteria mentioned above, and it offers advance features to schedule automatic bidding based on your business requirements as well as analytical tools to track your conversion and campaigns success. For more information regarding this bid management software, refer to http://www.apexpacific.com/bidmax.html. This tool will help you understand the whole process of designing and maintaining PPC campaigns so that you always manage to allocate your budgets cost-effectively and increase your revenue. It also allows you to create comprehensive reports at the click of a button, making it simple to manage your return on investment from your PPC campaign.

Paid Search Advertising presents an excellent opportunity to deliver results to your business immediately by targeting the right online audience. Focus on identifying highly targeted keywords that convert for your Web site. Calculate your bids so your sales justify the cost. This way you will maximize your return on investment and ensure your Web site's success with PPC advertising.

Poorani Prithiviraj is an Internet Marketing Manager at Apex Pacific Pty Ltd, pioneers of Internet marketing solutions to help companies boost online sales and profitability. Apex Pacific provides complete solutions covering Search- Engine Optimization and PPC Bid Management Software, service, and training. If you would like to learn more about paid search advertising, visit Apex Pacific at **www.apexpacific.com** or e-mail Poorani at poorani@apexpacific.com.

The Search Engine That Rewards

Tony Tateossian, Founder — Cosmodex, www.cosmodex.com

- Always use an analytics tool to calculate your ROI.

- When generating keywords, get into the minds of your target audience and come up with keyword phrases they would use to find your business.

- Start with minimum bids and move them up as you see sales increase for all keywords, separate most popular keywords, and target those with higher bids.

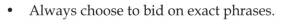

- Always choose to bid on exact phrases.

- Remove keywords that do get any conversions.

- Search for keyword phrases that have no competition.

- Use pricing in your title to stop users who are not willing to pay that amount and get your clicks from prospects who are ready to buy at the advertised price.

Tips & Tricks

Jeff Figueiredo, Senior Strategist, www.pointit.com

- Data analysis should not be limited to keywords, ad copy, and landing pages, but it must also take into account day of week, time of day, and network (content versus search).

- Test and then retest later. What worked today make not work in three months if your competitors copy you.

- Your PPC tracking can usually improve. If you are a B 2 C, can you currently track revenue to keyword match type, ad copy, and landing page? If you are a B 2 B, are you currently tracking by keyword into your SFA/CRM, such as Salesforce?

- Be aware of what your competitors are doing, but do not assume that they are successful. Test and retest according to your metrics.

- Use all match types. If you have all match types in an account and you are getting traffic on broad and phrasing match keywords, you are missing keyword variations and keyword negatives. Continue expanding.

Most people compete on head keywords because it is easy. Do the hard work and compete on the tail keywords.

- Managing SEO and PPC requires different skills. Treat them as such, regardless of whether you outsource or keep search in-house.

- If you are paying percentage of media of PPC management, start looking around at other agencies. Tripling the media expense seldom does triple work, so why do fees triple? Agencies should charge by the hour.

13 Quick Tips

Eric Layland, Senior Strategist, www.pointit.com

1. Conversion tracking to the keyword level is a must.

2. Reporting of key metrics (clicks, ctr, cost, avg cpc, conversions, conversion rate, cost per conversion) is a necessity.

3. A tool with the ability to check referring URLs enables the optimization of search and content networks.

4. It is imperative to understand the audience you are targeting and what drives their interest in the type of offer promoted. Appeal to the audience by using language they know.

5. Develop a campaign architecture that supports program goals and objectives.

6. Manage bids to the keyword level. Single bids for campaigns or groups of keywords is only viable in low volume tail terms.

7. Understand the behavior of your audience. Do they perform better on certain days? At certain times? Search management tools exist that allow for day parting. Successful leveraging of day-parting tools can be very effective at eliminating wasteful spending.

8. Landing pages that are aligned with the keywords and ad copy perform better. The conversion path needs to be optimized in its entirety from keyword to check out.

9. Understanding micro-conversions can reveal the true value of a visit. Micro-conversions are actions taken by a visitor that move them one step closer to completing a transaction. It begins with a click but may include page views of key pages, white papers, Webinars, and details on shipping and handling. Micro-conversions are particularly important for B 2 B clients but also have appeal to B 2 C.

10. ABT — Always be testing.

11. Continually add, subtract, and refine keywords. Test keywords in different positions as their performance may vary.

12. Use referral log data to add keywords and negatives.

13. Track which keywords generate phone calls from customers and prospects with call tracking technology. This is particularly important for B 2 B advertisers or those who deeply considered purchases.

Final Tips

Steve Tateossian, SEO Specialist, www.contentdomain.com

- PPC campaigns should be conducted in conjunction with an SEO campaign, meaning the keywords that you are purchasing placement for should be the most competitive, descriptive keywords (which often convert and thus monetize at higher rates).

- What can be classified as middle - ground words should be primarily focused on in an organic sense, i.e., SEO Web copy and content.

- Longer, three- to four-word keyword phrases are often typed following more one-word generic phrases. The user becomes savvy along the way and narrows the scope of search down to the specifics. SEO people should keep this in mind, but in terms of sheer traffic, the highest bid words are the way to go. Of course, this type of strategy alludes to a viable marketing budget, and if you cannot play big, you should likely not play at all and focus your efforts solely on organic referrals, which in 2006 were 80 percent of click-throughs via search engines.

Recommended Reference Library

You need to build a solid reference library to assist you with your PPC marketing campaign and your e-commerce online marketing portfolio. While there are plenty of excellent books on the market, I recommend you add the following to your library. All are available through Atlantic Publishing Company **www.atlantic-pub.com**, as well as **Amazon.com** and Barnes and Noble **bn.com**:

How to Use the Internet to Advertise, Promote and Market Your Business or Web Site — With Little or No Money

Interested in promoting your business and Web site but do not have the big budget for traditional advertising? This new book will show you how to build, promote, and make money from your Web site or brick and mortar store using the Internet with minimal costs. Let us arm you with the knowledge you need to make your business a success! Learn how to generate more traffic for your site or store with hundreds of Internet marketing methods, including many free and low-cost promotions.

This new book presents a comprehensive, hands-on, step-by-step guide for increasing Web site traffic and traditional store traffic by using hundreds of proven tips, tools, and techniques. Learn how to target more customers to your business and optimize your Web site from a marketing perspective. You will learn to target your campaign, use keywords, generate free advertising, search-engine strategies, learn the inside secrets of e-mail marketing, how to build Web communities, co-branding, auto-responders, Google™ advertising, banner advertising, eBay storefronts, Web design information, search-engine registration, directories, and real-world examples of what strategies are succeeding and what strategies are failing. ISBN-10: 0-910627-57-6 • ISBN-13: 978-0-910627-57-3 - 288 Pages • Item # HIA-01 • $24.95.

"It is easy to be confused about Internet marketing opportunities with a blend of fast-paced changes and tech terminology complicating the picture, but any small business owner seeking enlightenment need look no further than How to Use the Internet to Advertise, Promote and Market Your Business Web Site with Little Or No Money. It packs tried-and-tested marketing applications with easy explanations of Internet choices, pros and cons, and it covers everything from automating a Web site to optimizing a search-engine result. An essential guide any business needs for making a powerful Web presence."

Midwest Book Review

Online Marketing Success Stories: Insider Secrets from the Experts Who Are Making Millions on the Internet Today

Standing out in the turmoil of today's Internet marketplace is a major challenge. There are many books and courses on Internet marketing, but this is the only book that will provide you with insider secrets. We asked the marketing experts who make their living on the Internet every day — and they talked. Online Marketing Success Stories will give you real-life examples of how successful businesses market their products online. The information is so useful that you can read a page and put the idea into action — today!

With e-commerce expected to reach $40 billion and online businesses anticipated to increase by 500 percent through 2010, your business needs guidance from today's successful Internet marketing veterans. Learn the most efficient ways to bring consumers to your site, get visitors to purchase, to up-sell, to avoid oversights, and avoid years of disappointment.

We spent thousands of hours interviewing, e-mailing, and communicating with hundreds of today's most successful e-commerce marketers. This book not only chronicles their achievements but is also a compilation of their secrets and proven successful ideas. If you are interested in learning hundreds of hints, tricks, and secrets about how to make money (or more money) with your Web site, this book is for you.

Instruction is great, but advice from experts is even better, and the experts chronicled in this book are earning millions. This new exhaustively researched book will provide you with a packed assortment of innovative ideas that you can put to use today. It gives you proven strategies, innovative ideas, and actual case studies to help you sell more with less time and effort. ISBN-10: 0-910627-65-7 • ISBN-13: 978-0-910627-65-8 288 Pages • Item # OMS-02 • $21.95.

The eBay Success Chronicles: Secrets and Techniques eBay PowerSellers Use Every Day to Make Millions

There are many books about eBay; this is the only one that will provide you with insider secrets. We asked the PowerSeller experts who make their living on eBay every day — and they talked.

We spent countless hours researching, interviewing, and e-mailing eBay PowerSellers. This book is a compilation of their secrets and proven successful ideas. If you are interested in learning hundreds of hints, tricks, and secrets about how to make money (or more money) on eBay, this book is for you.

The experts chronicled in this book earn $1,000 to $150,000 per month through eBay. Inside the pages of this new exhaustively researched guide you will find a jam-packed assortment of innovative ideas that you can put to use today. This book gives you the proven strategies that you need to sell more with less time and effort.

With more than 430,000 sellers making a living off eBay today, there is no reason you should not become financially successful. This book will arm you with the knowledge to become an eBay PowerSeller. ISBN-10: 0-910627-64-9 • ISBN-13: 978-0-910627-64-1 - 408 Pages • Item # ESC-02 • $21.95.

eBay Income: How ANYONE of Any Age, Location and/or Background Can Build a Highly Profitable Online Business with eBay

eBay has changed the way products and services are purchased all over the world. Daily over 1.5 million online customers and providers log on to bid and sell virtually anything that can be bought or purchased. In 2006 eBay sellers are estimated to post $22 billion in sales. There are businesses earning $1 million a year selling products on eBay today. It is estimated that more than 500,000 people make full-time incomes just with their eBay business. eBay also allows you to run a business that requires no advertising costs. This expertly written new book will show you how to take advantage of this business phenomenon and arm you with the proper knowledge and insider secrets. Filled with actual examples and anecdotes from real eBay entrepreneurs, this book is as engaging as it is informational.

eBay is a level playing field. It does not matter how old you are, what nationality or income level, whether you own a business, what your background is, or where you are located. Start making money on eBay today!

The book starts with a complete overview of how eBay works. You are guided through the whole process of creating the auction and auction strategies. You will find everything you will ever need to get started making money on eBay! ISBN-10: 0-910627-58-4 • ISBN-13: 978-0-910627-58-0 • 288 Pages • Item # EBY-01 • $24.95.

How to get the Financing for your New Small Business: Innovation Solutions from the Experts Who Do it Every Day — With CD-ROM

This new book will provide you with a road map to securing financing by going into traditional financing methods and assisting the reader to set up proper financial statements and a proper business plan. It details the differences between debt and equity financing and how and why to use each. Valuation techniques are explained for determining what your business is truly worth. However, the book's real strength is in explaining alternative and creative methods of financing, such as SBA financing, investor angels, IPOs, limited public offerings, and venture capital.

Essential resources for finding the detailed information you need are included throughout. ISBN-10:0-910627-55-X • ISBN-13:978-0-910627-55-9 • 316 Pages • Item # HGF-01 $39.95.

2,001 Innovative Ways to Save Your Company Thousands by Reducing Costs: A Complete Guide to Creative Cost Cutting and Boosting Profits

For the small business owner, every dollar you can save by reducing costs goes directly to the bottom line in increased profits. This new book details more than 2,000 specific ways that your company can reduce costs today. This is not a "theory" book; there is practical advice on thousands of innovative ways to cut costs in every area of your business. Not only is the idea presented, but also the pertinent information is provided such as contacts and Web sites for companies, products, or services recommended.

We spent thousands of hours interviewing, e-mailing, and communicating with hundreds of today's most successful small business managers and owners. This book is a compilation of their secrets and proven successful ideas. If you are interested in learning thousands of hints, tricks, and secrets about how to reduce business expenses and increase your profits without increasing sales, this book is for you.

You will discover more than 2,000 practical insider techniques and tips that have been gleaned from successful business operators from around the world and tested in real-life business applications. You can put this information in place today to reduce expenses and expand profits. Easy to read and understand, this step-by-step guide will take the mystery out of how to reduce costs in several critical areas: office, operations, labor, cost of goods sold, advertising, marketing, human resources, insurance, employee benefits, compensation, pension plans, training, accounting, software, Web site, mailing, shipping and receiving, rent, interest and debt, utilities, and hundreds more. ISBN-10: 0-910627-77-0 • ISBN-13: 978-0-910627-77-1 352 Pages Item # IWS-02 • $21.95.

365 Foolish Mistakes Smart Managers Make Every Day: How and Why to Avoid Them

Here is a very surprising statistic: within the first 18 months on the job, 40 percent of all management newcomers fail by getting fired, quitting, or receiving a bad review, according to Manchester, Inc., a business consulting group. Some first-timers are overwhelmed by their newfound power while some are weighed down with responsibility, but for most, the overriding concern is to avoid personal failure.

This new ground breaking book will guide the new manager to success and avoid the many common mistakes and pitfalls along the way. You will learn how to face the unique challenges every day in your job and offer detailed and innovative solutions to help you achieve your potential. Learn how to become a true leader who commands respect, commitment, and credibility.

Topics include:

- What It Takes To Be a Manager,
- How to Take Charge
- How to Establish Your Authority
- Earn Respect and Credibility
- Deal With Social Issues
- How To Be A Leader
- Gain the Cooperation and Commitment of Others
- Manage Yourself
- Conduct Interviews
- Set Realistic Goals
- Implement Coaching Skills
- Commit to Creative Problem Solving
- Avoid Sexual Harassment Suits
- Manage Multiple Projects and Assignments
- Delegate Effectively
- Conduct Successful Meetings
- Break Down Communication Barriers
- Deal with Interruptions
- Develop Self-Confidence
- Turn Around Unacceptable Performance

- Deal with Stress
- Write Effectively and Clearly
- Use E-Mail Effectively
- Deal With Employees Who Complain or Are Disagreeable

In addition to the comprehensive content in the book, we spent thousands of hours interviewing, e-mailing, and communicating with hundreds of today's most successful managers. This book is a compilation of their secrets and proven successful ideas. If you are interested in learning hundreds of hints, tricks, and secrets about how to be a great first-time manager, this book is for you. ISBN-10: 0-910627-75-4 • ISBN-13: 978-0-910627-75-7 • 334 Pages • Item # FMS-02 • $21.95.

How to Write a Great Business Plan for Your Small Business in 60 Minutes or Less — With CD-ROM.

A business plan precisely defines your business, identifies your goals, and serves as your firm's résumé. The importance of a comprehensive, thoughtful business plan cannot be over-emphasized. So much hinges on it: outside funding, credit from suppliers, management of your operation and finances, promotion and marketing of your business, and achievement of your goals and objectives. Yet many small businesses never take the time to prepare one. Now it is easy — and you can do it in less than an hour. This new book and companion CD-ROM will demonstrate how to construct a current and pro-forma balance sheet, an income statement, and a cash flow analysis. You will learn to allocate resources properly, handle unforeseen complications, and make good business decisions. The CD-ROM, written in MIcrosoft® Word, allows you to plug in your own information while providing specific and organized information about your company. ISBN-10: 0-910627-56-8 • ISBN-13: 978-0-910627-56-6 • 288 Pages • Item # GBP-01 $39.95.

About the Author

Bruce C. Brown is the best selling author of *How to use the Internet to Advertise, Promote and Market Your Business or Web Site with Little or No Money.*Bruce is finishing his 23rd year as an officer in the United States Coast Guard and is looking forward to retirement when he can concentrate on helping others succeed with their online businesses and marketing campaigns. He uses his 20+ years of expertise in financial management in conjunction with more than 12 years as a web designer, business owner, e-marketing consultant, and hardware and software specialist. He completed college during his military career, earning degrees from the University of Phoenix and Charter Oak State College. He currently splits his time between Washington, DC, and Land O Lakes, Florida, with his wife Vonda, and youngest son, Colton. His oldest son, Dalton, is a full-time student at the University of South Florida in Tampa (Go Bulls!), and his middle son, Jordan, is a full-time student at the University of Florida in Gainesville (Go Gators!).

Author Dedication

This book is dedicated to my father and mother.

With special thanks to the love and support of my beautiful wife Vonda and our sons Dalton, Jordan, and Colton.

AD For Web advertising, an ad is usually a banner, a graphic image, or set of animated images (in a file called an animated GIF) of a designated pixel size and byte size limit. An ad or set of ads for a campaign is "the creative." Banners and other special advertising that include an interactive or visual element beyond the usual are "rich media."

AD IMPRESSION Also called an ad view, it occurs when a user pulls up a Web page through a browser and sees an ad that is served on that page. Many Web sites sell advertising space by ad impressions.

AD ROTATION Ads are often rotated into ad spaces from a list. This is usually done automatically by software on the Web site or at a central site administered by an ad broker or server facility for a network of Web sites.

AD SPACE A space on a Web page that is reserved for ads. An ad space group is a group of spaces within a Web site that share the same characteristics so that an ad purchase can be made for the group of spaces.

AD STREAM The series of ads viewed by the user during a single visit to a site.

AD VIEW Synonymous with ad impression, it is a single ad that appears on a Web page when the page arrives at the viewer's display. Ad views are what most Web sites sell or prefer to sell. A Web page may offer space for a number of ad views. In general, the term impression is more commonly used.

AFFILIATE The publisher/salesperson in an affiliate marketing relationship.

AFFILIATE DIRECTORY A categorized listing of affiliate programs.

AFFILIATE FORUM An online community where visitors may read and post topics related to affiliate marketing.

AFFILIATE FRAUD Bogus activity generated by an affiliate in an attempt to generate illegitimate, unearned revenue.

AFFILIATE MARKETING
Revenue sharing between online advertisers/merchants and online publishers/salespeople, whereby compensation is based on performance measures, typically in the form of sales, clicks, registrations, or a hybrid model. Affiliate marketing is the use by a Web site that sells products of other Web sites, called affiliates, to help market the products.

AMAZON.COM Book seller who created the first large-scale affiliate program. Hundreds of other companies have followed.

AFFILIATE MERCHANT The advertiser in an affiliate marketing relationship.

AFFILIATE NETWORK A value-added intermediary providing services, including aggregation, for affiliates and affiliate merchants.

AFFILIATE SOFTWARE
Software that, at a minimum, provides tracking and reporting of commission-triggering actions (sales, registrations, or clicks) from affiliate links.

BANNER Ad in the form of a graphic image that typically runs across a Web page or is positioned in a margin or other space reserved for ads. Banner ads are usually Graphics Interchange Format (GIF) images. In addition to adhering to size, many Web sites limit the size of the file to a certain number of bytes so that the file will display quickly. Most ads are animated GIFs since animation has been shown to attract a larger percentage of user clicks. The most common larger banner ad is 468 pixels wide by 60 pixels high. Smaller sizes include 125 X 125 and 120 X 90 pixels. These and other banner sizes have been established as standard sizes by the Internet Advertising Bureau.

BEYOND THE BANNER The idea that there are other ways in addition to banner ads to use the Internet to communicate a marketing message, including sponsoring a Web site or a particular feature on it; advertising in e-mail newsletters; co-branding with another company and its Web site; contest promotion; and, in general, finding new ways to engage and interact with the desired audience. "Beyond the banner" approaches can also include the interstitial and streaming video infomercial. The banner itself can be transformed into a small rich media event.

BEHAVIORALLY TARGETED ADVERTISING A method of compiling data on Web visitors such as surfing history, gender, age, and personal preferences, to target them with tailored ads.

BLACK LISTS Blocks mail from known spam sources.

BOOKED SPACE This is the number of ad views for an ad space that are currently sold out.

BRAND, BRAND NAME, AND BRANDING A product, service, or concept that is publicly distinguished from others so that it can be easily communicated and usually marketed. A brand name is the name of the distinctive product, service, or concept. Branding is the process of creating and disseminating the brand name. Branding can be applied to the entire corporate identity as well as to individual product and service names. In Web and other media advertising, it is recognized that there is usually some kind of branding value whether an immediate, direct response can be measured from an ad or campaign. Companies like Proctor and Gamble have made a science of creating and evaluating the success of their brand name products.

CACHING In Internet advertising, the caching of pages in a cache server or the user's computer means that some ad views will not be known by the ad counting programs, and it is a source of concern. There are several techniques for telling the browser not to cache particular pages. On the other hand, specifying no caching for all pages may mean that users will find your site to be slower than you would like.

CAMPAIGN One or more ad groups. The ads in a given campaign share the same daily budget, language, and location targeting, end dates, and distribution options.

CLICK According to ad industry recommended guidelines from FAST, a click occurs "when a visitor interacts with an ad." This does not apparently mean simply interacting with a rich media ad, but actually clicking on it so that the visitor is headed toward the advertiser's destination. It also does not mean that the visitor actually waits to arrive at the destination, but only that the visitor started to go there.

CLICK STREAM A click stream is a recorded path of the pages a user requested in going through one or more Web sites. Click stream information can help Web site owners understand how visitors are using their site and which pages are getting the most use. It can help advertisers understand how users get to the client's pages, which pages they look at, and how they go about ordering a product.

CLICK-THROUGH Count by the sponsoring site of ad clicks. In practice, "click" and "click-through" tend to be used interchangeably. A click-through, however, seems to imply that the user actually received the page. A few advertisers are willing to pay only for click-throughs rather than for ad impressions.

CLICK RATE Percentage of ad views that resulted in click-throughs. Although there is visibility and branding value in ad views that do not result in a click-through, this value is difficult to measure. A click-through has several values: it is an indication of the ad's effectiveness and it results in the viewers' getting to the advertiser's Web site where other messages can be provided. A new approach is for a click to result not in a link to another site but to an immediate product order window. Whether a click rate is successful depends on a number of factors, such as campaign objectives, how enticing the banner message is, how explicit the message is (a message that is complete within the banner may be less apt to be clicked), audience/message matching, how new the banner is, and how often it is displayed to the same user. In general, click rates for high-repeat, branding banners vary from 0.15 to 1 percent. Ads with provocative, mysterious, or other compelling content can induce click rates ranging from 1 percent to 5 percent and sometimes higher. The click rate for a given ad tends to diminish with repeated exposure.

CO-BRANDING Co-branding on the Web often means two Web sites or Web site sections or features displaying their logos (and thus their brands) together so that the viewer considers the site or feature to be a joint enterprise. (Co-branding is often associated with cross-linking between the sites, although it is not necessary.)

COOKIE A file on a Web user's hard drive kept in one of the subdirectories under the browser file directory that is used by Web sites to record data about the user. Some ad rotation software uses cookies to see which ad the user has just seen so that a different ad will be rotated into the next page view.

COST-PER-ACTION Cost-per-action is what an advertiser pays for each visitor who takes some specifically defined action in response to an ad beyond simply clicking on it. For example, a visitor might visit an advertiser's site and request to subscribe to their newsletter.

COST-PER-CLICK (CPC) The amount of money an advertiser will pay to a site each time a user clicks on an ad or link.

COST-PER-LEAD A more specific form of cost-per-action in which a visitor provides enough information at the advertiser's site (or in interaction with a rich media ad) to be used as a sales lead. Note that you can estimate cost-per-lead regardless of how you pay for the ad. In other words, buying on a pay-per-lead basis is not required to calculate the cost-per-lead.

COST-PER-SALE Sites that sell products directly from their Web site or can otherwise determine sales generated as the result of an advertising sales lead can calculate the cost-per-sale of Web advertising.

CPA Cost per action. The cost of one impression (the action of displaying a banner ad).

CPM Cost per thousand ad impressions, an industry standard measure for selling ads on Web sites. This measure comes from print advertising. The "M" has nothing to do with "mega" or million. It is taken from the Roman numeral for "thousand."

CREATIVE Ad agencies and buyers often refer to ad banners and other forms of created advertising as "the creative." Since the creative requires inspiration and skill that may come from a third party, it often does not arrive until late in the preparation for a new campaign launch.

CONVERSION RATE The percentage of site visitors who respond to the desired goal of an ad campaign compared with the total number of people who see the ad campaign. For example, the goal may be convincing readers to become subscribers, encouraging customers to buy something or enticing prospective customers from another site with an ad.

CTR Click-through rate. The cost of one click-through for a banner ad.

DEMOGRAPHICS Data about the size and characteristics of a population or audience (for example, gender, age group, income group, purchasing history, personal preferences).

DOMAINS Registered domain name (with name server record).

DOUBLE OPT-IN A message automatically sent to the person who has signed up for a mailing list, asking if he or she really wants to be added to the list. Unless the person actively replies positively, he or she never gets another message.

DYNAMIC AD PLACEMENT The process by which an ad is inserted into a page in response to a user's request.

ELECTRONIC MAILING LISTS Also referred to as listservs; sometimes used to send advertising messages because they reach a list of subscribers who have already expressed an interest in a topic.

ENTERTAINMENT POLLS Unscientific polls appearing on any manner of Web sites representing the collective opinions of people taking the poll.

FILTERING The immediate analysis by a program of a user Web page request to determine which ad or ads to return in the requested page. A Web page request can tell a Web site or its ad server whether it fits a certain characteristic such as coming from a particular company's address or that the user is using a particular level of browser. The Web ad server can respond accordingly.

FOLD "Above the fold," a term

borrowed from print media, refers to an ad that is viewable as soon as the Web page arrives. You do not have to scroll down (or sideways) to see it. Since screen resolution can affect what is immediately viewable, it is good to know whether the Web site's audience tends to set their resolution at 640 X 480 pixels or at 800 X 600 (or higher).

HARVESTING Using automated scripts known as "bots" to identify the correct syntax of e-mail addresses on Web pages and newsgroup posts and copy the addresses to a list.

HEADER ANALYSIS Identifies headers that do not conform to RFCs, a strong indication of spam.

HOSTS A computer system with registered IP address.

HIT Sending a single file, whether an HTML file, an image, an audio file, or other file type. Since a single Web page request can bring with it a number of individual files, the number of hits from a site is not a good indication of its actual use (number of visitors). It does have meaning for the Web site space provider, however, as an indicator of traffic flow.

IMAGE SCANNING Filters out offensive images before a user sees them.

IMPRESSION The count of a delivered basic advertising unit from an ad distribution point. Impressions are how most Web advertising is sold and the cost is quoted in terms of the cost per thousand impressions (CPM).

INSERTION ORDER A formal, printed order to run an ad campaign. Typically, the insertion order identifies the campaign name, the Web site receiving the order, the planner or buyer giving the order, the individual ads to be run (or who will provide them), the ad sizes, the campaign beginning and end dates, the CPM, the total cost, discounts to be applied, reporting requirements and possible penalties or stipulations relative to the failure to deliver the impressions.

INTERNET Millions of computers that are linked together around the world, allowing any computer to communicate with any other that is part of the network.

INVENTORY Total number of ad views or impressions that a Web site has to sell over a given period. Usually, inventory is figured by the month.

KEYWORD MATCHING OPTIONS There are four types of keyword matching: broad matching, exact matching, phrase matching, and negative keywords. These options help you refine your ad targeting on Google™ search pages.

"JUNK" E-MAIL E-mail messages

sent to multiple recipients who did not request them and are not in the right target audience.

KEYWORD A word or phrase that a user types into a search engine when looking for specific information.

KEYWORD SEARCHES Searches for specific text that identifies unwanted e-mail.

MAXIMUM COST-PER-CLICK (CPC) With keyword-targeted ad campaigns, you choose the maximum cost-per-click (Max CPC) you are willing to pay.

MAXIMUM COST-PER-IMPRESSION (CPM) With site-targeted ad campaigns, you choose the maximum cost per thousand impressions (Max CPM) you are willing to pay.

MEDIA BROKER Since it is often not efficient for an advertiser to select every Web site it wants to put ads on, media brokers' choose sites for advertisers and their media planners and buyers, based on demographics and other factors.

MEDIA BUYER Usually at an advertising agency, this person works with a media planner to allocate money provided for an advertising campaign among specific print or online media (magazines, TV, Web sites) and places the ad orders. On the Web, placing the order often includes requesting proposals and negotiating the final cost.

META TAGS Hidden HTML directions for Web browsers or search engines. They include important information such as the title of each page, relevant keywords describing site content, and the description of the site that shows up when a search engine returns a search.

NETWORKS Registered class A/B/C addresses.

NEWSGROUPS Topic-specific discussion and information exchange forums open to interested parties.

NON-PERMISSION MARKETING An e-mail message which is or appears to be sent to multiple recipients who did not request it, even though they may be in the right target market.

OPT-IN E-MAIL E-mail containing information or advertising that users explicitly request (opt) to receive. Typically, a Web site invites its visitors to fill out forms identifying subject or product categories that interest them and about which they are willing to receive e-mail from anyone who might send it. The Web site sells the names (with explicit or implicit permission from their visitors) to a company that specializes in collecting mailing lists representing different interests. Whenever the mailing list company sells its lists to advertisers, the Web site is paid a small amount for each name that it generated for the list.

You can sometimes identify opt-in e-mail because it starts with a statement that tells you that you have previously agreed to receive such messages.

PAGE IMPRESSIONS A measure of how many times a Web page has been displayed to visitors. Often used as a crude way of counting the visitors to a site.

PAGE REQUESTS A measure of the number of pages that visitors have viewed in a day. Often used as a crude way of indicating the popularity of a Web site.

PAID SEARCH The area of keyword, contextual advertising, often called PPC.

PAGE VIEW A common metric for measuring how many times a complete page is visited.

PPC The advertiser pays a certain amount for each click-through to the advertiser's Web site. The amount paid per click-through is arranged at the time of the insertion order and varies considerably. Higher PPC rates recognize that there may be some "no-click" branding value as well as click-through value provided.

PAY-PER-LEAD The advertiser pays for each sales lead generated. For example, an advertiser might pay for every visitor who clicked on a site and then filled out a form.

PAY-PER-SALE Not customarily used for ad buys. It is, however, the customary way to pay Web

sites that participate in affiliate programs, such as those of Amazon.com and Beyond.com.

PAY-PER-VIEW The prevalent type of ad-buying arrangement at larger Web sites. This term tends to be used only when comparing this most prevalent method with PPC and other methods.

PAYMENT THRESHOLD The minimum accumulated commission an affiliate must earn to trigger payment from an affiliate program.

PROOF OF PERFORMANCE Proof for advertisers that the ads they have bought have actually run and that click-through figures are accurate. In print media, tear sheets taken from a publication prove that an ad was run. On the Web, there is no industry-wide practice for proof of performance. Some buyers rely on the integrity of the media broker and the Web site. The ad buyer usually checks the Web site to determine the ads are actually running. Most buyers require weekly figures during a campaign. A few want to look directly at the figures, viewing the ad server or Web site reporting tool.

PSYCHOGRAPHIC CHARACTERISTICS Personal interest information gathered by Web sites by requesting it from users. For example, a Web site could ask users to list the Web sites that they visit most often. Advertisers could use this data to help create a demographic profile for that site.

REPORTING TEMPLATE
Although the media have to report data to ad agencies and media planners and buyers during and at the end of each campaign, no standard report is yet available. FAST, the ad industry coalition, is working on a proposed standard reporting template that would enable reporting to be consistent.

RICH MEDIA Advertising that contains perceptual or interactive elements more elaborate than the usual banner ad. Today the term is used for banner ads with popup menus that let the visitor select a particular page to link to on the advertiser's site. Rich media ads are generally more challenging to create and to serve. Some early studies have shown that rich media ads tend to be more effective than ordinary animated banner ads.

ROI Return on investment is "the bottom line" about how successful an ad or campaign was in getting returns (sales revenue) for the money expended (invested).

RUN-OF-NETWORK An ad that is placed to run on all sites within a given network of sites. Ad sales firms handle run-of-network insertion orders in such a way as to optimize results for the buyer consistent with higher priority ad commitments.

RUN-OF-SITE An ad that is placed to rotate on all non-featured ad spaces on a site. CPM rates for run-of-site ads are usually less than rates for specially-placed ads or sponsorships.

SEARCH-ENGINE MARKETING (SEM) Promoting a Web site through a search engine. This most often refers to targeting prospective customers by buying relevant keywords or phrases.

SEARCH ENGINE Provides an index of other Web site addresses listed according to key words and descriptions in the original page.

SEARCH-ENGINE OPTIMIZATION (SEO) Making a Web site friendlier to search engines, resulting in a higher page rank.

SPAM — An unwanted e-mail message sent in bulk to thousands of addresses to try to advertise something.

SPAM POSTS Messages posted to an e-mail discussion group, chat rooms, or bulletin boards that are "off topic" or distinctly promotional.

SPLASH PAGE Also known as an interstitial, it is a preliminary page that precedes the regular home page of a Web site and usually promotes a particular site feature or provides advertising. A splash page is timed to move on to the home page after a short period of time.

SPONSOR Depending on the context, it means an advertiser who has sponsored an ad and, by doing so, has also helped sponsor or sustain the Web site itself. It can also mean an advertiser who has a special relationship with the Web site and supports a special feature of it, such as a writer's column, a Flower-of-the-Day, or a collection of articles on a particular subject.

SPONSORSHIP An association with a Web site in some way that gives an advertiser some particular visibility and advantage above that of run-of-site advertising. When associated with specific content, sponsorship can provide a more targeted audience than a run-of-site ad buys. Sponsorship also implies a "synergy and resonance" between the Web site and the advertiser. Some sponsorships are available as value-added opportunities for advertisers who buy a set amount of advertising or more.

TARGETING Purchasing ad space on Web sites that match audience and campaign objective requirements. Techtarget.com, with more than 20 Web sites targeted to special information technology audiences, is an example of an online publishing business built to enable advertising targeting.

UNIQUE VISITOR Someone with a unique address who is entering a Web site for the first time that day (or some other specified period). Thus, a visitor who returns within the same day is not counted twice.

A unique visitors' count tells you how many different people there are in your audience during the period, but not how much they used the site during the period.

USER SESSION Sometimes determined by counting only those users who have not reentered the site within the past 20 minutes or a similar period. User session figures are sometimes used incorrectly to indicate "visits" or "visitors" per day. User sessions are a better indicator of total site activity than "unique visitors" are.

VIEW Depending on what is meant, either an ad view or a page view. Usually an ad view is intended. There can be multiple ad views per page views. View counting should consider that a small percentage of users choose to turn the graphics off (not display the images) in their browser.

VISIT A Web user with a unique address entering a Web site at some page for the first time that day -or for the first time in a lesser time period. The number of visits is roughly equivalent to the number of different people who visit a site. This term is ambiguous unless the user defines it, since it could mean a user session, or it could mean a unique visitor that day.

WHITE LISTS Guarantees delivery of known good addresses.

YIELD The percentage of clicks versus impressions on an ad within a specific page.

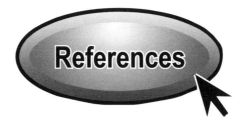

SOURCES FOR TERMS AND DEFINITIONS

http://searchcio.techtarget.com/sDefinition/0,,sid19_gci211535,00.html

http://adwords.Google.com

http://www.marketingterms.com/

http://www.wikipedia.com

RECOMMENDED RESOURCES

While this is certainly not an all-encompassing list, the following resources and their URLs are my "recommended" sources.

DOMAIN NAME REGISTRATION

GoDaddy.com: **http://www.godaddy.com**
Network Solutions: **http://www.networksolutions.com**
Register.com: **http://www.register.com**

WEB HOSTING COMPANIES

Readyhosting: **http://www.readyhosting.com**
Verio: **http://www.verio.com**
Rackspace: **http://www.rackspace.com**
You can obtain current reviews and rankings for Web Hosting Companies at: **http://www.hostaz.com, http://www.upperhost.com, or http:// www.tophosts.com/top25-web-hosts.html**

WEB SITE DESIGN

Gizmo Graphics Web Design: **http://www.gizwebs.com**

SECURE SERVER CERTIFICATES

GoDaddy: **http://www.godaddyssl.com**
Geotrust: **http://www.thawte.com/**

VeriSign: **http://www.verisign.com**

E-commerce Software

Monster Commerce: **http://www.monstercommerce.com/**

PDG Software: **http://www.pdgsoft.com**

PayPal: **http://www.paypal.com**

Rich Media Technologies: **http://www.justaddcommerce.com**

E-commerce Templates: **http://www.e-commercetemplates.com/**

DemandWare: **http://www.demandware.com/**

Another good review of Shopping Cart Software is available here:
http://shopping-cart-review.toptenreviews.com

Search-Engine Optimization

Google™: **http://www.Google.com/Web marketings/seo.html**

Intelligent Web Marketing: **http://www.i-web-marketing.com/**

CPM (costs per impression) Calculator

http://www.clickz.com/resources/adres/cpm_calculator/

Logo Design

Logo Twister: **http://www.logotwister.com/**

LogoWorks: **http://www.logoworks.com/**

Permission-Based E-mail/E-zine Management

Topica.com: **http://www.topica.com**

Affiliate Program

Affiliate Tracking Network**http://www.affiliatetracking.com**

PPC Program

Google™ AdWords: **http://adwords.Google.com**

Yahoo!® Search Marketing: **http://searchmarketing.yahoo.com/**

Microsoft® adCenter: **http://adcenter.Microsoft.com/**

Index